Praise for *Reframing Trauma*

"The strength of this volume lies in its insistence on the vitality of diverse communities responding to trauma. The authors resist the pathologizing narratives often associated with trauma, powerfully advocating for communities that are frequently overlooked in trauma literature. These unique essays showcase pastoral theologians as attentive educators and advocates for healing justice. Serving as a model for intercultural literacy, they make excellent additions to a variety of theological courses."

—**Shelly Rambo**, associate professor of theology, Boston University

"*Reframing Trauma* is a deeply thoughtful and compassionate exploration of how we understand and experience trauma. M. Jan Holton and Jill L. Snodgrass invite us to see suffering through a psychospiritual lens, offering insight and genuine hope for healing and growth. This book speaks to the heart and mind and is a must-read for those seeking to navigate the complexities of human distress with grace and wisdom."

—**John Swinton**, professor in practical theology and pastoral care, School of Divinity, History and Philosophy, King's College University of Aberdeen

"While I have long been skeptical of superficial applications of the concept of post-traumatic growth, I find in this book a sophisticated understanding of the coexistence of traumatic suffering with resilience. From a psychoanalytic perspective, I appreciate this as a move from unconscious splitting to greater possibilities for wholeness. By widening the lens in this approach to trauma beyond a purely medicalized conception, and beyond Western and Christian notions of trauma and healing, the authors offer an expanded and more contextualized understanding of how persons navigate both trauma and healing. By framing stress and trauma as a continuum, this volume invites readers to expand their thinking about how to address trauma, with implications for practice, in a world where global injustice and climate crisis have created a baseline of existential anxiety for us all."

—**Pamela Cooper-White**, Christiane Brooks Johnson Professor Emerita of Psychology and Religion, and dean and vice president emerita for academic affairs, Union Theological Seminary

reframing
TRAUMA

M. JAN HOLTON AND JILL L. SNODGRASS
EDITORS

reframing TRAUMA

A Psychospiritual Theory and Theology

Fortress Press
Minneapolis

REFRAMING TRAUMA
A Psychospiritual Theory and Theology

30 29 28 27 26 25 24 1 2 3 4 5 6 7 8 9

Library of Congress Cataloging-in-Publication Data

Names: Holton, M. Jan, editor. | Snodgrass, Jill Lynnae, editor.
Title: Reframing trauma : a psychospiritual theory and theology / M. Jan Holton, and Jill L. Snodgrass, editors.
Description: Minneapolis : Fortress Press, [2025] | Includes bibliographical references and index.
Identifiers: LCCN 2024040510 (print) | LCCN 2024040511 (ebook) | ISBN 9798889832942 (print) | ISBN 9798889832959 (ebook)
Subjects: LCSH: Spirituality--Psychological aspects. | Psychology and religion. | Minorities--Psychology. | Minorites--Religious life.
Classification: LCC BF51 .R39 2025 (print) | LCC BF51 (ebook) | DDC 201/.615--dc23/eng/20241024
LC record available at https://lccn.loc.gov/2024040510
LC ebook record available at https://lccn.loc.gov/2024040511

Cover design: LUCAS Art & Design, Jenison, MI
Cover illustration: Trees in Bird Garden, Iver Heath, 1913 by Paul Nash. Sourced from Birmingham Museums Trust/Unsplash

Print ISBN: 979-8-8898-3294-2
eBook ISBN: 979-8-8898-3295-9

CONTENTS

ACKNOWLEDGMENTS

All scholarly projects are the product of many hearts and minds, particularly a collaborative endeavor such as this. We are most appreciative to the volume's contributing authors—Eunil David Cho, John B. Freese, Nazila Isgandarova, Ryan LaMothe, Jessica Chapman Lape, Keith A. Menhinick, Hee-Kyu Heidi Park, and Cody J. Sanders—for their creative, critical, and expansive thought on trauma in contemporary contexts.

We are grateful to Carrie Doehring and Nancy Ramsay whose project on military moral injury inspired us to pursue a coedited issue of *Pastoral Psychology* followed by a monograph publication. We also wish to thank Kirk A. Bingaman, editor in chief of *Pastoral Psychology*, and Springer Publishing Company for their cooperative support in sharing permission to adapt material for this publication.

We are indebted to the Society for Pastoral Theology (SPT) 2023 Steering Committee—Jim Higginbotham, Hee-Kyu Heidi Park, Leanna Fuller, Eunil David Cho, and Jessica Chapman Lape—for the invitation to offer the Work-in-Progress presentation at the 2023 Annual Meeting. Our work is richer for the reflection and input of our brilliant colleagues, particularly Carrie Doehring, Leanna Fuller, Jeanne Stevenson-Moessner, Mary Moschella Clark, Brooke Petersen, Cedric Johnson, and Storm Swain.

Finally, we thank Duke Divinity School and the Center for the Humanities at Loyola University Maryland for financially supporting this project.

CONTRIBUTORS

Eunil David Cho is assistant professor of spiritual care and counseling and codirector of the Center for Practical Theology at Boston University School of Theology. His scholarship in practical theology and spiritual care, especially with immigrant and refugee communities, engages with narrative theories and therapy, social scientific studies of religion, and critical race theory. He is the author of *Undocumented Migration as a Theologizing Experience* (Brill 2024) and an ordained minister in the Presbyterian Church (USA).

John B. Freese is a professor of Buddhist studies, spiritual care, and contemplative studies at University of the West and Sakya Buddha University. His research focuses on Buddhist spiritual care based on early Buddhist and Daoist yogic teachings informed by somatic trauma therapy and depth psychology. He is the editor of *An Anthology of 50 Discourses from the Samyutta Nikaya* under the pen name Dhammabodhi. He is the author of the article "The Dependent Origination of Whiteness" from the ethnic studies journal *Kalfou*, which analyzes white supremacy from a trauma-informed early Buddhist perspective. He is a cofounder of, and minister in, the Dhamma Vinaya Order. He is the editor of *The New Order* on Substack and the host of the *Down with the Dharma* podcast.

M. Jan Holton is associate professor of the practice of pastoral theology and care at Duke University Divinity School. Her work focuses on the psychodynamic implications of trauma and forced displacement, the intercultural dynamics within pastoral care, and pastoral care to marginalized populations. She is the author of two books, *Building the Resilient Community* and *Longing for Home: Forced Displacement and Postures of Hospitality.* Jan is an ordained elder in the United Methodist Church.

Nazila Isgandarova has a PhD from the University of Toronto, a doctor of ministry degree in pastoral counselling, marriage, and family studies from Wilfrid Laurier University, and a master of social work from the University of Windsor. She is a Registered Psychotherapist at the College for Registered

Psychotherapists of Ontario and a Registered Social Worker at the Ontario College of Social Workers and Social Service Workers. Nazila is the recipient of the Champion of Diversity Award and Ontario Volunteer Service Award of the Ontario government, the Order of Vaughan, the Forum for Theological Exploration Research Award for her study on domestic violence against Muslim women, the Canadian Association for Spiritual Care Senior Research Award, and the Society for Pastoral Counselling Research Award. Nazila is an assistant professor at Emmanuel College of Victoria University in the University of Toronto. She is the author of *Muslim Women, Domestic Violence, and Psychotherapy: Theological and Clinical Issues* (Routledge 2018) and *Islamic Spiritual Care; Theory and Practice(s)* (Pandora Press 2019).

Ryan LaMothe is professor of pastoral care and counseling at Saint Meinrad Seminary and School of Theology. Ryan has authored numerous books and articles in the areas of political pastoral theology, psychoanalysis, and psychology of religion. His most recent monographs are *Care of Souls, Care of Polis: Toward a Political Pastoral Theology*, *The Coming Jesus and the Anthropocene*, *Pastoral Care in the Anthropocene Age*, and *A Political Psychoanalysis for the Anthropocene Age*.

Jessica Chapman Lape is a womanist pastoral theologian, clinically trained chaplain, and community trained birthworker. She is ordained in the United Church of Christ. Jessica has authored several peer-reviewed articles at the intersections of spirituality and public health. Her scholarship engages womanist pastoral methodologies to explore African American women's cultural and spiritual practices of health, health care, and healing justice.

Keith A. Menhinick is lecturer in religious studies at Georgia State University. His research focuses on lived religion, spiritual care, and trauma resiliency in marginalized communities, particularly the LGBTQ+ community. He is also a certified teacher of the Community Resiliency Model (CRM)® through the Trauma Resource Institute and an ordained minister in the Alliance of Baptists.

Hee-Kyu Heidi Park is an associate professor of practical theology and pastoral counseling in the Christian Studies Department at Ewha Womans University in Seoul. Her current research focuses on the boundary experiences of the empire, examined through a series of qualitative explorations. The postcolonial concept of spectrality plays a crucial role, both as a foundation for her research methodology and as a descriptive concept in her work. Her upcoming publication *The Movement of the Heart: Understanding Biblical Engagement for Transformation* examines evangelical laypersons' experiences of spiritual transformation in Bible reading through the lens of psychology and postcolonialism. Heidi is a teaching elder of the Presbyterian Church (USA) and an affiliate pastor of Hyanglin Church in Seoul.

Cody J. Sanders is associate professor of congregational and community care leadership at Luther Seminary, St. Paul, Minnesota, and a faculty member at the Center for Chaplaincy Studies. He is a former parish pastor and chaplain serving both Harvard and MIT. He has published several books, including *Spiritual Care First Aid: An All-Hands Approach for Church and Community*, *Corpse Care: Ethics for Tending the Dead*, and *A Brief Guide to Ministry with LGBTQIA Youth*. Cody is an ordained Baptist minister (Alliance of Baptists and American Baptist Churches).

Jill L. Snodgrass is professor of theology at Loyola University Maryland. Her research focuses on spiritual care and counseling with traditionally marginalized populations. She is the editor of *The Art of Spiritual Care Across Religious Difference*, coauthor of *Moral Injury After Abortion: Exploring the Psychospiritual Impact on Catholic Women*, author of *Women Leaving Prison: Justice-Seeking Spiritual Support for Female Returning Citizens*, coeditor of *Understanding Pastoral Counseling*, and author of numerous peer-reviewed articles. Jill is an ordained minister in the United Church of Christ.

INTRODUCTION

Expanding Psychospiritual Understandings of Stress, Trauma, and Growth

M. Jan Holton and Jill L. Snodgrass

PERCEPTIONS OF TRAUMA in US culture, and arguably across the world, employ a hyperfocused lens that problematizes individual symptoms and behaviors and resists any shift in our gaze. In the face of blatant forms of violence and aggression that seem ever-present, especially for people living on the margins, this focus may not seem unreasonable. But to examine the cultural pervasiveness of trauma as a concept, we must pull the lens back to a much wider view. There, on the periphery, begins to emerge a lurking shadow that is the legacies of colonialism and capitalism that shape the world, along with the norms, expectations, and injuries with which we contend today. This shadow informs our religious, political, and cultural beliefs and practices, which affect individuals and communities differently depending on our proximity to power and privilege; nonetheless, we are all deeply influenced by this reality.

Shadows, including the shadows of colonialism and capitalism, are only seen in relation to light and our relative location. For the most privileged, those who metaphorically live at high noon, the shadow can all but disappear, allowing them the possibility to never acknowledge its reality. For so many others, in fact most global inhabitants, the light reveals the lurking effects of oppression and greed, and a world on fire sparked by their continuing legacy.

Whether the chaos resulting from colonialism and capitalism is now more prevalent than ever before, or merely fewer of us can ignore its impact, is a matter of debate. Nonetheless, it is difficult to ignore the conflict and threat, armed and otherwise, reverberating across the globe, whether as efforts to reclaim domination or in resistance to it. We are overwhelmed. The increasing environmental and political ambiguities, not to mention those natural to the course of human life, continually stir anxieties that we are ill-prepared to tolerate. This inability to tolerate ambiguity leaves us grasping for ways to name what lurks behind the feelings.

Pastoral theologian Ryan LaMothe reminds us that we cannot ignore this global, macro view because "suffering and care are inextricably bound to political and economic realities," and failure to recognize the impact of these forces leaves us more likely to "collude unwittingly with these forces that lead to harm instead of devising interventions that are aimed at resisting and changing these forces and structures."[1] This complicity can magnify all our suffering and add to a sense of confusion and of feeling overwhelmed.

Naming the Feeling of Being Overwhelmed

When we put everyday distressing experiences in the context of ongoing and escalating existential threats unfolding around us, it can become more difficult for us to find the words to express the distress or suffering we feel. In her seminal work *The Body in Pain: The Making and Unmaking of the World*, Elaine Scarry, professor of aesthetics and general theory of value at Harvard University, examines the inexpressibility, linguistically speaking, of physical pain.[2] Pain creates a barrier between self and others because there are no words to join the suffering of one in pain with a sympathetic other. Scarry makes clear that she is speaking of physical pain, the pain of torture to be specific, rather than psychological pain such as grief and the like. And yet, one cannot help but see parallels with what seems a cultural inability to find a language to express the pain stemming from the broad types of distress experienced today. This dearth of distress language, accompanied by increasing distress, causes us to grasp for a concept that speaks sufficiently to the depth of our experience and validates our suffering, a psychological concept like trauma.

Here we find the paradox: left unnamed and unexamined, the imprint of stress and trauma not only shapes the lives of individuals and

---

1 Ryan LaMothe, *Care of Souls, Care of Polis: Toward a Political Pastoral Theology* (Eugene, OR: Cascade Books, 2017), 3–5. LaMothe is speaking here of ministers and by extension other spiritual caregivers, but his insight is applicable to us all.

2 Elaine Scarry, *The Body in Pain: The Making and Unmaking of the World* (New York: Oxford University Press, 1985).

communities but can continue, cascading through subsequent generations. Yet, naming experiences as traumatic *without discernment* can increase distress and impede the growth and wisdom needed to navigate the natural ambiguities of life, as well as those imposed upon us. Rebranding current or collective historical wounds according to a Western biomedical model can ignore or negate culturally specific traditions and languages for distress, which can potentially create harms of another kind. *Reframing Trauma* explores the need to reconceptualize trauma and reframe it as part of a stress-trauma continuum, particularly given the way trauma can engender great suffering as well as resistance, and even the possibility of transformation.[3] Our desire is to better interpret and convey the effects of suffering that lead to distress of all kinds without over-legitimizing trauma and minimizing distress.

The Manifestation of the Experience

Regardless of the embedded legacies that lead to this point, or how we describe them, experiences of stress and trauma do not affect only one part of us. The complexity of being human is that distress and suffering impact the cross section of our spirits, minds, and bodies. The context and shape of these experiences are so various that we cannot possibly name them all. *Reframing Trauma* explores traditions and practices that interpret trauma through a somatic lens of regeneration and growth as well as the intentional degradation imposed across cultures when sexual violence against the female body is used as a tool of war. We examine a non-Western cultural struggle with particularities of collective historical violence as well as those generated by the legacy of enslavement and ongoing oppression. Examining these manifestations of distress and trauma leads us to reclaim the spiritual flourishing and growth such experiences can engender, while still honoring the internal "dis-ease" within individuals and communities that so often results.

---

3 Catherine N. Dulmus and Carolyn Hilarski, "When Stress Constitutes Trauma and Trauma Constitutes Crisis: The Stress-Trauma-Crisis Continuum," *Brief Treatment and Crisis Intervention* 3, no. 1 (2003): 27–35, https://doi.org/10.1093/brief-treatment/mhg008.

Psychospiritual Wisdom and the Dis-ease of Stress and Trauma

Experiences such as those noted above that fall along a stress-trauma continuum frequently result in spiritual dis-ease, a lack of harmony in our relationships with self, others, creation, and—for followers of the Abrahamic traditions—God. *Reframing Trauma* considers the nature and the impact of spiritual dis-ease by drawing upon wisdom proffered by several spiritual and religious traditions including Christianity, Buddhism, and Islam. Each of the book's contributing authors occupies a distinctive religious location, and the ways we engage these traditions or locations psychospiritually is deeply informed by matters of race, ethnicity, gender, sexual orientation, age, socioeconomic status, and geographic home.[4]

We (Jan and Jill), along with many of the book's contributing authors, are members of the Society for Pastoral Theology (SPT), "a community of scholars, teachers, students, and practitioners of care committed to enriching the discipline of pastoral theology and advancing its role in equipping people for ministry."[5] Members and friends of SPT have worked to foster greater religious and spiritual diversity and inclusion in the Society and the discipline, yet the Christocentric roots of "pastoral" theology continue to privilege hegemonic Christian theologies and worldviews. Despite our best efforts, we find this troublesome dynamic replicated in this volume. *Reframing Trauma* aims to shift the discussion of stress and trauma and incorporate diverse theological and psychospiritual perspectives, yet it falls short of the goal. Even our best efforts are inadequate. It is against this backdrop that we (Jan and Jill), as practicing Christians, draw from Christian theological language and constructs,[6] turning particularly to the wisdom of existential theologian Paul Tillich,

---

4 Kathleen J. Greider, "Religious Location and Counseling: Engaging Diversity and Difference in Views of Religion," in *The Art of Spiritual Care Across Religious Difference*, rev. ed., ed. Jill L. Snodgrass (Minneapolis: Fortress Press, 2024), 17–53.

5 "About Us," Society for Pastoral Theology, accessed March 28, 2024, https://societyforpastoraltheology.org/about-us/.

6 Our distinctive religious locations bias our perspectives on the psychospirituality of trauma. In chapter 1, further insight into Jan's and Jill's respective religious locations is offered to demonstrate the privileges that bias our perspectives on making meaning from affliction and seeking hope.

to frame the spiritual dis-ease that can result from experiences of stress and trauma.[7]

Experiences of stress and trauma can bring us face-to-face with our finitude. We encounter our finite nature in multiple ways, not the least of which is when we encounter what Tillich calls the threat of nonbeing.[8] The most obvious threats of nonbeing are felt via "actual or threatened death, serious injury, or sexual violence" (Criterion A in the definition of post-traumatic stress disorder in the *Diagnostic and Statistical Manual of Mental Disorders*[DSM-5-TR].)[9] But nonbeing also arises in the form of emptiness and meaninglessness, and in guilt and moral self-reproach. We see this when we experience distress while participating in the suffering and extinction of nonhuman species (see chapter 4), in the effects of violence passed down by generations of African American women (see chapter 2), and in the effects of genocidal rape (see chapter 6). Encountering our finitude results in uncertainty, angst, and existential anxiety, or what social work scholar Allan Hugh Cole Jr. termed the *disquieted soul.*[10]

Dis-ease, or the disquieted soul, threatens our rootedness in God, the Ground of Being.[11] Experiences of stress and trauma can compromise or disrupt our spiritual lives in four foundational realms: our understanding of God, our relationship with God, our personal purpose or *tikkun*, and fear of death (mortal concerns).[12] When spiritual dis-ease arises in one or more of these four realms, our rootedness in God can be injured to such an extent that it feels irreparable. The world, with its hyper-focused lens attuned to symptoms and behaviors of "trauma," proffers countless forms of unhelpful "treatment," or ways to manage such damaged roots: drugs and alcohol, excessive sleeping or eating, isolation, conspicuous consumption, and more. St. Ignatius of Loyola referred to these as unhealthy or disordered

7 Paul Tillich, *Systematic Theology*, vol. 1 (Chicago: University of Chicago Press, 1951).

8 Tillich, *Systematic Theology*.

9 American Psychiatric Association, *Diagnostic and Statistical Manual of Mental Disorders*, 5th ed., Text Revision (Washington, DC: American Psychiatric Association, 2022), https://doi.org/10.1176/appi.books.9780890425787.

10 Allan Hugh Cole Jr., *Be Not Anxious: Pastoral Care of Disquieted Souls* (Grand Rapids, MI: Eerdmans, 2008).

11 Tillich, *Systematic Theology*.

12 Cole Jr., *Be Not Anxious*, 14.

attachments, things and relationships we attach to that keep us from authentic connection with God.[13] Disordered attachments can include people, material objects, titles and occupations, physical states, and more, many of which have trickled down through the legacies of colonialism and capitalism. Disordered attachments only deepen our estrangement from self, other, and God. When experiences of stress and trauma bring us face-to-face with our finitude and resulting dis-ease, the only way to repair the damage and re-root oneself in God is by embracing hope.

The Hope to Face Dis-ease

Too often trauma and resilience are framed as dichotomous constructs and experiences. Resilience is considered the defeat of trauma—that is, an outcome—when, according to both scriptural and spiritual wisdom, resilience is also a process that co-occurs alongside adversity.[14] Psychospiritual wisdom from various traditions details what it means to experience, often simultaneously, trauma and resilience, despair and hope. Examples of such wisdom are provided in chapter 1.

Consider even now, for example, how Tillich unpacked an understanding of the anxiety produced when we confront our nonbeing and finitude as well as the need to embrace such anxiety with courage.[15] When humans experience the anxiety of nonbeing, anxiety grounded in our mortality, meaninglessness, and immorality, our spiritual response should not be to dispel, disregard, or deaden the anxiety but to embrace it with courage. Such courage is rooted in a hope made possible by the Ground of Being, by God. According to Tillich, when humans have the courage to be amid the anxiety that so often emerges from experiences of stress and trauma, the true power of being is revealed. The hope to face dis-ease, the courage to be, cannot be found in disordered attachments. It is found in God and manifests as the co-occurrence of resilience amid adversity, growth amid trauma.

---

13 Louis J. Puhl, *The Spiritual Exercises of St. Ignatius: Translation Based on Studies in the Language of the Autograph* (Chicago: Loyola Press, 2021).

14 Mary Beth Werdel and Robert J. Wicks, *Primer in Posttraumatic Growth: An Introduction and Guide* (Hoboken, NJ: Wiley, 2012).

15 Paul Tillich, *The Courage to Be*, 2nd ed. (New Haven, CT: Yale University Press, 2000).

The nine chapters of *Reframing Trauma* demonstrate how hope amid the dis-ease that can result from experiences of stress and trauma is found in the Ground of Being—variously conceptualized in different psychospiritual wisdoms. However, given that current psychological conceptualizations of trauma are deeply rooted in the legacies of colonialism and capitalism, and the way such definitions are exported globally, we seek to guard against enforcing a universal, hegemonic theory of trauma as hope-filled. Rather, we wish to give language to those who, as an outgrowth of their psychospiritual commitments, wish to shift their narratives of stress and trauma by recognizing the authentic goodness that can exist amid the evil.

Dialogue Partners

Scholars in the disciplines of pastoral psychology, pastoral care and counseling, and spiritually integrated psychotherapy have, for many years, been working to name what is distinctive about these disciplines' perspectives on trauma. Shelly Rambo's perspectives on trauma elevate the growth and new life that can emerge from the wounding of trauma.[16] Storm Swain's contributions on the potential for transformation amid trauma invite readers to consider the potential for transformation amid trauma in situations of moral and natural evil, including natural disasters, acts of terror, and the recent Covid-19 pandemic.[17] Jennifer Baldwin employs somatic studies and internal family systems (IFS), a psychotherapeutic model, to posit ways of thinking theologically about trauma that honor resilience and recovery.[18] Brooke Petersen elevates the experience of religious trauma among queer people in nonaccepting faith communities and the potential for post-traumatic growth (PTG).[19] Chanequa Walker-Barnes reveals the deep harms to Black women

16 Shelly Rambo, *Spirit and Trauma: A Theology of Remaining* (Louisville, KT: Westminster John Knox Press, 2010); Shelly Rambo, *Resurrecting Wounds: Living in the Afterlife of Trauma* (Waco, TX: Baylor University Press, 2017).

17 Storm Swain, *Trauma and Transformation at Ground Zero: A Pastoral Theology* (Minneapolis: Fortress Press, 2011); Storm Swain, "Embodied Coping in COVID 19 Crisis," YouTube video, 19:38, March 26, 2020, https://www.youtube.com/watch?v=a5QESAGOPJo.

18 Jennifer Baldwin, *Trauma-Sensitive Theology: Thinking Theologically in the Era of Trauma* (Eugene, OR: Cascade Books, 2018).

19 Brooke N. Petersen, *Religious Trauma: Queer Stories in Estrangement and Return* (Lanham, MD: Lexington Books, 2022).

when the stereotype of the strong Black woman perpetuates existing trauma while creating new ones.[20] Mary Beth Werdel incorporates the role of meaning making that can be life giving as part of the fundamental framework of trauma and growth.[21] Cody J. Sanders names the theological narratives that violate queer souls and contribute to suicide among LGBTQ+ people as well as the practices of care that support resilience and resistance.[22] *Reframing Trauma* contributes to an enduring theological narrative of trauma that honors the co-occurring realities of woundedness and growth.

An Overview of the Book

Reframing Trauma includes nine chapters that paradoxically expand and narrow our conceptions of trauma by attending to experiences of stress and trauma in various contexts, cultures, and peoples. Each contribution is grounded in a strength-based approach to trauma that contextualizes our societal negativity bias within spiritual values of hope, (post-traumatic) growth, and (possibly) resilience while not diminishing the very real suffering, even despairing effects, that emerge from stress and trauma of all kinds. Each chapter supports the following three core assertions: (1) trauma is an ever-evolving concept, therefore, indiscriminately describing everything from the world's response to the Covid-19 pandemic to a mass shooting as traumatic is arcane, inaccurate, and unhelpful; (2) notwithstanding the Western belief in the supremacy and universality of biomedical models of trauma, other cultures have valid ways of understanding and addressing the effects of extreme experiences—what we would call traumatic—as well as ways of fostering resilience and growth; and (3) theological and spiritual wisdom offers insight into how stressful and traumatic experiences can be both life-limiting and life-giving, both despairing and the impetus for growth and resilience.

Chapter 1, "Psychospirituality and Trauma: A Theoretical and Theological Foundation," interrogates and reframes overly narrow, life-limiting

---

20 Chanequa Walker-Barnes, *Too Heavy a Yoke: Black Women and the Burden of Strength* (Eugene, OR: Cascade Books, 2014).

21 Mary Beth Werdel, *The Paradox of Trauma and Growth in Pastoral and Spiritual Care: Night Blooming* (Lanham, MD: Lexington Books, 2024).

22 Cody J. Sanders, *Christianity, LGBTQ Suicide, and the Souls of Queer Folk* (Lanham, MD: Lexington Books, 2020).

conceptions of trauma. Although biomedical definitions of trauma are essential for diagnosis and treatment, they are necessarily designed to serve the larger biomedical system. We (Jan and Jill) argue that the medicalization of distress as a cultural phenomenon both influences, and is influenced by, Christian theological anthropology. This theology is one that makes distress and trauma not just unfortunate but a punishment to be avoided at all costs, and it contributes to the Christian tradition's sometimes narrow focus on the woundedness and suffering of Christ and his followers. A reframed psychospiritual theology of trauma recognizes that the cross is only one end of a continuum of suffering reflected in the life of Jesus. Christians must also honor the resilience in the face of traumatic experience that leads to hope, meaning, and even new life in a postcrucifixion world.

In chapter 2, "A Womanist Psychospirituality: Gendering and Racializing Trauma and Resilience," Jessica Chapman Lape details the interconnected nature of African American women's trauma and resilience, and its relation to white supremacy. Lape argues that trauma hinders or destroys African American women's psychospirituality; however, it is because of African American women's intersecting identities that they maintain unique mechanisms for resisting and confronting stress and trauma. Such acts of resilience are adaptive and generative, and maintain the potential to preserve, protect, and, at times, reinforce a psychospirituality in the intergenerational, communal, and individual lives of African American women.

In chapter 3, "The Psychospiritual Trauma of LGBTQ+ People and Communities: Depathologizing Queer Lives and Experiences," Keith A. Menhinick and Cody J. Sanders explore how family rejection, religious/spiritual violence, homelessness, adverse school experience, interpersonal violence, and related experiences are common among LGBTQ+ people and communities. The very conditions of sexual and gender "deviance" (queerness and transness) can give rise to a kind of chronic stress, liable to turn traumatic, as a kind of regulatory and disciplinary function of society's intent to annihilate or assimilate LGBTQ+ life. Menhenick and Sanders demonstrate how collective efforts in the LGBTQ+ community to demedicalize and depathologize trauma help to externalize the source of violence from a problem of the individual to a problem of the social environment.

In chapter 4, "Ontological Psychospirituality: The Stress and Trauma of Other Species," Ryan LaMothe argues that more-than-human species have continuously experienced suffering, stress, and trauma at the hands of human beings, and that the experience will only increase as the effects of climate change worsen. Abrahamic scriptures along with Western political philosophies and theologies have served as apparatuses to produce and maintain an ontological rift between human beings and other species. This rift leads to the exclusion of other species from political questions of human dwelling, which then legitimates the instrumental and callous exploitation of other species and results in their sufferings and traumas. LaMothe posits the notion of an inoperative pastoral care as a counter to the ontological rift, inviting more empathic, compassionate, and inclusive relations with more-than-human species.

In chapter 5, "Psychospiritual Stress, Trauma, and Migration: Understandings for Displaced Communities," Eunil David Cho argues that as migrants flee their homelands due to wars, poverty, natural disasters, political violence, social injustice, and colonial oppressions, migration stress and trauma are inherently collective, cumulative, and intercultural experiences. According to Cho, the prevailing model of trauma is insufficient to examine and address these dimensions of migration. In addition, the current biomedical model of trauma often overlooks the significance of religion and spirituality in people's experience of transnational migration. Thus, intercultural understanding and treatment of migrants' traumatic experience requires a sociocultural analysis to understand how migrants, individually and collectively, engage resources, such as religious rituals and indigenous spiritualities, to cope with their losses and make new meaning toward recovery and healing.

In chapter 6, "Psychospirituality and Genocidal Rape: Stress, Trauma, and Post-Traumatic Growth in Victim-Survivors," Nazila Isgandarova addresses the topics of genocidal rape and war. She argues that the threat to life also enhances the will to live because humans have the capacity to respond to everyday life with its challenges and adversities in a positive, resilient way. Resilience and PTG show that health can co-occur with, and follow, trauma. The chapter features stories of resilient women who suffered genocidal rape amid wars and reveals the transformative power of resilience in women who are victims of war. These women find ways to transcend their experience of trauma and find new meaning in life. Spirituality often plays a role in PTG, and likewise, pharmacotherapy and other sources can help women to stimulate the resilience process.

In chapter 7, "The Psychospirituality of Historical Trauma in South Korea: Mapping the Colonial Legacy," Hee-Kyu Heidi Park posits that the impact of historical traumas like colonization and wars haunts the lives of individuals, families, and communities across the generations. There are multiple efforts to define such trauma experiences apart from the medical model. However, the particularities of historical trauma sometimes create dissonance in such understandings, calling for further articulation. The collective trauma and communal experiences in South Korea highlight the tensions in understanding historical trauma. Yet, spectrality, acknowledgment of or engagement with ghosts and spirits, can help to address the subjectivities of the complex personhood emerging out of stress and trauma. Such spectrality moves the subjects toward the future, offering a psychospiritual way of proceeding.

In chapter 8, "A Buddhist Psychospirituality of Trauma: A Critical Correlation of Vipassana Meditation and Somatic Experiencing," John B. Freese contends that Buddhism and trauma therapy in the United States largely focus on insight, or *vipassana*, meditation as taught by the Insight Meditation Society and Spirit Rock. Freese argues that current theories can be advanced by incorporating somatic experiencing therapy and the *vipassana* teachings of Goenka Vipassana as they are strikingly similar. Exploring the distinctions between early Buddhist yogic, later Buddhist scholastic, and modern scientific scholastic traditions of theory and practice evidences the similarities between Goenka Vipassana and somatic experiencing theory and practice. Such insights lay the groundwork for a revised theory of trauma-informed Buddhist spiritual care and counseling.

In chapter 9, "A Reframed Psychospirituality of Stress and Trauma: Honoring the Complexity of Lived Experience," we (Jan and Jill) posit revised understandings of God, creation, and humans, while incorporating the wisdom of other religious and spiritual traditions, to offer an expanded understanding of the psychospirituality of trauma and resilience. This reframed theology rejects the notion that suffering, stress, and trauma are rooted solely in human moral failings and a subsequent divine punishment. Rather, it explores the relational ruptures associated with stress and trauma and the various ways belonging is lost as a result. Yet even amid a loss of belonging, resilience—rooted in God who is the relational center for all belonging—can co-occur with stress and trauma. We argue that resilience amid stress and trauma can be enhanced through trauma narratives, somatic practices, meaning making, and post-traumatic growth.

The book's conclusion, "Moving from Theory to Practice," offers four case studies that invite the reader to consider the implications of this reframed psychospirituality of stress and trauma for spiritual caregiving. The case studies privilege an intercultural approach, stressing the importance of contextual caregiving that values multiple perspectives and authentic participation. Each case study focuses on one of the following distinctive contexts and modalities of care: hospital chaplaincy, congregational care, spiritually integrated psychotherapy, and nonprofit/non-governmental organization (NGO) care. The case studies highlight the theological implications of a theoretical reframing of trauma.

An Invitation

Reframing Trauma: A Psychospiritual Theory and Theology reframes trauma as a stress-trauma continuum that eschews the sentiment, ubiquitous in popular culture, that everything stressful is traumatic as well as the notion that so-called true trauma is defined by the DSM-5-TR. As you consider this reframed understanding of trauma, and the way it is demonstrated amid contemporary global challenges of racism, eco-violence, and myriad sociopolitical and interpersonal injustices, we invite you to engage this as a work in progress and to claim the contributions made by your own theoretical insights, lived experiences, and pastoral and clinical engagement. While theoretical conceptions of trauma grounded in the stress-trauma continuum offer a positive reframing of the construct, psychospiritual wisdom continues to inform how such understandings might continue to be reframed and refined in a manner that honors experiences of stress and trauma alongside the co-occurring realities of resilience and growth.

1

PSYCHOSPIRITUALITY AND TRAUMA

A Theoretical and Theological Foundation

M. Jan Holton and Jill L. Snodgrass

TRAUMA HAS MANY types, and it is variously defined according to differences in discipline and context. Definitions of trauma are intended to describe a phenomenon or lived experience, yet they also inform how humans experience the self, relationships, events, and the world. The American Psychological Association (APA) defines trauma, in a general sense, as "an emotional response to a terrible event such as an accident, rape, or natural disaster."[1] All aspects of creation, including but not limited to humans, endure terrible events. The pervasiveness of such terrible events seemingly supports the attitude, rather ubiquitous in the United States, that everything stressful is traumatic. Yet, not every terrible event is traumatic simply because it is distressing. Many medical and mental health professionals argue that only experiences that entail "actual or threatened death, serious injury, or sexual violence" constitute *real* trauma.[2] Racism, eco-violence, and myriad sociopolitical and interpersonal injustices continuously injure individuals, communities, and the planet, thereby challenging existence. Even so, the biomedical model of trauma put forth in the DSM-5-TR with its emphasis on pathology fails to acknowledge the traumatic nature of these many diffuse and persistent injuries that humans endure.[3] Amid the varying conceptualizations of trauma, the disciplines of pastoral theology, spiritual care,

1 *American Psychological Association Dictionary of Psychology Online*, "Trauma," accessed January 9, 2024, https://dictionary.apa.org/trauma.

2 American Psychiatric Association, *Diagnostic and Statistical Manual of Mental Disorders*, 5th ed., Text Revision (Washington, DC: American Psychiatric Association, 2022), https://doi.org/10.1176/appi.books.9780890425787.

3 American Psychiatric Association, *Diagnostic and Statistical Manual.*

and spiritually integrated psychology are uniquely poised to reconceptualize trauma and reframe it as part of a stress-trauma continuum, particularly given the way trauma can engender great suffering as well as resistance and even the possibility of transformation.[4]

It is important to acknowledge some of the tensions faced in endeavoring to reconceptualize and reframe trauma. At its core, this is an epistemological enterprise that requires more holistic understandings of "how we know what we know."[5] It requires thinking more broadly as well as more narrowly about how trauma is defined, but most importantly, thinking *differently.* Most essential is that we value ways of knowing that are central to non-Western, Black, Indigenous, and people of color (BIPOC), even if those ways of knowing are in tension with the medicalization of trauma privileged in the United States. While biomedical definitions of trauma are essential for diagnosis and treatment, they are necessarily narrow, limited, and designed to serve the larger biomedical system. Our aim is not to alter how trauma is defined in the DSM-5-TR. Nonetheless, we find it imperative to push against definitions of trauma that fail to acknowledge insidious terrible events such as those stemming from racism in the United States or the resilience via resistance that so often co-occurs. The effort to reframe understandings of trauma and push beyond the medical model is rooted in theoretical research as well as empirical research.[6]

---

4 Catherine N. Dulmus and Carolyn Hilarski, "When Stress Constitutes Trauma and Trauma Constitutes Crisis: The Stress-Trauma-Crisis Continuum," *Brief Treatment and Crisis Intervention* 3, no. 1 (2003): 27–35, https://doi.org/10.1093/brief-treatment/mhg008.

5 bell hooks, *Teaching to Transgress: Education as the Practice of Freedom* (New York: Routledge, 1994), 174.

6 George A. Bonanno and Anthony D. Mancini, "Beyond Resilience and PTSD: Mapping the Heterogeneity of Responses to Potential Trauma," *Psychological Trauma: Theory, Research, Practice, and Policy* 4, no. 1 (2012): 74–83, https://doi.org/10.1037/a0017829; B. Christopher Frueh et al., "Documented Combat Exposure of US Veterans Seeking Treatment for Combat-Related Post-Traumatic Stress Disorder," *British Journal of Psychiatry* 186, no. 6 (2005): 467–472, https://doi.org/10.1192/bjp.186.6.467; Valery Krupnik, "Trauma or Adversity?," *Traumatology* 25, no. 4 (2019): 256–261, http://dx.doi.org/10.1037/trm0000169; Anthony J. Marsella et al., "Ethnocultural Aspects of PTSD: Some Closing Thoughts," in *Ethnocultural Aspects of Posttraumatic Stress Disorder: Issues, Research, and Clinical Applications*, ed. Anthony J. Marsella, Matthew J. Friedman, Ellen T. Gerrity, and Raymond M. Scurfield, (Washington, DC: American Psychological Association, 1996), 529–538,

Method and Positionality

Pastoral theology, spiritual care, and spiritually integrated psychology are inherently interdisciplinary. Theorists and practitioners in the fields aim to be "bilingual" in the "languages" of psychology and theology/religious studies.[7] Questions of how these disciplines are integrated have endured for decades and present epistemological challenges.[8] Theologian Ian Barbour posited four common methods for managing the epistemic tension between science and religion: conflict, independence, dialogue, and integration.[9] In seeking to reconceptualize and reframe trauma, we employ an integrative method wherein we view psychology and theology/religious studies as allied, mutually informing disciplines. Coherence between the two is possible because knowledge is always both constructed and revealed. The psychological sciences, and some may argue theology, aim for objectivity and neutrality, yet both are culturally informed and constructed. Therefore, we do not place primacy upon biomedical/psychological insight nor upon theological/religious wisdom. Rather, we aim to understand how the wisdom from each can be integrated toward a coherent conception of trauma that is both culturally relevant and liberative.

Although we take an integrative approach, our religious locations and other aspects of our social identities and lived experiences dispose us to view the psychological with a hermeneutic of hope.[10] As two white, cisgender, heterosexual females, we each experience myriad privileges in the United States. We are both ordained in Christian denominations (Jan in the United

---

https://doi.org/10.1037/10555-022; Michelle R. Spoont et al., "From Trauma to PTSD: Beliefs about Sensations, Symptoms, and Mental Illness," *Qualitative Health Research* 19, no. 10 (2009): 1456–1465, https://doi.org/10.1177/1049732309348370; Bessel A. van der Kolk et al., "Disorders of Extreme Stress: The Empirical Foundation of a Complex Adaptation to Trauma," *Journal of Traumatic Stress* 18, no. 5 (2005): 389–399, https://doi.org/10.1002/jts.20047.

7 Carrie Doehring, "The Challenges of Being Bilingual: Methods of Integrating Psychological and Religious Studies," in *Understanding Pastoral Counseling*, ed. Elizabeth A. Maynard and Jill L. Snodgrass (New York: Springer, 2015), 87–99.

8 Loren Townsend, *Introduction to Pastoral Counseling* (Nashville: Abingdon Press, 2009).

9 Ian Barbour, *Religion and Science* (San Fransisco: HarperSanFrancisco, 1990).

10 Kathleen Greider, "Religious Location and Counseling: Engaging Diversity and Difference in Views of Religion," in *Navigating Religious Difference in Spiritual Care and Counseling: Essays in Honor of Kathleen J. Greider*, ed. Jill L. Snodgrass (Claremont: Claremont Press, 2019), 11–44.

Methodist Church and Jill in the United Church of Christ), which biases us toward making deliberative meaning from affliction and seeking hope, practices most surely facilitated in part by our privileges.

My (Jan's) worldview is strongly impacted, personally and professionally, by my research over the years in refugee camps and conflict areas (in South Sudan and the Democratic Republic of the Congo) with persons who have experienced war, famine, and violence in many forms. From them I have learned much about what we would call trauma as well as the many ways that people are resilient in the face of circumstances that cause despair. I am resolute in the inclusion of a cultural (and intercultural) lens through which to ask questions of God, faith, and the human predicament. I attempt, though imperfectly to be sure, to live into a vigilant stance of practicing and building social empathy in the world I inhabit.

My (Jill's) perspectives on trauma are influenced, in part, by my own experiences of distress that are often classified in US culture, accurately or not, as traumatic. My experience teaching undergraduate students amid the Covid-19 pandemic has shown me that the mental health crisis facing youth and emerging adults in the United States is indisputable, yet students frequently consider their distress to be symptomatic of trauma.[11] Certainly, their psycho-social-emotional development impacts how they appraise and construct their experiences. But culture also seems to support distorted appraisals of distress and coping.

Current Cultural Constructions of Trauma

The use of the term *trauma* to describe personal distress has become so ubiquitous as to cause a recent *New York Times* opinion editor to ask: If everything is "trauma," is anything?[12] Trauma, much like depression and anxiety,

11 "US Surgeon General Issues Advisory on Youth Mental Health Crisis Further Exposed by COVID-19 Pandemic," US Department of Health & Human Services (Washington, DC: GPO, 2021), https://www.hhs.gov/about/news/2021/12/07/us-surgeon-general-issues-advisory-on-youth-mental-health-crisis-further-exposed-by-covid-19-pandemic.html.

12 Jessica Bennett, "If Everything is 'Trauma,' is Anything?," *New York Times*, February 4, 2022, https://www.nytimes.com/2022/02/04/opinion/caleb-love-bombing-gaslighting-trauma.html.

has become a catchall term for distress. We find ourselves in a vocabulary desert when it comes to words that describe difficult events and the feelings they evoke. What most people today do know, put simply, is that post-traumatic stress disorder (PTSD) is caused by terrible events that the mind cannot wrap itself around. Of course, the clinical language for PTSD and other stressors in the DSM-5-TR is much more complex. Nonetheless, in this current era when extraordinary events seem to be outcompeting themselves, colloquial practice has come to depend heavily on the use of the term *trauma* to describe these distressing experiences. Our "idioms of distress" have narrowed to the point that any distress can be labeled traumatic.[13]

While it is easy to blame the dearth of linguistic agility on popular culture, the truth is much more complicated. Our cultural dependency on trauma language to describe psychological distress has been shaped by decades of increasing dependence on biomedical models for mental illness. In any given culture, a variety of ways exist to express distress. Expressive modes are culturally constituted in the sense that they initiate particular types of interaction and are associated with culturally pervasive values, norms, generative themes, and health concerns.[14]

In the United States and arguably in most Western societies, we depend on the formula of medical diagnosis, treatment, and cure to address our modern ills, be they physical or mental. The popular perception of mental disorders and language with which we describe them have been shaped by these clinical models to such a degree that we have lost our ability to describe them otherwise.[15] This trauma language serves to validate suffering of all kinds, particularly that over which we have little control.[16] Yet when our sole language for understanding trauma is bound by this biomedical model, we unnecessarily limit our understanding of which experiences are considered

---

13 Mark Nichter, "Idioms of Distress: Alternatives in the Expression of Psychosocial Distress—A Case Study from South India," *Culture, Medicine and Psychiatry* 5, no. 4 (1981): 379–408, https://doi.org/10.1007/BF00054782.

14 Nichter, "Idioms of Distress," 379.

15 Joseph E. Davis, *Chemically Imbalanced: Everyday Suffering, Medication, and Our Troubled Quest for Self-Mastery* (Chicago: University of Chicago Press, 2020).

16 Didier Fassin and Richard Rechtman, *The Empire of Trauma: An Inquiry into the Condition of Victimhood*, trans. Rachel Gomme (Princeton: Princeton University Press, 2009).

traumatic, what the effects of that trauma might look like in the lived experience, and even to whom (or to what creatures) we may apply the notion of trauma in the first place.

Language informs how we construct, narrate, and understand our experiences. Theorist, educator, and social critic bell hooks noted that "shifting how we think about language and how we use it, necessarily alters how we know what we know."[17] If what we come to know in the context of distressing experiences, especially in uncertain times when one seems to have no control, is consistently constructed as traumatic, it reduces the propensity toward resilience and growth. Naming all our experiences as traumatic can be life-limiting. Paradoxically, biomedical constructions of trauma limited to events that entail "actual or threatened death, serious injury, or sexual violence" can invalidate the enduring distress that some humans experience in the face of systemic oppression or multiple stresses stemming from ongoing planetary devastation.[18] In these and other situations, naming such experiences as traumatic can be a life-giving witness to the damage and strain endured. Practicing "language care" is essential to reconceptualizing trauma and reframing it as part of a stress-trauma continuum.[19] Caring for the language we employ and taking care to define that language precisely can be both a pastoral practice (or discipline) and a pastoral intervention.

The Seeming Pervasiveness of Trauma

In many ways, the Covid-19 pandemic represents a turning point in the human experience of terrible events. Though not experienced on an equal level by all globally, the awareness of the potential for illness, the ever-increasing death toll, and the accompanying deleterious racial, economic, and political repercussions are unparalleled in recent memory, if not beyond. Concurrently, the media and popular culture has magnified the traumatic potential of myriad life experiences, including identifying as LGBTQ+, running while Black, gun violence, school shootings, interpersonal violence,

---

17 hooks, *Teaching to Transgress*, 174.

18 American Psychiatric Association, *Diagnostic and Statistical Manual.*

19 Laura D. Bueckert and Daniel S. Schipani, "Interfaith Spiritual Caregiving: The Case for Language Care," in *Spiritual Caregiving in the Hospital: Windows to Chaplaincy Ministry* (Kitchener, ON: Pandora Press, 2006), 245–263.

and other terrible events.[20] The traumatic potential of everyday life has, some argue, shaped an entire generation. Maxwell Alejandro Frost, a twenty-five-year-old running for Congress in Florida's Tenth Congressional District, told an NPR interviewer, "Our generation [Gen Z] has been born into a lot of trauma and a lot of civil unrest around people being frustrated with things. And I think because of that, our generation naturally thinks about things in a bit of a different way."[21] Assertions such as these are often attempts to witness and honor suffering, but an unintended consequence can be the medicalization or the pathologizing of distress.

Over twenty years ago, psychiatrist and philosopher Patrick Bracken argued against the "trauma industry."[22] According to Bracken, biomedical conceptualizations of trauma erroneously reify universal truths about terrible events by positing that the mind, regardless of whose mind, will process such events in the same general way. Yet, not all humans' autonomic nervous systems function the same, and meaning-making is highly subjective and contextual. Humans most often make meaning of distressing events in community, not in isolation. Individuals, families, and communities conceptualize experiences of distress as traumatic in part because such conceptualizations are culturally supported in cultures where distress has been medicalized.[23]

Individually and collectively, many in the United States, particularly in this current time, seem to be struggling to cope with and manage their

20 Kurt Streeter, "Running While Black: Our Readers Respond," *New York Times* (New York City, NY), May 18, 2020; Michelle Blake, "U.S. Children Carry a Double Burden for Gun Violence and Policy Gaps," *Newsweek*, August 8, 2022, https://www.newsweek.com/us-children-carry-double-burden-gun-violence-policy-gaps-opinion-1730617; Christa Hillstrom, "The Hidden Epidemic of Brain Injuries from Domestic Violence," *New York Times Magazine*, March 1, 2022, https://www.nytimes.com/2022/03/01/magazine/brain-trauma-domestic-violence.html.

21 Elena Moore, "The First Gen Z Candidates are Running for Congress—and Running Against Compromise," All Things Considered, *National Public Radio*, July 6, 2022, https://www.npr.org/2022/07/06/1109193929/the-first-gen-z-candidates-are-running-for-congress-and-running-against-compromi.

22 Patrick Bracken, *Trauma: Culture, Meaning & Philosophy* (Hoboken, NJ: Wiley, 2002).

23 Ross G. White, Sumeet Jain, David M. R. Orr, and Ursula M. Read, eds., *The Palgrave Handbook of Sociocultural Perspectives on Global Mental Health* (New York: Palgrave Macmillan/Springer Nature, 2017).

emotions of distress. Yet paradoxically, the medicalization of distress contributes to and supports a low tolerance of distress, which ultimately impedes our ability to cope. This is particularly problematic given that "low tolerance to distress is an important predictor of psychopathology and maladaptive health behaviors, including anxiety, depression, substance abuse, eating disorders, and borderline personality disorder," the experience of which can contribute to our self-appraisal as being "traumatized."[24]

The Movement for Global Mental Health and contemporary psychological aid to refugees exemplify the problems that Bracken raised regarding the medicalization of distress.[25] Humanitarian psychiatry has over the last twenty years exported the Western medical model of PTSD and the consequent dependence on trauma language to refugee and internal displacement camps, disaster zones, and conflict areas around the world.[26] Interestingly, there is very often a notable absence of an indigenous word for trauma or even some of the common responses to the effects of traumatic events in these other cultures. For example, there is no indigenous word for trauma in South Sudan even though they have been engaged in some level of conflict for many decades or longer.[27] Rather, as with Arabic words and cultural concepts subsumed into tribal languages, PTSD has likewise been imported to describe the specific clinical symptoms of trauma. It is difficult to believe that a people at war for decades would not have their own words to describe what are considered in the biomedical model to be universal emotions and behaviors associated with the effects of war. Some have made the argument that the South Sudanese were simply unaware of what responses one might expect from the trauma of war, a perspective that

24 Roger McIntosh, Gail Ironson, and Neal Krause, "Keeping Hope Alive: Racial-Ethnic Disparities in Distress Tolerance are Mitigated by Religious/Spiritual Hope among Black Americans," *Journal of Psychosomatic Research* 144, no. 110403 (2021): 2, https://doi.org/10.1016/j.jpsychores.2021.110403.

25 White et al., *The Palgrave Handbook*; Bracken, *Trauma: Culture, Meaning & Philosophy*.

26 Bracken, *Trauma: Culture, Meaning & Philosophy*; Fassin and Rechtman, *The Empire of Trauma*; Derek Summerfield. "A Critique of Seven Assumptions Behind Psychological Trauma Programmes in War-Affected Areas," *Social Science and Medicine* 45, no. 10 (1999): 1449–1462, https://doi.org/10.1016/s0277-9536(98)00450-x.

27 Jan Holton, *Building the Resilient Community: Lessons from the Lost Boys of Sudan* (Eugene, OR: Cascade Books, 2011).

negates the wisdom of the culture and fails to embrace the concept that the meaning of such experiences is constructed rather than a foregone outcome of a terrible event like war.

The medicalization of distress and the proliferation of the trauma industry are also evident in the qualifications for refugees seeking asylum in the United States. Refugees are required to show evidence of trauma, particularly by means of a psychiatric assessment but also through photographs of wounds and other sources of documentation.[28] This demonstrates not only the medicalization of distress but also its politicization. It is not without some degree of irony that while asylum seekers are required to be trauma victims to receive asylum, the experiences of many BIPOC, who have endured arguably the greatest degree of racism, violence, and ongoing uncertainty in the United States, do not satisfy cultural or biomedical conceptions of trauma. There is power in determining whose suffering is legitimated, or not, as being deemed trauma induced. Privileged authorities exercise this power, and we cannot escape the reality that many individuals are eager to have their experience validated and thereby be designated a trauma survivor.

From Adverse Childhood Experience to Trauma-Informed

In 1966, the National Academy of Sciences identified trauma as the most "neglected disease of our society," rendering trauma a central focal point for research across disciplines.[29] This sentiment set the groundwork for the Adverse Childhood Experiences (ACE) study, a seminal study conducted from 1995 to 1997 by the Centers for Disease Control and Prevention and Kaiser Permanente Health System that resulted in pivotal information about the correlation between the effects of various early-in-life stressors and outcomes later in life. The study has proven indispensable for large-scale public health planning and policy even today. Over the last twenty years, however, the results of the ACE study also have been pushed to the frontlines in medical, social work, and other contexts on an individual level through the use of the ACE-10 questionnaire, a ten-question assessment that attempts to measure the number

---

28 Fassin and Rechtman, *The Empire of Trauma*.

29 Committee on Trauma and Committee on Shock, *Accidental Death and Disability: The Neglected Disease of Modern Society* (Washington, DC: National Academies Press, 1966), https://www.ncbi.nlm.nih.gov/books/NBK222962/.

of specific stressors in childhood. In doing so, advocates for its use imply a causal relationship between early trauma and detrimental effects later in life. Public health researchers have strongly criticized these ACE screenings, the algorithms used to assess risk, and how they are utilized, saying:

> *Projecting the risk of health or social outcomes based on any individual's ACE score by applying grouped (or average) risk observed in epidemiologic studies can lead to significant underestimation or overestimation of actual risk; thus, the ACE score is not suitable for screening individuals and assessing risk for use in decision making about need for services or treatment [and further,] although the health conditions listed within the [ACE score] algorithm have been associated with ACEs in epidemiologic studies, most occurrences of many listed conditions are caused by factors other than ACEs.*[30]

The ACE study has also raised the question of how to train professionals to be aware of significant stressors, including trauma, in the lives of those to whom they offer services. From this has emerged a trauma-informed paradigm that now shapes the training of professionals across multiple disciplines, including health care, social work, church, and education, to name a few. Clinical psychologists Maxine Harris and Roger D. Fallot, early leaders in trauma-informed mental health practice, advocate for "administrators [to] declare their intent to make an understanding of the impact of violence and victimization an integral part of the mission of their agencies."[31] It would be difficult to argue that methods of improving the understanding of people's lives and the events that shape them is not a good thing, but, like the use of ACE testing, the push for trauma-informed services has frequently become overly reductive as it has spread beyond the mental health context.

---

30 Robert F. Anda, Laura E. Porter, and David W. Brown, "Inside the Adverse Childhood Experience Score: Strengths, Limitations, and Misapplications," *American Journal of Preventive Medicine* 59, no. 2 (2020): 293–294, https://doi.org/10.1016/j.amepre.2020.01.009.

31 Maxine Harris and Roger D. Fallot, "Envisioning a Trauma-Informed Service System: A Vital Paradigm Shift," in *Using Trauma Theory to Design Service Systems*, ed. Maxine Harris and Roger D. Fallot (Hoboken, NJ: Jossey-Bass/Wiley, 2001), 6.

Ultimately, the over-popularization of the ACE study, ACE scoring, and trauma-informed paradigms, especially through social media during the recent years of the pandemic, make us aware of the tension always at play when discerning the value and use of large-scale studies and all that trickles down from them. Surely, professionals of all sorts and the citizens they serve benefit alike from being better informed. We must stay vigilant, however, for the increasing and unhelpful ways that distortions and unexamined overuse of these same tools shape and misshape trauma discourse among the general public.

Theologies of Trauma

The medicalization of distress, a cultural phenomenon, both influences and is influenced by Christian theological anthropology as well as understandings of God and Jesus. Whether we heard it from a grandmother or a seminary professor, many of us have been deeply shaped by the notions of humankind's fallen, sinful nature and the idea that, were it not for human disobedience, human existence would be perfect, immortal, and, most importantly, free of suffering and distress. This theology makes suffering not just unfortunate but a punishment to be avoided at all costs. It is a de facto theology of distress in which we can easily become perpetually caught between what should be and what is. The theological narrative we hear less often is one in which we are created by God as the finite creatures that we are and are celebrated as good, even within all our limitedness.[32] In this view suffering, while not something to be celebrated, is still an experience of the human condition but one that comes to us without an implicit moral failing. This perspective does not mean that we do not also recognize the ways that humans always fail (in our finitude) to perfectly live into the love, expectations, and unlimited possibilities offered to us by a redeeming, loving, and grace-filled God. These are not just abstract philosophical musings. Our understanding of who we are in our naked creatureliness has practical consequences in feet-on-the-ground everyday living and particular consequences in how we shape a theology of trauma.

32 Edward Farley, *Good and Evil: Interpreting a Human Condition* (Minneapolis: Fortress Press, 1990); Paul Tillich, *Systematic Theology*, vol. 1 (Chicago: University of Chicago Press, 1951).

The emphasis on humanity's fallen nature also contributes to the Christian tradition's focus on the woundedness and suffering of Christ and his followers. Paul attributed his own woundedness, a "thorn in the flesh," to God that he might be "made perfect in weakness."[33] The belief that wounds are a conduit to faith pervaded the life of the early church, particularly when many followers endured persecution. In much of Christian theology, woundedness not only binds humans with one another in a common experience but connects humans to the suffering Christ and God. Historically, connection with the suffering Christ emboldened Christians to cope with life in a fallen world. For those who have suffered at the hands of others, the notion of living in the woundedness of Christ can draw one closer to God.

The notion that suffering and trauma are inherent to the Christian journey is part of many Christians' embedded theology.[34] Regrettably, such theological perspectives are often used to normalize distress and trauma among contemporary Christians. Similar to the way that trauma language can validate our suffering, enduring suffering can be used to validate our faithfulness as Christians. Identifying with the suffering Christ in such a manner can be helpful but in the long term can also leave sufferers stalled in victimhood and unable to envision horizons of hope. Life-limiting theological perspectives on suffering have been employed to justify violence, abuse, and oppression. Conversely, the medicalization of distress has contributed to both implicit and explicit encouragement to take pride in the "privilege to suffer as Christians . . . [for such] trials and tribulations in connection with the Savior are honorable and profitable."[35]

---

33 2 Cor. 12:9 (NSRV).

34 Howard W. Stone and James O. Duke, *How to Think Theologically*, 3rd ed. (Minneapolis: Fortress Press, 2013); Carrie Doehring, "Spiritual Care After Violence: Growing from Trauma with Lived-Theology," Biola University Center for Christian Thought, *The Table*, June 23, 2014, para. 8, https://cct.biola.edu/spiritual-care-violence-growing-trauma-lived-theology/. Drawing on the work of Stone and Duke, Carrie Doehring defines embedded theology as the "beliefs and values instilled throughout childhood, which exert an unconscious influence and surface under stress. Embedded theologies are those pre-critical and often unexamined beliefs and practices that have become a habitual part of one's worldview and practices."

35 Jenny Walker, "Suffering with Christ," *Tabletalk* 53 (2020): para. 2–3, https://tabletalkmagazine.com/article/2020/10/suffering-with-christ/.

The valorization of trauma is problematic, especially when emphasized over and above God's transforming power in a manner that leads Christians to seek suffering.[36] "That Jesus suffered and died for others to bring about salvation models behavior that Christians seek to follow," thus communicating the message that "suffering is redemptive."[37] Rather than focusing on the uniqueness of Jesus's suffering, some Christians are misguidedly emboldened to "take up their cross and follow" Jesus, sanctifying their own suffering and trauma and, in some cases, colluding with the abusive acts of perpetrators and transgressors.[38] In contrast, exhortations on suffering such as those found in Hebrews were meant to help Christians resist evil, not to condone it.[39] Rather than perpetuating evil via life-limiting theologies, Christians can act with compassion toward the transformation of trauma and suffering.[40] Shifting problematic, embedded theologies of trauma to more deliberative, life-giving theologies is necessary but can be tremendously difficult. Nonetheless, Scripture and the Christian tradition offer profound wisdom for engaging in this task.

Reframing Theologies of Trauma

Too often trauma and resilience are framed as dichotomous constructs and experiences. Resilience is considered the defeat of trauma—an outcome—when, according to both scriptural and psychological wisdom, resilience is also a process that co-occurs alongside adversity.[41] Scriptural examples of this abound. Consider how Jacob wrestled with the angel as recounted in Genesis. Jacob wrestled the angel, physically toiling throughout the night,

---

36 Bryan R. Dyer, "'A Great Conflict Full of Suffering': Suffering in the Epistle to the Hebrews in Light of Feminist Concerns," *McMaster Journal of Theology and Ministry* 12 (2010–2011): 179–198, http://www.mcmaster.ca.proxy-ln.researchport.umd.edu/mjtm/.

37 Dyer, "'A Great Conflict Full of Suffering,'" 181.

38 Matt. 16:24 (NSRV)

39 Jeanne Stevenson-Moessner, "The Road to Perfection: An Interpretation of Suffering in Hebrews," *Interpretation* 57 (2003): 280–290, https://link.gale.com/apps/doc/A105160684/AONE?u=googlescholar&sid=googleScholar&xid=23be684a.

40 John Swinton, *Raging with Compassion: Pastoral Responses to the Problem of Evil* (Grand Rapids, MI: Eerdmans, 2007).

41 Mary Beth Werdel and Robert J. Wicks, *Primer in Posttraumatic Growth: An Introduction and Guide* (Hoboken, NJ: Wiley, 2012).

until the angel departed at daybreak. Jacob received a blow to the hip that wounded him, crippling him for the rest of his life. But, despite the scars, Jacob also received a new name, Israel, meaning "one who struggles with God."[42] Amid the trauma of his battle, a metaphorical and literal confrontation with his own growing edges and with God, Jacob was simultaneously wounded and blessed by the struggle.

Likewise, the New Testament portrays Jesus, time and time again, with his "back against the wall."[43] In *Jesus and the Disinherited*, pastor, theologian, and civil rights leader Howard Thurman reminds us of the essential fact that Jesus grew up and lived as a dark-skinned Jew under the oppression of empire. Among all the interpretations of Jesus's life and death, the most important speak "to those who stand, at a moment in human history, with their backs against the wall."[44] God did not take on human form as a Roman elite but as a poor Jew. Jesus lived as an outcast facing injustice daily. But Jesus's life is ultimately one that demonstrates resilience amid oppression. He exercised power by choosing his response to the distresses of this world. Jesus taught that the alleviation of distress or the eradication of injustice would not be enacted by laws but by the ethical practice of love grounded in love of God, other, and self.

Although Jesus did not call Christians to seek trauma and suffering, the Scriptures offer numerous examples of Jesus speaking transparently about the simultaneously arduous and blessed nature of discipleship. Consider, for example, the Beatitudes recounted in Matthew. When Jesus stated, "Blessed are those who hunger and thirst for righteousness, for they will be filled," he was not foreshadowing an eschatological, otherworldly blessing.[45] It was not that the hungry *will be* blessed; they already are. The struggle for right relationship and justice is both inherently distressing and generative.

Despite these scriptural examples of co-occurring resilience and adversity, many Christian theologies of trauma focus most closely, if not entirely, on how the suffering associated with PTSD is reflected in the wounds of

---

42 Daniel J. Elazar, "Jacob and Esau and the Emergence of the Jewish People," *Judaism* 43, no. 3 (1994): 295.

43 Howard Thurman, *Jesus and the Disinherited* (New York: Beacon, 1996).

44 Thurman, *Jesus and the Disinherited.*

45 Matt. 5:6 (NRSV)

Jesus at the end of his life as he hung on a cross. This can undoubtedly be a great comfort to victims of PTSD, especially those just recognizing themselves as such, who feel alone, abandoned, and misunderstood. To stay in this place of woundedness, though, risks condemning victims of trauma to a life of victimhood and undermines the power of ongoing resurrection that recognizes moments of growth amid suffering. Identifying solely with Christ's wounded nature prevents one from becoming a victim-survivor.

The cross is only one end of a continuum of suffering and stresses for Jesus and for all those who live under the thumb of oppression. A theology of trauma cannot overlook the ways that Jesus speaks into the lives of all who live on a continuum of traumatic injuries. In the secular context, we as a Western culture have held to the particular diagnostic truth that PTSD is the ultimate plumb line by which real trauma is determined. It is true that any theology of trauma must acknowledge that not all distress is traumatic; our finitude ensures that struggle is a part of life. A reframed pastoral theology of trauma, however, must recognize that the life spirit of those with their backs against the wall is a spirit that is denied its freedom and dignity and carries a trauma no less wounding than biomedically sanctioned PTSD. From his earliest days as a refugee through his life as a dark-skinned man living under the foot of empire, Jesus's life reflects the suffering of people the world over who face injustice and oppression as their daily reality. His life and ministry offer a way of knowing about the world and the struggle it brings. A Christian trauma theology must be inclusive of Jesus's life as a continuum in which persons of color, those living in poverty, and others see and find hope for their own traumatic struggle, even if it is not reflected in the DSM-5-TR diagnostic criteria for PTSD.

Psychological Theories of Trauma

Contemporary psychological wisdom is heavily informed by the *Diagnostic and Statistical Manual of Mental Disorders* (DSM), first created by the American Psychiatric Association in the early 1950s to establish a common nomenclature around psychological pathology and distress that located its origins in biological causes. The advantages of a biomedical diagnostic model for the treatment and care of persons with mental disorders, including PTSD, has been substantial but is not without cost. Locating clinical psychology and diagnosis within a medical framework has legitimized mental illness not only for treatment purposes but also for health care reimbursement, pharmaceutical intervention (though dependence on pharmaceuticals may also tip over into a harmful trend), and, importantly, as areas of concern in the eyes of the public. This deductive model, however, also narrows how we conceive of illness and diagnoses, thereby employing a deficit-based approach that eschews other important social influences that shape life experiences, health and unhealth, and the resourcefulness of individuals. It is these aspects that are especially relevant to expanding our understanding of trauma and that we bring into focus in this chapter.

There have been several touchstones along the way to a developed psychology of what today is termed *trauma*. Trauma, called in more recent decades shell shock, war neurosis, or combat fatigue, has been well recognized over the centuries as a response to the experiences of war and combat.[46] The psychiatric treatment of "post-Vietnam syndrome" in Vietnam War veterans arguably served as an entryway into what became the DSM diagnosis of PTSD.[47] The focus then broadened in subsequent years to include the traumatic experiences of children and eventually of women. Perhaps most notable in this regard was the seminal work of psychiatrist Judith Herman.[48] Regardless of the era or the population, psychological theories of trauma reflect and are embedded in the sociocultural context.

The United States is unique among other countries in its use of the DSM-5-TR as the diagnostic tool for mental health conditions, including PTSD. Although Australia is rapidly also switching to its use, other member states of the World Health Organization adhere to the International Classification of Diseases (ICD) system, now in its eleventh version, for the centralized classification of all diseases, including mental illnesses. Therefore, it is helpful to consider how the diagnosis of mental health disorders such as PTSD has been framed in this country and globally.

---

46 Marc-Antoine Crocq and Louis Crocq, "From Shell Shock and War Neurosis to Posttraumatic Stress Disorder: A History of Psychotraumatology," *Dialogues in Clinical Neuroscience* 2, no. 1 (2000): 47–55, https://doi.org/10.31887/DCNS.2000.2.1/macrocq.

47 Fassin and Rechtman, *The Empire of Trauma*.

48 Judith Herman, *Trauma and Recovery: The Aftermath of Violence—From Domestic Abuse to Political Terror* (New York: Basic Books, 1992).

Trauma neurosis, the experience of psychological and physical distress stemming from disasters and other experiences, has had a global presence in the treatment of psychiatric conditions for more than a century and in Japan as early as the 1870s.[49] The tragic event and consequence of the atomic bombings at Hiroshima and Nagasaki in 1945 were unprecedented in every way, including that of understanding the psychological response to catastrophic traumas. Interestingly, it was not until after the training of Japanese mental health professionals by the US Community Crisis Response Team (CCRT) in response to a 1995 earthquake that PTSD became well known and ultimately the primary frame for understanding the effects of traumatic experience in Japan.[50]

However, indigenous and traditional ways of understanding distress are generally disregarded within contemporary psychological theories of trauma. The violence and cultural degradation experienced within many Indigenous communities and among marginalized peoples throughout history and the world has an intergenerational impact.[51] Distress and trauma do not result from cognitive appraisals made by disembodied organisms, nor are they primarily emotional responses. Distress and trauma are passed among people, including from one generation to the next. The DSM-5-TR diagnostic criteria for PTSD do not reflect this indigenous/traditional wisdom.

In authoring the DSM-5, the American Psychiatric Association did attempt to acknowledge how distress and trauma are cultural constructions. To aid clinicians in considering the impact of culture when diagnosing clients, they added a "Glossary of Cultural Concepts of Distress" in an appendix.[52] The glossary lists nine common cultural syndromes of

---

49 Toyomi Goto and John P. Wilson, "A Review of the History of Traumatic Stress Studies in Japan: From Traumatic Neurosis to PTSD," *Trauma, Violence, & Abuse* 4, no. 3 (2003): 195–209, https://doi.org/10.1177/1524838003004003001.

50 Goto and Wilson, "A Review of the History of Traumatic Stress Studies in Japan."

51 Yael Danieli, ed., *International Handbook of Multigenerational Legacies of Trauma* (New York: Plenum Press, 1998); Resmaa Menakem, *My Grandmother's Hands: Racialized Trauma and the Pathway to Mending Our Hearts and Bodies* (Las Vegas, NV: Central Recovery Press, 2017); Ellen Pinderhughes, "The Multigenerational Transmission of Loss and Trauma: The African-American Experience," in *Living Beyond Loss: Death in the Family*, 2nd ed., ed. Froma Walsh and Monica McGoldrick (New York: W. W. Norton, 2004), 161–181.

52 American Psychiatric Association, *Diagnostic and statistical manual.*

distress. For example, *khyal cap*, or a *wind attack*, "is a syndrome found among Cambodians in the United States and Cambodia" that includes symptoms of "dizziness, palpitations, shortness of breath, and cold extremities, as well as other symptoms of anxiety and autonomic arousal."[53] The belief that wind may arise within the body and blood, thus causing such symptoms, is acknowledged as a culturally distinctive manifestation of distress. However, *khyal cap* is then linked back to disorders in the main body of the DSM-5, including distinctly Western perceptions of distress such as panic attack and panic disorders. Therefore, while recent editions of the DSM have given a nod to the impact of social and cultural influences, these have been far outpaced by the rise of neuroscience and the search for neurological evidence of mental health pathology. The failure to integrate various social stressors such as racism, persecution of LGBTQ+ persons, economic oppression, and other such factors into the diagnostic model means we often dismiss the severity and impact of having to endure these lifelong threats.

Contemporary means of conceptualizing trauma, both clinical and popular, also fail to acknowledge the human tendency to focus on the negative. We "display a negativity bias, or the propensity to attend to, learn from, and use negative information far more than positive information."[54] Humans' negativity bias serves adaptive purposes from an evolutionary perspective, but it also means that negative events have greater psychological, and arguably spiritual, impact than positive events. Conceptualizing all stressful events as traumatic is both an outgrowth of, and fuel for, our negativity bias. The pathology-focused clinical diagnostic frame only further reinforces both. Overemphasizing the negative to the point of normalizing trauma disposes us to minimize our ability to cope and supports deficit-based rather than strength-based self-assessments. Consider, for example, the way violence and mass shootings have been normalized within US culture. The

---

53 Tim Thornton, "Cross-Cultural Psychiatry and Validity in DSM-5," in *The Palgrave Handbook of Sociocultural Perspectives on Global Mental Health*, ed. Ross G. White, Sumeet Jain, David M. R. Orr, and Ursula Read (New York: Palgrave Macmillan/ Springer Nature, 2017), 55.

54 Amrisha Vaish, Tobias Grossmann, and Amanda Woodward, "Not All Emotions Are Created Equal: The Negativity Bias in Social-Emotional Development," *Psychological Bulletin* 134, no. 3 (2008): 383, https://doi.10.1037/0033-2909.134.3.383.

widespread nature of such events caused the American Psychological Association to publish a cover story in *Monitor on Psychology* entitled "Stress of Mass Shootings Causing Cascade of Collective Traumas."[55] Is the United States, as a nation, collectively traumatized by mass shootings? Though they are tragic events to be sure, clinical psychologist Sarah R. Lowe and physician and epidemiologist Sandro Galea reviewed forty-nine studies on the impact of mass shootings on mental health and found that PTSD prevalence was as low as 3 percent and as high as 91 percent, raising significant methodological concerns.[56] Perhaps it is our negativity bias that causes us to conflate stress and trauma and fear in ways that diminish our ability to cope with distressing events.

The Stress-Trauma Continuum

Social work scholars Catherine N. Dulmus and Carolyn Hilarski sought to aid researchers and practitioners in accurately defining the terms *stress*, *trauma*, and *crisis* with the goal of improved assessment and intervention.[57] Toward this end, they conceptualized the stress-trauma-crisis continuum to explain the uniqueness of, and relationship among, these constructs, each of which results from the perception of an event, not the event itself. Although crisis is outside the focus of this volume, reconceptualizing a psychospiritual theory and theology of trauma is founded upon the stress-trauma continuum. To reiterate, we are not suggesting a continuum that reflects progressive phases of stress that ends at its ultimate, and thus most clinically legitimate, form of PTSD.

First, it is essential to remember that not all stress is distress. "Eustress" is a positive stress response that is not only helpful but necessary for optimal performance. Eustress is "a type of stress that results from challenging but attainable and enjoyable or worthwhile tasks (e.g., participating in an athletic

---

55 Zara Abrams, "Stress of Mass Shootings Causing Cascade of Collective Traumas," *Monitor on Psychology* 53, no. 6 (2022): 20, https://www.apa.org/monitor/2022/09/news-mass-shootings-collective-traumas.

56 Sarah R. Lowe and Sandro Galea, "The Mental Health Consequences of Mass Shootings," *Trauma, Violence, & Abuse* 18, no. 1 (2015): 62–82, https://doi.org/10.1177/1524838015591572.

57 Dulmus and Hilarski, "When Stress Constitutes Trauma and Trauma Constitutes Crisis."

event, giving a speech)."[58] Eustress differs from distress, which is a negative stress response and involves "negative affect and physiological reactivity: a type of stress that results from being overwhelmed by demands, losses, or perceived threats. It has a detrimental effect by generating physical and psychological maladaptation and posing serious health risks for individuals."[59] The same event—for example, giving a major speech—can cause one person eustress and another distress based upon their perception. Like eustress and distress, trauma also results from perception. "The bomb dropped on Hiroshima may be a trauma-producing event, a military victory, or a divine retribution depending on the individual's . . . attribution and perception of the occurrence."[60] While distress and trauma can produce the same physiological responses (e.g., hypertension, migraines), the acute and long-term neurological impact of trauma is distinct. Because personality and culture influence our perceptions and appraisals of events, and because our spiritual and religious beliefs and practices influence our perceptions, religious leaders and practitioners of spiritually integrated psychotherapy should utilize the stress-trauma continuum in assessing any and every care receiver's or client's presentation of distress.

Reframing a Psychospiritual Theory and Theology of Trauma

The exploration of theological and psychological conceptions of trauma evidences why pastoral theology, spiritual care, and spiritually integrated psychology as subdisciplines should be invested in reconceptualizing and reframing understandings of trauma. Our strength-based, reframed understanding of trauma is built upon the following four working principles:

- Not all distress is trauma, nor should all distress be avoided.
- PTSD, as defined in the DSM-5-TR, does not encompass all categories of traumatic distress.

58 *American Psychological Association Dictionary of Psychology Online*, "Eustress," accessed January 9, 2024, https://dictionary.apa.org/eustress.

59 *American Psychological Association Dictionary of Psychology Online*, "Distress," accessed January 9, 2024, https://dictionary.apa.org/distress.

60 Dulmus and Hilarski, "When Stress Constitutes Trauma and Trauma Constitutes Crisis," 29.

- Stress and trauma can co-occur with growth and resilience, as evidenced in the wisdom of Scripture and tradition.
- Stress and trauma exist on a continuum not a hierarchy, and both are deserving of care.

Centering and privileging Jesus' crucifixion as the Christian example of trauma is a disservice to all those whose own experiences along the stress-trauma continuum leaves them longing to see their own life reflected in the life of Jesus. A deliberative Christian theology recognizes that the cross is only one end of a continuum of suffering reflected in the life of Jesus. Further, life for Jesus began on the margins of society, much as it does for many today living under the thumb of oppression. We ought not rush too quickly to resurrection, yet we must honor the resilience many enact in the face of traumatic experience that leads them to find hope, meaning, and even new life in a post-crucifixion world.[61]

Jesus's ministry reflects the complex tensions of living in the unpredictable world of empire with hope constantly under threat. God's grace revealed in Jesus Christ shows us that it is never either/or but always both/and. The wounds of the world are real, and yet a faith built upon the promise of an always faithful God opens the possibility to choose hope even while experiencing our woundedness. Built upon the promises of God, we are always living in the potential for being simultaneously broken and redeemed. Our distress and traumas alike offer the potential for resilience and, at times, post-traumatic growth (PTG). This reconceptualized and reframed psychospiritual theory and theology of trauma is evident in contemporary examples of distress across myriad cultures.

Implications for Spiritual Care and Counseling

Religious leaders, spiritual caregivers, and clinicians offering spiritually integrated psychotherapy and care can benefit from grounding their perceptions,

61 Socially and historically, the trauma of being Black in the United States is unique. Oppressions quite often compound, making it even more challenging to cope, and yet people keep going. People learn to struggle well, and often it is in resisting that people become resilient.

assessments, and interventions in a reframed psychospiritual theory and theology of trauma. This framework invites professionals to:

- Recognize the broad range of care receivers' and clients' needs, whether their experiences are most aptly termed distress or trauma. Both necessitate intervention and care.
- Assist care receivers and clients in identifying language that accurately reflects their distress beyond the biases and fixed terminology of trauma culture.
- Acknowledge that oppression can, but does not always, have a traumatic effect and that we need to create space for naming and experiencing it as such when relevant.
- Avoid exporting Western, biomedical conceptions of trauma and colonizing them within other cultures and contexts. We would do well to be mindful of this caution in our everyday discourse, in how we talk about events occurring in other contexts or cultures and also within intercultural relationships.
- Provide care receivers and clients with space to shift embedded theological understandings of trauma that center distress to the exclusion of hope as well as understandings that center hope to the exclusion of distress and help guide them in constructing more deliberative theologies of trauma.

The work of reconceptualizing and reframing understandings of trauma is imperative. But, theories and theologies must be practiced and enacted in order to foster resistance and the possibility of transformation.

2

A WOMANIST PSYCHOSPIRITUALITY

Gendering and Racializing Trauma and Resilience

Jessica Chapman Lape

IN THE WINTER of 1856, enslaved Margaret "Peggy" Garner attempted to find freedom for herself and her family. At twenty-two years old, Peggy, along with her husband, his parents, and their four children, escaped their plantation in Boone County, Kentucky. After crossing the Ohio River into Ohio, a free state, the family took shelter at the home of Peggy's free cousin, Elijah Kite. In the middle of the night, slave catchers surrounded Elijah's home. Fearing for her life and the lives of her children, Peggy quickly chose to slit the throat of Mary, her two-year-old daughter, to prevent her from returning to slavery. Peggy attempted to do the same with all her other children as well as herself but was stopped by Elijah's wife, Mary. Moments later, US marshals entered the home.

Peggy was taken to jail, and a trial ensued. During the trial, Mary served as a witness. She recounted finding Peggy standing next to her slain daughter wrapped in a sheet and preparing to slit the throat of her son. As Mary attempted to stop the murder, Peggy exclaimed that she would rather kill all her children than have them taken back over the river. Peggy's lawyer, abolitionist John Jolliffe, advocated for her to be tried for murder. In doing so, Jolliffe would have set a civil rights precedent as murder charges would suggest that Peggy be tried as a human being killing another human being rather than a slave killing a slave. Such a murder conviction would also prevent Peggy from returning to slavery. However, his attempt failed. Peggy was instead charged with damage of property—the property being her two-year-old daughter. Her family was then reinstituted into the domestic slave trade and sold to the brother of their former enslaver

Archibald Gaines, who was reportedly the father of Peggy as well as of two of her children.[1]

The story of Peggy Garner is one of tragedy and desperation. It captures the trauma experienced by African American women during slavery. Enslaved women of all ages experienced outrageous forms of sexual, psychological, spiritual, and physical violence at the hands of their enslavers. Their lives were under constant surveillance, and danger existed around every corner. Women's bodies were used as mechanisms of production, labor, and scientific research, and their humanity was eclipsed by their caricatures as either submissive asexual caregivers or licentious hypersexual seductresses. Peggy opted to ensure that her daughter would never experience such trauma again.

When we consider trauma and its impact on African American women, we must begin with stories like Peggy's. US chattel slavery attempted to strip Africans of their languages, their religions, their tribal lineages, and other key aspects of cultural identity so that they lost that which constituted their humanness. Relationships to land, spirit, and culture were severed by white supremacy and capitalism. Cultural particularities among tribal and geographically similar groups coalesced into a conglomeration of American Blackness. From this new composite identity, ways of being, worldviews, and spiritualities emerged. The African American woman was born from this traumatic conglomeration. This is where our trauma begins yet also where our resilience is birthed.

While Peggy's story is one of trauma, it is also one of resistance. Rather than enduring the enslavement of their children or witnessing their daughters become subject to sexual violence, many enslaved mothers practiced reproductive resistance such as avoiding sexual intercourse, terminating pregnancies, and infanticide.[2] Such resistance demonstrates the extreme and catastrophic insidiousness of chattel slavery and the sheer determination of African American women to transcend it for themselves and their families.

---

1 "Reproduction and Resistance," *Hidden Voices: Enslaved Women in the Lowcountry and U.S. South*. Lowcountry Digital History Initiative, https://ldhi.library.cofc.edu/exhibits/show/hidden-voices/resisting-enslavement/reproduction-and-resistance; "The Slave Trageoy in Cincinnati," *New York Times*, February 2, 1856, https://www.nytimes.com/1856/02/02/archives/the-slave-trageoy-in-cincinnati.html.

2 Lowcountry Digital History Initiative, "Hidden Voices."

Positionality of a Womanist Pastoral Theologian

Because of their identities as both women and Black, African American women experience gender-based and race-based stress and trauma induced by white supremacy. This stress and trauma aims to hinder or destroy African American women's psychospirituality. Yet, it is because of their intersecting identities that African American women maintain unique mechanisms of resilience in confronting such stress and trauma. This resilience is adaptive and generative and maintains the potential to preserve, protect, and, at times, reinforce African American women's psychospirituality—and has done so for generations.

A womanist psychospiritual analysis of African American women's intersectional experiences explores the peculiar and reciprocal relationship between stress, trauma, and resilience in the intergenerational, communal, and individual lives of African American women. Womanist psychospirituality involves a metatheoretical integration of womanist psychology, African American psychology, and womanist pastoral theology to explore the meaning-making processes of African American women. As clinical psychologist Martha E. Banks and pastor Stephanie Lee avowed, "womanism encompasses the spiritual, communal, and psychological aspects of a woman."[3] *Womanism*, a term coined by Alice Walker in 1983, further describes a philosophical and ethical commitment to witnessing the capacity for flourishing among African American women and those in their circles. Psychologist Janis V. Sanchez-Hucles suggested that womanism is rooted in Black women's folk culture and, therefore, "offers a model that is committed to survival and wholeness and addresses all of the oppression experienced by [Black women]."[4] As such, womanism is a phenomenological lens through which to consider how African American women, despite the destructive

---

3 Martha E. Banks and Stephanie Lee, "Womanism and Spirituality/Theology," in *Womanist and Mujerista Psychologies: Voices of Fire, Acts of Courage*, ed. Thema Bryant-Davis and Lillian Comas-Díaz (Washington, DC: American Psychological Association, 2016), 124.

4 Janis V. Sanchez-Hucles, "Womanist Therapy with Black Women," in *Womanist and Mujerista Psychologies: Voices of Fire, Acts of Courage*, ed. Thema Bryant-Davis and Lillian Comas-Díaz (Washington, DC: American Psychological Association, 2016), 72.

trauma caused by white supremacism, continue to make a way out of what seems like no way for themselves and their families.

I am a womanist. I am a womanist pastoral theologian committed to an ethic of care that seeks to support African American women forced to navigate white supremacist systems with tools and resources of their ancestors and with hope and optimism for their future generations. I am an African American mother, partner, sister, daughter, auntie, and sisterfriend who navigates white supremacist systems. I wonder how I and my circle might transcend such harrowing attempts to thwart our flourishing in this world. I approach this womanist psychospiritual work holding my ethical commitments, intersectional identities, and social location in tandem with my scholarly curiosities.

Defining the Problem

Peggy's story, and the story of many African American women that came before and after her, is a story of white supremacy rearing its head in the lives of African American women. I argue that white supremacy is the root cause of intergenerational, communal, and individual race-based and gender-based trauma for African American women. White supremacy is a system that infects all American systems through inequitable distribution of resources, racial hierarchy, and unjust policies and practices. As a systematic process, white supremacy upholds every iteration of oppression and contributes to a complex matrix of limitations to the survival, liberation, and flourishing of those whose identities intersect in myriad ways—namely, poor African American women.

African American women encounter white supremacy through the deleterious effects of racism and gender oppression. Racism entails "multiple types of ethnic discrimination in which an ethnic group in power supports scripts of superiority/inferiority and corresponding policies and practices that reinforce the domination/subjugation of the ethnic groups in all public and private spheres."[5] Racism occurs throughout society—within

5 Helen A. Neville and Alex L. Pieterse, "Racism, White Supremacy, and Resistance: Contextualizing Black American Experiences," in *Handbook of African American Psychology*, ed. Helen A. Neville, Brendesha M. Tynes, and Shawn O. Utsey (Thousand Oaks, CA: Sage Publishing, 2009), 160.

interpersonal relationships, institutional practices and policies, and cultural practices and values. Gender oppression intersects with racism to further complicate the lives of African American women. Gender oppression "limits or prohibits one's freedom, dignity, or subjectivity on the basis of one's gender expression, identity, and/or role."[6] African American women experience gender oppression in wider American society as well as within African American communities. Like racism, gender oppression impacts women through interpersonal interactions, institutional practices and policies, and cultural values and practiced beliefs. Gender oppression and other oppressions or *-isms*, including sexism, classism, and heterosexism, join racism as components or consequences of white supremacy.

For this discourse, I focus on the experience of African American transwomen and cisgender women vis-à-vis their relationship to cisgender men of all races and the societal privileging of men over women. For such women, intersectional oppression by way of white supremacy is a psychologically, spiritually, and often physically violent act in that it attempts to corrode the identity, spirit, and health of its targets. Such violence begets stress and trauma. Stress and trauma can be experienced as independent phenomena. Stress involves external and internal factors influencing a person's behavior, feelings, and emotionality.[7] Trauma consists of external factors aimed to negatively impact the psychospirituality of individuals and communities.[8] The stress-trauma continuum offers a means to conceptualize African American women's experience of white supremacy, and its iterations of racism and gender oppression, in individual, collective, and intergenerational ways.

---

6 Jennifer C. Ingrey, "Gender Oppression," in *The Wiley Blackwell Encyclopedia of Gender and Sexuality Studies*, ed. Wai Ching Angela Wong, Maithree Wickramasinghe, Renée C. Hoogland, and Nancy A. Naples (Hoboken, NJ: Wiley, 2016), 1, https://doi.org/10.1002/9781118663219.wbegss324.

7 American Psychological Association, "Stress," *APA Dictionary of Psychology* (Washington, DC: American Psychological Association, 2022), https://dictionary.apa.org/stress.

8 Danielle Drake-Burnette, BraVada Garrett-Akinsanya, and Thema Bryant-Davis, "Womanism, Creativity, and Resistance: Making a Way Out of 'No Way,'" in *Womanist and Mujerista Psychologies: Voices of Fire, Acts of Courage*, ed. by Thema Bryant-Davis and Lillian Comas-Díaz (Washington, DC: American Psychological Association, 2016), 173–194, https://doi.org/10.1037/14937-008.

Shawn Arango Ricks, scholar and licensed mental health counselor, advocated for an expanding redefinition of trauma that considers Black women's lived experiences.[9] She noted that trauma "includes fighting every day to have your voice heard. It includes fighting for your child(ren) to ensure their psychological development. Trauma is putting on the mask and cape before you walk out of the door and hoping that no one sees your tears or your fears—for if they smell weakness, they will pounce."[10] The stressors of white supremacy contribute to trauma while intergenerational and collective knowledge of trauma contribute to chronic stressors.

The continual vacillation along the stress-trauma continuum has adverse consequences for African American women's psychospirituality. Psychospirituality, in this case, describes the emotional, spiritual, and cognitive processes involved in making meaning of lived experiences.[11] A healthy and robust psychospirituality connects African American women to their sense of self, their sense of humanity, their sense of the sacred, and their community. When stress and trauma occur, these processes of connection are potentially disrupted, leading to adverse effects on emotional, spiritual, and psychological health. Race-based and gender-based stress and trauma potentiate such a catastrophic impact on African American women's psychospirituality because they are unceasing and target a person's inherent humanity. As long as African American women live, work, love, learn, play, get sick, and parent in American society, they will never avoid white supremacist culture.

Gendering Trauma's Psychospiritual Impact

Psychologist Shelly P. Harrell defines racism-related stress as "race-related transactions between individuals or groups and their environment that emerge from the dynamics of racism and that are perceived to tax or exceed

9 Shawn Arango Ricks, "Normalized Chaos: Black Feminism, Womanism, and the (Re)definition of Trauma and Healing," *Meridians* 16, no. 2 (2018): 343–350, https://doi.org/10.2979/meridians.16.2.15.

10 Ricks, "Normalized Chaos," 346.

11 Jessica Chapman Lape, "A Pandemic of Mistreatment: Theories, Practices, and Convergences in Womanist Clinical Pastoral Theology and Black Maternal Healthcare Curing Covid-19," *Journal of Pastoral Theology* 31, no. 2–3 (2021): 128–144, https://doi.org/10.1080/10649867.2021.1929712.

existing individual and collective resources or threaten well-being."[12] Harrell identifies multiple forms of racism-related stress with individual, communal, and generational impacts. Clinical psychologists Riana Elyse Anderson and Howard C. Stevenson situate Harrell's racism-related stress framework as racism-related trauma.[13] Research on racism-related stress and trauma focuses on the correlation of traumatic stress with racism experienced among entire groups of people, regardless of gender or gender expression.[14]

Yet, these frameworks are rarely conceptualized to include the particularities of gendered racism.[15] Gendered racism describes the intersectional experience of gender oppression and racism for women of color. At times, African American women encounter racism in similar ways to African American men and non-cisgender African Americans, but there are often distinct ways African American women experience racism due to their simultaneous experience of gender oppression (much like there are distinct ways non-cisgender African Americans experience racism due to their simultaneous experience of heterosexism).

Through a lens of gendered racism, I explore racism-related stress and trauma by elevating examples that illustrate various forms of stress and trauma for African American women today. I consider the psychospiritual ramifications of stress and trauma by turning to a pivotal text in womanist god-talk—the story of Hagar in Genesis of the Hebrew Bible. In the text, Genesis 16–21, Hagar is a young African enslaved woman who serves as the surrogate for her owner, Sarai. While enslaved in Sarai's home, Hagar experiences extreme mistreatment. Womanist theologian Delores S. Williams situates Hagar's poverty, socioeconomic status as a slave, foreignness as African,

---

12 Shelly P. Harrell, "A Multidimensional Conceptualization of Racism-Related Stress: Implications for the Well-Being of People of Color," *American Journal of Orthopsychiatry* 70, no. 1 (2000): 44, https://doi.org/10.1037/h0087722.

13 Riana Elyse Anderson and Howard C. Stevenson, "RECASTing Racial Stress and Trauma: Theorizing the Healing Potential of Racial Socialization in Families," *American Psychologist* 74, no. 1 (January 2019): 63–75, http://doi.org/10.1037/amp0000392.

14 Robert T. Carter, "Racism and Psychological and Emotional Injury: Recognizing and Assessing Race-Based Traumatic Stress," *The Counseling Psychologist* 35, no. 1 (2007): 13–105, http://doi.org/10.1177/0011000006292033; Harrell, "A Multidimensional Conceptualization of Racism-related Stress"; Neville and Pieterse, "Racism, White Supremacy, and Resistance."

15 Philomena Essed, *Understanding Everyday Racism: An Interdisciplinary Theory* (Thousand Oaks, CA: Sage, 1991).

and female body at the center of her problems.[16] I turn to Hagar because, as Williams suggests, Hagar's experience as an oppressed African woman resonates deeply with African American women today.

Gendered Racism and the Individual

In the public sphere, Black women experience higher rates of psychological abuse such as insults, coercive control, humiliation, and name-calling than all women, regardless of race and ethnicity.[17] Dehumanizing caricatures of African American women as, for example, a hypersexualized Jezebel[18] or an "angry Black woman" position African American women as subjects of an objectifying and ridiculing gaze. The image of the Jezebel has persisted for generations, painting African American women as licentious sexual deviants.[19] The notion that African American women cannot control their sexual appetites contributes to public opinion around reproductive control while simultaneously contributing to disproportionate experiences of sexual trauma. Meanwhile, an estimated 40 to 60 percent of Black women are coerced to have sexual contact by age eighteen, and 38 percent of Black women experience sexual violence in a form other than rape during their lifetime.[20] Sexual trauma by way of sexual harassment and coercion illustrates the insidious interconnection of racism and gender oppression.

Like the Jezebel, the angry Black woman trope also illustrates gendered racism. In two studies conducted by management and organizations scholars Daphna Motro, Jonathan B. Evans, Aleksander P.J. Ellis, and Lehman Benson, III, the researchers found that despite anger being a common expression in the workplace, "when some people see a Black woman become

---

16 Delores S. Williams, *Sisters in the Wilderness: The Challenge of Womanist God-Talk* (Maryknoll, NY: Orbis Books, 1993).

17 Jameta Nicole Barlow, "Black Women, the Forgotten Survivors of Sexual Assault," *American Psychological Association*, February 1, 2020, https://www.apa.org/pi/about/newsletter/2020/02/black-women-sexual-assault.

18 Patricia Hill Collins, *Black Feminist Thought: Knowledge, Consciousness, and the Politics of Empowerment* (New York: Routledge, 2000), 86.

19 Collins, *Black Feminist Thought*, 86.

20 National Center on Violence Against Women in the Black Community, *Black Women and Sexual Assault* (Washington, DC: National Center on Violence Against Women in the Black Community, 2018), https://ujimacommunity.org/wp-content/uploads/2018/12/Ujima-Womens-Violence-Stats-v7.4-1.pdf.

angry, they're likely to attribute that anger to her personality—rather than an inciting situation."[21] The angry Black woman trope, often maintained through the media such as Tyler Perry's *Diary of a Mad Black Woman*, is used to justify and uphold society's perception of African American women's anger as an inherent personality trait that negates society's involvement in unjust sexist and racist practices that should reasonably be expected to anger Black women. Such characterizations potentially lead to microaggressions or microstressors.[22] Educational psychologists Helen A. Neville and Alex L. Pieterse define microaggressions as "unintentional behaviors consistent with avoidance and minimization of racial others."[23] When internalized, microaggressions lead to distress, low self-esteem, and a sense of inferiority.[24] Microaggressions are common but rarely confronted and thus significantly contribute to a person's stress level over time.[25]

These tropes constitute a stressful hyperawareness. African American women exist in a society that requires them to constantly hold their identities in question and wonder how they are perceived by those with societal power. To be perceived as a Jezebel potentiates the experience of sexual trauma. To be perceived as angry potentiates the experience of underhanded discrimination in the workplace or society at large—perhaps leading to the traumatic experience of overtaxing one's allostatic load. Gendered racism impacts the stress and trauma of individual African American women in ways that neither gender oppression nor racism can do alone.

The impact of these tropes are examples of the catastrophic nature of gendered racism on the lives of individual African American women whose psychospirituality is disrupted when gendered racism produces stress and trauma. During her enslavement, Hagar found herself alone in the home of Sarai and Abram. Sarai found herself unable to bear children, which endangered the

21 Daphna Motro, Jonathan B. Evans, Aleksander P. J. Ellis, and Lehman Benson, III, "The 'Angry Black Woman' Stereotype at Work," *Harvard Business Review*, January 31, 2022, para. 6, https://hbr.org/2022/01/the-angry-black-woman-stereotype-at-work.

22 Harrell, "A Multidimensional Conceptualization of Racism-Related Stress."

23 Neville and Pieterse, "Racism, White Supremacy, and Resistance," 165.

24 Wendy Ashley, "The Angry Black Woman: The Impact of Pejorative Stereotypes on Psychotherapy with Black Women," *Social Work in Public Health* 29, no. 1 (2014): 27–34, http://doi.org/10.1080/19371918.2011.619449.

25 Harrell, "A Multidimensional Conceptualization of Racism-Related Stress."

prominent legacy promised to Abram by God. This led Sarai to take matters into her own hands. Williams notes that because Hagar was Sarai's slave, Abram had no power over her until Sarai consented.[26] Therefore, in desperation, Sarai relinquished control over Hagar and handed that control to Abram. Shortly after the exchange of control, Hagar conceived and Abram's opportunity to live into God's promise of a legacy was restored. Hagar then grew contemptuous toward Sarai. Sarai, in turn, sought ways to punish Hagar for her derision, overlooking reasons for the derision itself. As a slave, Hagar was powerless over her sexuality, and it was in turn used by her owners for their own potential gain.

Hagar's body and sexuality were objects to be bartered with, controlled, manipulated, and exploited with no consideration of her potential lived experiences of subjugation, humiliation, and decreasing sense of self-esteem. She was then treated as an angry Black woman by Sarai, who ignored her own responsibility and the traumatic impact of the surrogacy and enslavement system in which Hagar was entrapped. Hagar was objectified in the eyes of her owners and left alone to contend with her experiences of oppression. Her precarious experience of objectification left her to grapple with a dangerous decision—whether to flee from her enslavement and face uncertainty and danger outside of Sarai and Abram's home or stay with her enslavers and face Sarai's disdain and perhaps subsequent mistreatment by the family. As Williams notes, African American women's oppression mirrors Hagar's in that their identities as both women and ethnically other are at the center of their stress and trauma experiences.[27] Like Hagar, African American women contending with gendered racism potentially experience subjugation, humiliation, and a decreasing sense of self-esteem. Their harrowing experiences of objectification complicate their relationships with those holding societal power. They are left to navigate systems of oppression and to consider their options for survival amid uncertainty.

Gendered Racism and the Collective

"Cultural-symbolic and sociopolitical manifestations of racism" are collective experiences that impact the well-being of entire racialized communities.[28]

---

26 Williams, *Sisters in the Wilderness.*

27 Williams, *Sisters in the Wilderness.*

28 Harrell, "A Multidimensional Conceptualization of Racism-Related Stress," 46.

Economic injustice is an illustration of gendered racism with consequences for African American women and their families as a collective entity. The culturally symbolic story of Breonna Taylor, an African American woman who was killed inside her home by police officers in 2020, is another illustration of gendered racism with consequences for African American women as a collective whole. Economic injustice disproportionately impacts African American women. In 2019, Black women represented 22.3 percent of women in poverty but only 12.8 percent of women in the US.[29] This economic disparity is due in part to the wage gap. In 2020, African American women earned 38 percent less than white men while doing the same work.[30]

The stereotypical image of a mammy endorses African American women's economic injustice. The mammy represents the stereotyped Black woman's self-sacrificial vocational commitments during slavery and the Jim Crow era. The mammy is often portrayed as submissive and docile within her domestic role, and this image continues to contribute to society's perception of Black women in the workplace by suggesting that Black women are content with economic disparity.[31] When African American women economically support their families, their chronic experience with poverty is a form of gendered racism with consequences for entire family systems. Furthermore, this gendered racism contributes significantly to chronic stress. Chronic stress contributes to low self-esteem and self-worth as well as physical consequences including obesity, diabetes, and chronic pain.[32] Economic injustice is an insidious cycle with complex ramifications on persons and communities.

Gendered racism impacting Black women in community also includes vicarious racism.[33] Vicarious racism is the experience of racism originally

---

29 Amanda Fins, *National Snapshot: Poverty Among Women & Families* (Washington, DC: National Women's Law Center, 2020), https://nwlc.org/wp-content/uploads/2020/12/PovertySnapshot2020.pdf.

30 American Association of University Women, *Systemic Racism and the Gender Pay Gap: A Supplement to The Simple Truth* (Washington, DC: American Association of University Women, 2021), https://www.aauw.org/app/uploads/2021/07/SimpleTruth_4.0-1.pdf.

31 Collins, *Black Feminist Thought*.

32 Chanequa Walker-Barnes, *Too Heavy a Yoke: Black Women and the Burden of Strength* (Eugene, OR: Cascade Books, 2014).

33 Harrell, "A Multidimensional Conceptualization of Racism-Related Stress."

directed toward others in one's community. An example of vicarious gendered racism for African American women as a collective is the media-amplified murder of Breonna Taylor in March 2020. Taylor was a twenty-six-year-old, unarmed, Black health care worker whose life was taken by Louisville police officers possessing a no-knock warrant for a home raid. The involved officers were not charged with her murder by the state of Kentucky, and charges would not have been brought forward had the federal government not intervened many months later. To the state, Taylor was seen as a threat, at worst, or collateral damage, at best. The relatability to Taylor's experience as a young, professional Black woman had significant impact for African American women and girls across class and geographical distance. After witnessing the criminal justice system neglecting to function as a mechanism for justice, African American women grew increasingly fearful of, and disillusioned with, criminal justice systems and their treatment of Black women.[34] Vicarious identification with the trauma of one's community results in anger, rumination, hypervigilance, withdrawal from the community, and avoidance of similar environments.[35] Police brutality against African American women and the subsequent lack of justice is both communal stress and communal trauma.

African American women are hard hit in white supremacist systems and institutions that uphold both racist and patriarchal ideologies. Economic injustice and police brutality are cultural and sociopolitical collective experiences of gendered racism. These iterations of gendered racism perpetuate chronic stress and poor health among African American women situated in family systems or communal systems impacted by societal institutions such as the justice system. Of course, there are exceptions to Black women trapped in cyclical poverty and economic injustice as well as exceptions to the collective disillusionment with systems following Taylor's murder. These are only examples of collective stress and trauma chipping away at the spirit and health of African American women. Yet, despite the inducing

34 Donna M. Owens, "Breonna Taylor and Hundreds of Black Women Have Died at the Hands of Police: The Movement to Say Their Names is Growing," *USA Today*, March 11, 2021, https://www.usatoday.com/in-depth/news/investigations/2021/03/11/sayhername-movement-black-women-police-violence/6921197002/.

35 Anderson and Stevenson, "RECASTing Racial Stress and Trauma"; Harrell, "A Multidimensional Conceptualization of Racism-Related Stress."

circumstances, African American women and those in their circles navigate the stress-trauma continuum as a collective endeavor by forming communities to endure marginalization, injustice, and oppression.

No stranger to economic disparity and disillusionment with systems, Hagar chose to escape her enslavement. In this effort, she met God in the wilderness, who, out of concern for her survival in the desert, told Hagar to return to her enslaver's home. Hagar's initial escape was a decision that had an impact on the collective entity of her family—herself and her unborn child. She recognized that to stay in the home of Sarai was to stay in a system with catastrophic consequences that would result not only in her own trauma but perhaps that of her child as well. Likewise, through God's intervention, Hagar recognized that being alone in the wilderness could also pose dangers to herself and her family. As she navigated oppressive and dangerous forces, she weighed the impact on the collective.

After her return to Sarai's home, Hagar gave birth to Ishmael. Tensions ran high in the home, and Hagar and Ishmael were thrown out when they were no longer beneficial to Abram and Sarai. Now collectively in the wilderness, Hagar and Ishmael navigated danger, scarce resources, and hopelessness. A depressed and disparaged Hagar met God once more when all hope seemed lost. God intervened with resources and reiterated the promise of a legacy if Hagar and Ishmael could endure their hardship for just a bit longer. Hagar's desperation, hopelessness, and uncertainty mirrors that of African American women navigating systems of injustice for the collective good. Like African American women today, Hagar navigated oppression while considering the collective well-being of herself and her family. With full awareness that her stress and trauma impacted her child, Hagar sought to transcend oppression and find liberation outside of a system of injustice.

Gendered Racism Across Generations

The transgenerational transmission of racism encompasses the historic racialized experiences of entire peoples and the stories of race and racism they pass down through the generations. These experiences and stories bind stress and trauma to families and communities.[36] For example, Black

36 Harrell, "A Multidimensional Conceptualization of Racism-Related Stress."

women's iatrophobia, or distrust of the US health care system, represents gendered racism at work across generations. The legacy of eugenics contributes to this transgenerational transmission of distrust. Eugenics is premised upon the socially elite determining who in society is worthy of reproductive rights. As a result, beginning in the twentieth century, the United States began a concerted effort to mass sterilize minorities, including African Americans, Indigenous persons, the disabled, and the poor.[37] By 1983, African American women made up 43 percent of the women sterilized through government-sponsored family planning programs despite comprising only 6 percent of the American population.[38] Activist Fannie Lou Hammer coined the term *Mississippi appendectomy* to describe the widespread experience of anesthetized African American women who unknowingly received hysterectomies.[39] The communal knowledge of such gendered racist practices was transmitted over generations, contributing to collective and intergenerational iatrophobia as well as a general avoidance and distrust of institutions and systems.[40]

Today, this distrust is evident in many African American women's perspectives toward maternal health care. Black women's pregnancy-related mortality rate is three times higher than that of white women, and when controlled for factors such as class and education, race remains the primary determinant of this gendered disparity.[41] Biases against African American women among health care providers also contribute to this collective experience.[42] Furthermore, stereotypical tropes such as the mammy, the angry

---

37 Loretta J. Ross, "Trust Black Women: Reproductive Justice and Eugenics," in *Radical Reproductive Justice: Foundations, Theory, Practice, Critique,* ed. Loretta J. Ross, Lynn Roberts, Erika Derkas, Whitney Peoples, and Pamela Bridgewater Toure, 58–85 (New York: Feminist Press at the City University of New York, 2017).

38 Harriet A. Washington, *Medical Apartheid: The Dark History of Medical Experimentation on Black Americans from Colonial Times to the Present* (New York: Harlem Moon, 2006).

39 Washington, *Medical Apartheid.*

40 Chapman Lape, "A Pandemic of Mistreatment."

41 Chapman Lape, "A Pandemic of Mistreatment;" Liz Hamel, Lunna Lopes, Cailey Muñana, Samantha Artiga, and Mollyann Brodie, *Race, Health, and Covid-19: The Views and Experiences of Black Americans* (San Fransicsco: Kaiser Family Foundation, 2020), https://files.kff.org/attachment/Report-Race-Health-and-COVID-19-The-Views-and-Experiences-of-Black-Americans.pdf.

42 Chapman Lape, "A Pandemic of Mistreatment."

Black woman, the strong Black woman,[43] and the Jezebel all work to dehumanize Black women within health care systems, resulting in subpar care. This collective experience of mistreatment in conjunction with the legacy of eugenics further contributes to communal iatrophobia. A 2020 Kaiser Family Foundation study found that 37 percent of African American mothers felt that when seeking health care they were treated unfairly based on their race.[44] African American women intergenerationally transmit stories of mistreatment, thus significantly influencing the perception of health care systems among those in their circles of influence.[45]

Incidents of mistreatment and the subsequent intergenerational transmission of these incidents construct the collective memory of stress and trauma within African American women. We hold in our bodies, our spirits, and our memories the gendered racism of those who came before us. Our ancestors, mothers, grandmothers, and aunts transmit their pain, their distrust, and their weariness into the collective memory of our people as cautionary tales, attempting to mitigate the mistreatment of generations to come. Because mistreatment endures in systems like health care that are necessary for our survival, incidents of mistreatment continue to be transmitted into our collective memory. The ironic consequence of this transmission that aims to disrupt mistreatment is that it often leads to collective iatrophobia, contributing to the avoidance of health care systems, which ultimately has adverse effects on physical and mental health.[46]

Delores Williams posits that God's intervention in the wilderness during Hagar's initial escape was perhaps due to God's awareness of the high rate of infant mortality during Hagar's life in the ancient Near East.[47] God, as Hagar's community, attempted to mitigate a potentially catastrophic health experience for Hagar, recognizing that this experience had caused pain for generations of women before her. The transmission of this traumatic experience eventually shaped Hagar's decision to return to Sarai's home for Ishmael's birth.

---

43 Walker-Barnes, *Too Heavy a Yoke.*

44 Hamel et al., *Race, Health, and Covid-19.*

45 Chapman Lape, "A Pandemic of Mistreatment."

46 Chapman Lape, "A Pandemic of Mistreatment"; Walker-Barnes, *Too Heavy a Yoke.*

47 Williams, *Sisters in the Wilderness.*

The legacy of mistreatment in the health care system is but one example of generational transmitted trauma. Other iterations of stress and trauma enduring for generations undoubtedly enter into the collective memory of African American women and inform their decision-making. Much like God's concern for Hagar as she navigated danger and uncertainty, African American women's ancestors express concern for their future generations as they share stories of stress and trauma in an attempt to support women navigating their own dangerous systems.

These varied examples of gendered racism-related stress and trauma are intergenerational, communal, and individual. Such stress and trauma have a significant impact on the psychospirituality of African American women because they challenge, question, or threaten their very humanity. White supremacy benefits from controlling images of Black women as individuals such as the Jezebel, the mammy, and the angry Black woman to justify its violence. These controlling images invite society to dehumanize African American women by representing them as single stories without complexity and intersection. The pervasive communal and intergenerational injustice within the criminal justice system and the health care system (and others) determinedly threatens African American women by treating them as subhuman—as if their lives or reproductive freedom do not matter. African American women are reliant on these systems through their US citizenship and participation in society. Yet, these systems demonstrate methods of individual, collective, and intergenerational oppression and subjugation. US society and the systems within in it perpetuate the dehumanization of African American women on various levels and thus disrupt their psychospirituality.

According to counseling psychologist Robert T. Carter, "race-based events that may be severe or moderate, and daily slights or microaggressions, can produce harm or injury when they have memorable impact or lasting effect or through cumulative or chronic exposure to the various types or classes of racism."[48] Carter categorized race-based stress and trauma as racial harassment, racial discrimination, and discriminatory harassment. Racial harassment includes exclusionary practices and the avoidance of racialized groups (such as economic injustice), racial discrimination includes being

48 Carter, "Racism and Psychological and Emotional Injury," 88.

stereotyped as well as physical or verbal assault (such as sexual assault or the angry Black woman microaggression), and discriminatory harassment involves interlocking experiences of both avoidance and hostility toward racialized groups (such as mistreatment in criminal justice and health care systems). When these experiences are considered negative, memorable, sudden, or uncontrollable, a cluster of stressful and traumatic reactions can ensue, including depression, poor relationships, and withdrawal.

When facing gendered stress and trauma, one coping method employed by African American women is normalized chaos.[49] Cyclical and ongoing trauma is justified, minimized, or otherwise normalized as common, insignificant cultural experiences.[50] The strong Black woman archetype and the culturally embedded stigma regarding mental health care contribute to Black women coping with gendered racism by normalizing its pervasiveness among Black women and girls, allowing stress and trauma to pass as cultural norms and values.[51] This process of maladaptive coping through denial and self-minimization undergirds white supremacy's intent to hinder African American women's psychospirituality. Through constant negative, memorable, sudden, or uncontrollable external actions of gendered racism targeting both individuals and communities and the normalization of chaotic, unceasing trauma, a person's psychospirituality receives repeated, severe, violent blows. White supremacy aims to destroy us, yet we are still here.

African American Women's Resilience

Alternative coping methods to normalized chaos exist. Williams frames the Hagar story as illustrative of the ability of African American women to "make a way out of no way" amid multiple oppressions.[52] Like Hagar, African American women find themselves in the wilderness of unjust systems, oppression, marginalization, uncertainty, and dangerous environments. In the wilderness, their psychospirituality endures moments of despair,

49 Ricks, "Normalized Chaos."

50 Ricks, "Normalized Chaos."

51 Nina A. Nabors and Melanie F. Pettee, "Womanist Therapy with African American Women with Disabilities," *Women & Therapy* 26, no. 3–4 (2003): 331–341, https://doi.org/10.1300/J015v26n03_10.

52 Williams, *Sisters in the Wilderness.*

hopelessness, isolation, and loss of self. Yet it is precisely in the wilderness that Hagar met God. It is precisely in the wilderness that Hagar's identity as a woman, as a poor person, and as an ethnically othered person was affirmed by the divine. Williams named Hagar "the first female in the Bible to liberate herself from oppressive power structures."[53] Her resilience in the wilderness mirrors African American women's resilience in their own wilderness experiences of gendered racism.

African American women's intrinsic sense of resilience adapts over generations in response to stress and trauma and aids us in navigating white supremacy in creative, generative, and resourceful ways. N. Lynne Westfield, scholar of religious education, describes resilience as African American women's spiritual tenacity.[54] Resilience is what encourages African American women to live full lives and continue birthing and nurturing whole communities despite the white supremacy-induced trauma experienced over generations. Resilience differs from strength, which often stems from external sociocultural expectations that African American women should develop emotional fortitude, superhuman caregiving responsibilities, and self-sabotaging independence.[55] Rather, resilience thrives through emotional vulnerability, humanization of self and community, and interdependence. Resilience also differs from survival. Survivalism implies African American women engage in competition for limited resources, contend with a sense of loneliness, and intentionally distance themselves from others.[56] Resilience, however, is premised upon sharing resources and a communal sense of flourishing and belonging. For African American women, resilience is an intergenerational, relational, and spiritual practice. Although methods of resilience adapt over time to meet the varied needs of diverse generations of African American women, its persistence relies on maintaining a series of relationships: relationship with community, relationship with Spirit or the sacred, relationship with self, relationship with ancestors, and relationship with cultural practices.

---

53 Williams, *Sisters in the Wilderness*, 18.

54 N. Lynne Westfield, *Dear Sisters: A Womanist Practice of Hospitality* (Cleveland, OH: Pilgrim Press, 2007).

55 Nabors and Pettee, "Womanist Therapy"; Walker-Barnes, *Too Heavy a Yoke*.

56 Westfield, *Dear Sisters*.

Relationship with community promotes resilience in the face of gendered racism as it offers African American women space for self-realization and self-definition,[57] builds collective resilience,[58] and counters the trauma response of withdrawal and disconnection.[59] African American women in community define themselves with the fullness of their layered identities and shed controlling pejorative images such as the angry Black woman, the Jezebel, and the mammy. Their intersectional identities are mirrored among their peers, and no longer are they bound to traumatic tropes. Community cultivates connection, which, in turn, builds collective resilience, an effective coping mechanism for those from collectivist cultures like the African diaspora.[60] A 2002 study found that women of color experiencing higher collective resilience maintained increased positive mental and emotional health outcomes than those with little experience of collective resilience.[61] Finally, in community, African American women share needs, express feelings, and name their suffering free from the white gaze. They receive affirmation and support and foster trusting relationships with other women, family, faith communities, peers, and colleagues.[62] White supremacy–induced trauma encourages African American women to internalize negative stereotypes and withdraw from society. Community, therefore, is a tool for resilience and resistance against such aims.

Relationship with Spirit is both personal and communal. African American women have diverse expressions of spirituality and religiosity and hold a myriad of spiritual and religious belief systems, from organized religions such as Christianity to African diasporic traditions such as hoodoo. All forms of practiced spirituality significantly contribute to the physical and mental well-being of African American women and serve as a protective

---

57 Walker-Barnes, *Too Heavy a Yoke*.

58 Thema Bryant-Davis, Bemi Fasalojo, Ana Arounian, Kirsten L. Jackson, and Egypt Leithman, "Resist and Rise: A Trauma-Informed Womanist Model for Group Therapy," *Women & Therapy* (July 2021), http://doi.org/10.1080/02703149.2021.1943114.

59 Bryant-Davis et al., "Resist and Rise"; Sanchez-Hucles, "Womanist Therapy with Black Women."

60 Bryant-Davis et al., "Resist and Rise."

61 Bryant-Davis et al., "Resist and Rise," 7.

62 Walker-Barnes, *Too Heavy a Yoke*; Sanchez-Hucles, "Womanist Therapy with Black Women."

factor against the effects of oppression.[63] For generations, African American women engaged in personal spiritual practices and communal religious rituals to form and sustain a sense of faith, hope, accompaniment, liberation, and protection. Scholars of education and psychology Thema Bryant-Davis, Bemi Fasalojo, Ana Arounian, Kirsten L. Jackson, and Egypt Leithman note, "Spirituality affects almost every aspect of life for African American women and has shown to influence health, with research supporting that spiritual and religious coping is highly effective for African Americans with bereavement, illness, trauma, and stress."[64] A relationship with Spirit fosters resilience, encouraging African American women to make a way out of no way by transcending exclusionary and insidious barriers crafted by white supremacy and by centering a sense of connection and purpose.

Relationship with self resists white supremacy through fostering self-definition and self-empowerment.[65] Self-empowerment invites African American women to advocate for themselves and trust their intuition when confronting racism and gender oppression. Much like in community, African American women in relationship with their selves claim and name the fullness of who they are. An appreciation for the complexity of their layered and full lives compels them to resist external forces aiming to thwart any sense of self-love and self-care.[66] In her observations of Black women healing from trauma and normalized chaos, Ricks avers that rest, self-love, and self-care are counternarratives to the self-inflicted violence of burnout and acquiescence to the trope of superhuman strength.[67] A recent trend emerging on social media involves Black women embracing the soft life. The soft life encourages Black women to shed the burden of having to be strong and instead indulge in luxury and abundant self-care.

A relationship with ancestors is an integral practice of resilience. Resilience is reinforced through a constant forward movement by African American women encountering oppression and navigating relational practices

---

63 Banks and Lee, "Womanism and Spirituality/Theology."

64 Bryant-Davis et al., "Resist and Rise," 15.

65 Thema Bryant-Davis and Lillian Comas-Díaz, eds. *Womanist and Mujerista Psychologies: Voices of Fire, Acts of Courage* (Washington, DC: American Psychological Association, 2016).

66 Sanchez-Hucles, "Womanist Therapy with Black Women."

67 Ricks, "Normalized Chaos."

through it. Theologian Monica A. Coleman writes, "We can creatively transform the past to decide how we should move into the future. We can also draw power from the lives of those who have come before us. As we learn from the past, our ancestors have their own kind of immortality."[68] African American women learn from their ancestors' modeling of resilience and faith, serving as teachers and guides through ritual and intergenerational storytelling.[69] Their stories and experiences tell of overcoming remarkable circumstances and thus map out pathways for building resilience among future generations. Relationship with ancestors connects to relationship with Spirit as Black women engage African diasporic traditions, such as hoodoo, to heal from generational trauma and connect with their ancestral practices.

A relationship with cultural practices includes a relationship with intergenerational resources such as storytelling and ancestry. Storytelling is a central cultural practice for African American women as it resists traditions and expectations of silence.[70] Storytelling develops cultural consciousness by relating women to African American oral culture, providing a sense of belonging and participation in cultural history. Storytelling also develops self-confidence and agency as African American women choose how to design and craft the stories they tell.[71] An appreciation for, and relationship with, cultural practices has emerged alongside Black women's connection to African diasporic traditions.

These relational practices bolster resilience against the gendered racism experienced by African American women. The fostering of these relationships looks different over the course of generations, but there remains a throughline of hope, connection, and cultural awareness. African American women today would not have awareness of these relational resources for resilience if it were not for the generations before them who navigated gendered racism and white supremacy–induced trauma and passed along their stories of making a way out of no way.

---

68 Monica A. Coleman, *Making a Way Out of No Way: A Womanist Theology* (Minneapolis: Fortress Press, 2008), 101.

69 Stephanie M. Crumpton, *A Womanist Pastoral Theology against Intimate and Cultural Violence* (London: Palgrave Macmillan, 2014); Sanchez-Hucles, "Womanist Therapy with Black Women."

70 Bryant-Davis and Comas-Díaz, *Womanist and Mujerista Psychologies.*

71 Bryant-Davis and Comas-Díaz, *Womanist and Mujerista Psychologies.*

Where Do We Go from Here?

While white supremacy dehumanizes African American women, resilience supports African American women's psychospirituality, reminding them of their full humanity. While trauma is certainly a theme in the storied lives of African American women, it is not the entirety of their narrative. African American women are not merely victims of trauma but are agential beings with substantial power to write their own stories of emotional, spiritual, physical, and psychological health. Stories of women like Peggy, who took extreme measures to release her own narrative and her family's narrative from the control of white supremacy, illustrate women taking their future into their own hands. Despite their dire circumstances, many enslaved women pieced together relational resources to transcend the psychospiritual bondage of white supremacy. They pieced together their community, Spirit, themselves, their ancestors, and their cultural practices to tell their full stories of resilience and resistance despite the trauma that was designed to destroy them. These stories are told across the generations, offering hope and guidance to African American women facing their own contemporary iterations of white supremacy and trauma. Stories of resilience of today's African American women navigating gendered racism will certainly inform generations to come.

3

THE PSYCHOSPIRITUAL TRAUMA OF LGBTQ+ PEOPLE AND COMMUNITIES

Depathologizing Queer Lives and Experiences

Keith A. Menhinick and Cody J. Sanders

FROM THE CHURCH, the school, the courthouse to the family—the explicit message to an overwhelming number of queer and trans people is clear: *You are not welcome here, not wanted, not cherished, not loved.*[1] This message is repeated not only in myriad acts of abuse, rejection, and violence against the mind-body-spirits of LGBTQ+ people and communities, it is also encoded into the political discourses and social structures that organize our life together, including the "family" and even the "future."

Data about potentially traumatic and adverse experiences common to LGBTQ+ life in the US context unveils the deception in society's myth of inevitable progress. This myth ironically employs LGBTQ+ rights as *evidence* of progress while simultaneously working to undermine those rights and elide LGBTQ+ history. For example, research into the lived experience of rejection due to being LGBTQ+ correlates with societal attempts to erase queerness and transness from the school's curriculum, the government's history, the church's community, and even the family's name and lineage. Some will counter, of course, with citations of the growing number of affirming

1 Throughout this chapter, we use "queer and trans" as well as "LGBTQ+" to index the vast array of identifications, embodiments, and relationalities outside of the prescriptions of cisgender heterosexual patriarchy (*cis-heteropatriarchy*), including but not limited to those who identify as lesbian, gay, bisexual, transgender, two-spirit, gender-nonconforming, or queer, as well as those who choose to live against identificatory labels. We also use "queer and trans" interchangeably with "LGBTQ+" as this reflects common cultural usage within these communities. As we trace common patterns and experiences, however, by no means do we mean to imply a homogeneity to the queer and trans experience.

LGBTQ+ representations in media or perhaps with the growing number of affirming faith communities. Such invocations of progress, however, function to obscure the continued attacks on LGBTQ+ life. For example, over 510 anti-LGBTQ+ bills were introduced to state legislatures in 2023 alone.[2] This led the Human Rights Campaign (HRC) to declare a "state of emergency" for LGBTQ+ people living in the United States.[3]

Statistics like these serve not as self-evident *facts* but as glimpses into an unfolding picture of the patterns of violence against LGBTQ+ personhood and community. We argue that the range of responses to social pressures and violences falls along a continuum of *stress and trauma* and is significantly related to one's context, culture, and support system.[4] However, unlike other cultural violences, the attacks on LGBTQ+ life and community frequently emerge from "inside the house"—i.e., from the site of the *family*, including the *family of faith*. Attending to the Black gay and lesbian experience, Episcopal priest and pastoral theologian Horace L. Griffin writes,

> *Lesbians and gays generally emerge from heterosexual parents and families strongly opposed to them. Lesbians and gays enter the world of invisibility, not knowing other lesbian and gay people, and most times find themselves battling not only society, but the very communities that most oppressed groups have counted on to help them confront injustice: their own families, churches, and communities.*[5]

2 "Mapping Attacks on LGBTQ Rights in U.S. State Legislatures in 2023," American Civil Liberties Union, December 21, 2023, https://www.aclu.org/legislative-attacks-on-lgbtq-rights-2023.

3 "For the First Time Ever, Human Rights Campaign Officially Declares 'State of Emergency' for LGBTQ+ Americans; Issues National Warning and Guidebook to Ensure Safety for LGBTQ+ Residents and Travelers," Human Rights Campaign, June 6, 2023, https://www.hrc.org/press-releases/for-the-first-time-ever-human-rights-campaign-officially-declares-state-of-emergency-for-lgbtq-americans-issues-national-warning-and-guidebook-to-ensure-safety-for-lgbtq-residents-and-travelers.

4 Catherine N. Dulmus and Carolyn Hilarski, "When Stress Constitutes Trauma and Trauma Constitutes Crisis: The Stress-Trauma-Crisis Continuum," *Brief Treatment and Crisis Intervention* 3, no. 1 (2003): 27–35, https://doi.org/10.1093/brief-treatment/mhg008.

5 Horace L. Griffin, *Their Own Receive Them Not: African American Lesbians and Gays in Black Churches* (Cleveland, OH: Pilgrim Press, 2006), 156.

For pastoral theologians and spiritual care providers working with queer and trans folks, the *family* cannot be unproblematically cited or celebrated as a primary mediator of other sociopolitical oppressions but rather becomes revealed in many cases as a traumatic extension and expression of these oppressions.

Importantly, what is at stake for queer and trans people is not only the care and belonging of family but also the assets, resources, and supports tied to lineage, social network, and inheritance. These inner and outer resources are integral to surviving and coping with the anti-queer stressors and violences embedded in a white cis-heterosexist capitalist world order. They are also vital for imagining a family and a future with queer people in it.

Spiritual care with LGBTQ+ people requires responding to the range of disruptions and dysregulations experienced by the individual and the community—which fall on a continuum of stress and trauma—as well as intervening in the conditions of society and family that make being queer so precarious and potentially traumatic in the first place. Importantly, this work entails building up the relational, material, and even temporal resources for LGBTQ+ people to survive, cope, and connect *here and now* as well as *there and then*. Holistic spiritual care is thus a search for the resources, families, communities, histories, and futurities necessary for the full flourishing of all life.

Surveying the Lived Conditions of LGBTQ+ Life

The National Child Traumatic Stress Network published a two-part resource calling for all care providers and organizations to use a screener to assess for trauma exposure and post-traumatic stress symptoms when working with LGBTQ+ youth.[6] The rationale is that LGBTQ+ youth are disproportionately exposed to a range of adverse childhood experiences (ACEs) and potentially traumatic events (PTEs) compared with their cisgender,

6 Antonia Barba, Megan A. Mooney, Kalie Giovanni, Megan Clarke, Jennifer Brizzie Grady, and J.A. Cohen, *Identifying the Intersection of Trauma and Sexual Orientation and Gender Identity*, Part 1, *Key Considerations* (Los Angeles: National Child Traumatic Stress Network, 2021), https://www.nctsn.org/resources/identifying-the-intersection-of-trauma-and-sexual-orientation-and-gender-identity-key-considerations.

heterosexual peers. Consequently, these adverse and potentially traumatic experiences correlate with an increased risk for a range of mental and physical health challenges (e.g., depression, addiction, homelessness, suicidality) and an increased risk for relying on desperate coping methods (e.g., substance abuse, risky sexual behavior).

In part 1 of *Identifying the Intersection of Trauma and Sexual Orientation and Gender Identity*, the National Child Traumatic Stress Network surveyed data from a range of studies to posit four primary areas of research into the connection between LGBTQ+ experience and trauma: a sense of safety (in school), physical and sexual harassment and abuse, family rejection, and mental health.[7] We can map these four categories as the primary arenas of violence against the personhood and community of LGBTQ+ children and youth. In this study, we also begin to see a picture of how queer, trans, and ally communities are making sense of this violence through the category of traumatization.

A sense of safety is fundamental for optimal development of the child's nervous system, brain, personality, and community. The GLSEN (pronounced "glisten"; formerly the Gay, Lesbian, and Straight Education Network) National School Climate Survey reported that 59.5 percent of LGBTQ+ students felt unsafe at school due to their sexual orientation and 44.6 percent due to their gender expression.[8] Additionally, 62.2 percent of LGBTQ+ students experienced discriminatory policies at school, and an overwhelming percentage of LGBTQ+ students reported hearing homophobic and transphobic remarks from peers and teachers (98.5%) with 91.8 percent feeling distressed afterwards.[9]

Hearing violent language about one's own emerging sense of self in the very place where one is expected to gain an education and learn how to function in society negatively impacts the mind-body-spirit of an LGBTQ+ child. We can only postulate about the multiple educational disparities for

---

7 Barba et al., *Identifying the Intersection*, 2.

8 Joseph G. Kosciw, Emily A. Gretak, Adrian D. Zongrone, Caitlin M. Clark, and Nhan L. Truong, *The 2017 National School Climate Survey: The Experiences of Lesbian, Gay, Bisexual, Transgender, and Queer Youth in Our Nation's Schools* (New York: GLSEN, 2018), xviii, https://www.glsen.org/sites/default/files/2019-10/GLSEN-2017-National-School-Climate-Survey-NSCS-Full-Report.pdf.

9 Kosciw et al., *The 2017 National School Climate Survey*, xviii.

hypervigilant and stress-aroused LGBTQ+ students, whose sense of threat and ensuing stress can impair their cognitive abilities to concentrate, participate, learn, and retain.

The violence against LGBTQ+ children and youth in school also appears in the omission of LGBTQ+ history and comprehensive sex education from the school curriculum, which is also a refusal to teach LGBTQ+ students that they have a community. According to research published in the *Columbia Law Review*, "a comprehensive survey shows that anti-gay curriculum laws actually exist in twenty states."[10] This *absenting* of community and history is ultimately the denial of belonging—to a history; to an ancestry; to a present, alive, and vibrant community of diversity. Given the numerous overt attacks and censorship, the evidence is clear: "Schools nationwide are hostile environments for a distressing number of LGBTQ students."[11]

Thus, it is no wonder that, as a response to feeling unsafe amid the increased risk of threat and harm, a majority of LGBTQ+ youth avoided extracurricular activities (70.5%), one-third (34.9%) skipped at least one day of school in the past month, and 10.5 percent skipped four or more days.[12] Skipping school and extracurricular activities does not necessarily mean staying home for many LGBTQ+ children and youth. The Trevor Project, a non-profit with the mission of ending suicide among LGBTQ+ young people, reported fewer than one in three transgender and nonbinary youth feel affirmed in their home.[13] According to a national study by the Human Rights Campaign, 78 percent of LGBTQ+ youth are not out to their parents due to fears of repercussions, most specifically of abuse or rejection.[14] Familial rejection is no mere threat as 29 percent of LGBTQ+ youth have experienced being unhoused,[15] and, among that population, 75 percent of LGB youth and 90 percent of transgender and nonbinary youth link their

---

10 Clifford Rosky, "Anti-Gay Curriculum Laws," *Columbia Law Review* 117, no. 8 (2017), 1465, https://columbialawreview.org/content/anti-gay-curriculum-laws/.

11 Kosciw et al., *The 2017 National School Climate Survey*, xviii.

12 Kosciw et al., *The 2017 National School Climate Survey*, xviii.

13 The Trevor Project, *National Survey*, 4.

14 Human Rights Campaign Staff, *Human Rights Campaign Working to Defeat 340 Anti-LGBTQ+ Bills*, 4.

15 The Trevor Project, *National Survey*, 4.

homelessness directly to the experience of family abuse or rejection.[16] Experiences of abuse and rejection haunt many queer and trans people well past childhood and adolescence. The Pew Research Center found that about 39 percent (4 out of 10) of LGBTQ+ adults stated that they had been rejected by a close family member or close friend.[17]

The relational cutting off by family and close friends is simultaneously *spiritual* and *material*, entailing the removal of care and belonging as well as the withdrawal of social networks, political protections, cultural assets, and familial resources (e.g., land, housing, wealth, and inheritance). As a result, LGBTQ+ folks who experience family rejection are even more at risk for a variety of other challenges—food insecurity, homelessness, victimization, self-harm, suicidal ideation and attempt, and a range of mental health disorders. The removal of support networks and material resources also makes LGBTQ+ folks more vulnerable to a variety of communal and environmental stressors: the Covid-19 pandemic, natural disasters due to climate change, systemic racism and oppression, and a number of other crises. As agronomist Pablo Servigne, eco-adviser Raphaël Stevens, and agricultural engineer Gauthier Chapelle make clear, "It is well established that the most important factor for resilience (from the first minutes after the tragedy) is the closeness and helpfulness of family and neighbors (or even strangers) who can aid in overcoming fear, give care and bring touches of joy and optimism."[18] The quality and efficacy of such support is dependent upon the existence of a social network *before* the communal or environmental disaster occurs. For many young queer and trans people, these networks are precarious.

Data also shows that when LGBTQ+ youth reach out for help and services (e.g., government programs, housing shelters, lending services, health care), they are frequently met with higher rates of stigma and discrimination

---

16 Soon Kyu Choi, Bianca D. M. Wilson, Jama Shelton, and Gary Gates, *Serving Our Youth 2015: The Needs and Experiences of Lesbian, Gay, Bisexual, Transgender, and Questioning Youth Experiencing Homelessness* (Los Angeles: The Williams Institute with True Colors Fund, 2015), 5, https://williamsinstitute.law.ucla.edu/wp-content/uploads/Serving-Our-Youth-Update-Jun-2015.pdf.

17 Pew Research Center, *A Survey of LGBT Americans: Attitudes, Experiences and Values in Changing Times* (Washington, DC: Pew Research Center, 2013), 1, https://www.pewresearch.org/social-trends/2013/06/13/a-survey-of-lgbt-americans/.

18 Pablo Servigne, Raphaël Stevens, and Gauthier Chapelle, *Another End of the World is Possible: Living the Collapse* (Medford, MA: Polity Press, 2021), 42.

than the general population. Service discrimination becomes not only another source of violation and stress but also another cause of the economic, employment, health, and housing disparities for LGBTQ+ youth, especially those who are Black or Indigenous.[19] The shortage of culturally specific understandings and services then compounds the alienation for those brave enough to reach out for help, setting up LGBTQ+ folks to experience cycles of abuse, neglect, retraumatization, and isolation.

Of course, these accounts are largely silent about harm done to LGBTQ+ people in the church and other religious communities, which frequently sacralize the exclusions and abuses of the family and state. More specifically, religiosity is frequently the common denominator of households that exile their queer children.[20] Harmful religious narratives and theologies thus are a factor in interpersonal and intrapsychic violence, for these narratives "set life on edge, make life seem unlivable, and often lead to suicide."[21] One study concluded that 9.3 percent of LGBT youth met DSM-5 criteria for PTSD in the previous twelve months, and the rates exponentially increased for youth forced into conversion therapy.[22] Within-group differences in these studies are rarely accounted for, meaning these numbers may be higher, the risk much more severe, for LGBTQ+ folks of color and of varying physical abilities and immigration status.

There are few spaces of respite for a large percentage of LGBTQ+ people and even fewer for children and youth. Whether in the home, school, community, or church, many LGBTQ+ folks find themselves unable to escape hostile social environments. This inescapability reveals the very structures and institutions of life to be dehumanizing, deforming, and often

---

19 Caitlin Rooney and Laura E. Durso, *The Harms of Refusing Service to LGBTQ People and Other Marginalized Communities*, November 29, 2017 (Washington, DC: Center for American Progress). https://www.americanprogress.org/article/harms-refusing-service-lgbtq-people-marginalized-communities/.

20 Dirk-Jan Janssen and Peer Scheepers, "How Religiosity Shapes Rejection of Homosexuality across the Globe," *Journal of Homosexuality* 66, no. 14 (2019): 1974–2001, https://doi.org/10.1080/00918369.2018.1522809.

21 Cody J. Sanders, *Christianity, LGBTQ Suicide, and the Souls of Queer Folk* (Lanham, MD: Lexington Books, 2020), 1.

22 Brian S. Mustanski, Robert Garofalo, and Erin M. Emerson, "Mental Health Disorders, Psychological Distress, and Suicidality in a Diverse Sample of Lesbian, Gay, Bisexual, and Transgender Youths," *American Journal of Public Health* 100, no. 12 (2010): 2426–2432, https://doi.org/10.2105/ AJPH.2009.178319.

destructive for those whose lives, loves, and bodies deviate from the social norms and expectations of the dominant society and its mirror—the nuclear family.

In the 2022 National Survey on LGBTQ Youth Mental Health, 45 percent of LGBTQ+ youth reported they "seriously considered attempting suicide in the past year," and the rates were much higher for LGBTQ+ youth of color.[23] When LGBTQ+ children and youth are abused by, or cut off from, primary relationships and meaningful community, including the material resources tied to those connections, they are thereby cut off from a vision of the future with them in it. This is not an incidental violence but an intentional one. It is the systemic and structural intent of a cis-heteropatriarchal society to either assimilate or eradicate queerness from all facets of our shared life together: the family, school, community, and church, as well as the mind-body-spirit of the person.

The Crises of Trauma in/as Queerness

Obviously not every LGBTQ+ person experiences the range of stressors and potentially traumatic events surveyed. A variety of factors influence not only risk exposure but also the resources for coping and managing stress and trauma—the primary resource being a robust and holistic social support system. But again, for queer and trans folks, rejection from social networks and community is a frequently shared and common experience, even if not a universal one.

Several important patterns can be distilled from the above reporting. First, LGBTQ+ people are extremely vulnerable to a range of violent experiences throughout life. Second, the withdrawal of social support marks an ongoing fear and threat for LGBTQ+ folks. Third, organizations like the National Child Traumatic Stress Network, the Trevor Project, and the Human Rights Campaign, like many local queer communities, name these violences against LGBTQ+ folks as traumas.

These patterns evidence a collective urge from within the LGBTQ+ and ally communities to count the adversities and violences they experience as *traumas*. We suggest that the purpose is less about pinpointing trauma

---

23 The Trevor Project, *National Survey*, 4.

in empiricisms and more about charting collective and cultural patterns of violence and then naming (i.e., validating) those experiences through the very diagnostic category used against them historically in psychological and cultural discourses: the category of *trauma*.

The instinct to inventory patterns of violence and name them as traumas must be understood in the context of the historical perpetration of violence against LGBTQ+ personhood and community and the systematic undervaluing or elision of LGBTQ+ suffering altogether. In such instances, the source of trauma becomes located in events (e.g., community harassment and assault, family rejection) and in institutions (e.g., the family, the school), which constrict the diversity and expansiveness of human potentiality and relationality to binary gender and monogamous heterosexuality. Pastorally, this naming externalizes the sources (blame) of stress and trauma onto events and institutions, locating them outside the personhood of the LGBTQ+ individual and community. Such a shift is vital for creating community and for bringing a sense of comfort and agency to hurting souls.

Yet, in response to these formulations, some scholars and professionals may worry about the slippage between trauma as response to an event versus trauma as the event itself or even as descriptive of an entire culture. Elaine Miller-Karas, developer of the Trauma and Community Resiliency Models (TRM and CRM)®, embodies a way to hold both approaches together: thinking about trauma in terms of events that culture deems "traumatic" while also recognizing trauma as a neurobiological perception and response to an event or accumulation of events (though culturally we may or may not acknowledge the *event* nor the *accumulation* as traumatic).[24] Miller-Karas's work invites us to think about the politics of communally naming certain shared experiences, cultural discourses, and social institutions as *traumatic*.[25] Additionally, we can understand the queer person's response to such attacks as one that is neurobiologically, emotionally, and socially specific (even mediated), expressing itself in a range of potential responses along a continuum of stress and trauma.

24 Elaine Miller-Karas, *Building Resilience to Trauma: The Trauma and Community Resiliency Models* (New York: Routledge, 2015).

25 Miller-Karas, *Building Resilience.*

Many LGBTQ+ people are trying to survive, to love themselves and make new families, to find a place to belong and rest their tired heads. They are also searching for a language to make sense of their suffering and their pride. There are defensive reasons why LGBTQ+ communities find themselves using trauma language to describe frequently shared experiences. One important reason is to acknowledge and condemn the multivariate ways in which white cis-heteropatriarchy deforms the mind-body-spirits of queer folks in patterned ways, ways intended to maintain societal and familial homeostasis. Psychiatrist Murray Bowen would remind us that the two stases are intimately comingled, even coconstitutive.[26] From "Don't Say Gay" bills in schools to fundamentalist religious movements like Focus on the Family, the attack on LGBTQ+ life comes from multiple vectors and is systematically aimed at the erasure of our community, history, and future. How else to collectively imagine that violence aimed at "the destruction of experience" except as a kind of collective *trauma*?[27]

In the history of psychology, theories of trauma and sexuality have long been entangled. Sigmund Freud famously explored the connection between psychological states and somatic symptoms, linking the "symptom(s)" with not just *one* traumatic event but a "series of associatively linked episodes, beginning in early childhood, all of which needed to be exhumed."[28] For Freud, trauma indexes the repetition and reenactment of unclaimed and unassimilated experiences, particularly those that completely overwhelm and impair one's abilities to self-regulate, cope, connect, and make meaning. Freud's conception of trauma as repetition and reenactment has since received sustained attention, but less attention has been directed toward the context in which his theories of the unconscious and trauma emerged—namely, in the analysis of infantile seduction, childhood sexuality, repressed sexual and identificatory fantasies, and adult sexual perversity.

---

26 Michael E. Kerr and Murray Bowen, *Family Evaluation* (New York: W. W. Norton, 1988).

27 Vincenzo Di Nicola, "Two Trauma Communities: A Philosophical Archaeology of Cultural and Clinical Trauma Theories," in *Trauma and Transcendence: Suffering and the Limits of Theory*, ed. Eric Boynton and Peter Capretto (New York: Fordham University Press, 2018), 19, https://doi.org/10.1515/9780823280292-002.

28 Stephen A. Mitchell and Margaret J. Black, *Freud and Beyond: A History of Modern Psychoanalytic Thought* (New York: Basic Books, 2016), 10.

As Diana Fuss, professor of literature, film, and feminist studies, elaborates, "it is Freud who gives us our most familiar and denigrating sexual typologies, most memorable among them 'the male homosexual' . . . and 'the female homosexual.'"[29] Freud maintained that homosexuality "cannot be classified as an illness," yet he also declared it to be "a variation of the sexual function produced by a certain arrest of sexual development."[30] Despite Freud's own nuanced attention to sexuality, the ways that psychoanalytic and psychological ideas have been picked up culturally and politically have historically conflated trauma and unhealth with queerness itself, as if the roots of all psychic traumas are sexual perversity or gender incertitude.

While current medical, psychological, and social scientific discourses now work to decouple queerness from illness, defect, and perversity, the association between queerness and unhealth persists in the ways that the "homosexual," the "transgender," and the "queer" are still reproduced in cultural and political discourses not as persons but as figures of rupture, break, and discontinuity, marking a crisis and threat to the family, to democracy, and to children, which, as literary critic Lee Edelman famously argued, is a threat to the future itself.[31]

For LGBTQ+ and ally communities to count the common adversities and attacks on LGBTQ+ life as *traumas* (or potentially traumatic events) is thus an intervention to disassociate the rupture of queerness from the split of trauma. The inherent risk of this strategy is to make trauma "thinkable" and to "lose the spectrality, rupture, nonlinearity, and non-integrability that mark the traumatic as such."[32] Yet, if any community can simultaneously mobilize a category, critique it, and keep its signification open, it is the queer community. Psychologist and psychiatrist Vincenzo Di Nicola writes that "trauma" is not a master term but a flawed one, with a complicated history

29 Diana Fuss, "Pink Freud," *GLQ: A Journal of Lesbian and Gay Studies* 2 (1995): 1–2, https://doi.org/10.1215/10642684-2-1_and_2-1.

30 Sigmund Freud, "A Letter to an American Mother," *American Journal of Psychiatry* 105 (1935/1951): 787, https://doi.org/10.1176/ajp.107.10.786.

31 Lee Edelman, *No Future: Queer Theory and the Death Drive* (Durham, NC: Duke University Press, 2004).

32 Mary-Jane Rubenstein, "Afterword—The Transcendence of Trauma: Prospects for the Continental Philosophy of Religion," in *Trauma and Transcendence: Suffering and the Limits of Theory*, ed. Eric Boynton and Peter Capretto (New York: Fordham University Press, 2018), 286.

and no "unified discourse."[33] The same can be said of queerness itself. As with the term *queer*, queer and trans communities have been reclaiming the word *trauma* from its solely individual and pathological roots to index sociocultural processes of identity formation, which reveals how a violent world order stresses, traumatizes, and deforms the mind-body-spirits of LGBTQ+ folks by conscripting white cis-heterosexual roles, embodiments, and relations. (It is worth noting that we believe cis-heteropatriarchy harms all people—queer and straight alike—though that harm registers differently for those whose lives rub against the norms and thereby refuse cis-heteronormative assimilation.)

The collective efforts in the LGBTQ+ community to demedicalize and depathologize trauma, and to now use this language more broadly to describe a culture, is ultimately a strategy to externalize the source of violence from a problem of the individual to a problem of the social environment.[34] In this sense, LGBTQ+ stress and trauma may be read as appropriate and even adaptive responses to a violent context that seeks to do them harm—again, through strategies like assimilation, abuse, exclusion, silencing, or eradication. Throughout LGBTQ+ history, depathologizing trauma has been a consistent and reliable strategy for establishing queerness on new terms—which is not to deny that trauma may have pathological dimensions. By externalizing the source of their suffering (e.g., I am not the problem. The white cis-heteropatriarchal capitalist world order is.), LGBTQ+ folks claim a kind of community, agency, and resistance from within the site of violence. They open new space for rethinking the terms of queer and trans subject formations apart from the ways they have been deformed—i.e., the possibility of queer continuums of resilience-growth-hope in response to, but not totalized by, queer continuums of stress and trauma.

Queer Continuums of Stress and Trauma

Addressing concerns about oppression and trauma more broadly, feminist psychologist Maria Root expands traditional notions of trauma to include

33 Di Nicola, "Two Trauma Communities," 18.

34 Ann Cvetkovich, *An Archive of Feelings: Trauma, Sexuality, and Lesbian Public Cultures* (Durham, NC: Duke University Press, 2003), 25.

the "traumatogenic effects of oppression that are not necessarily overtly violent or threatening to bodily well-being at the given moment but that do violence to the soul and spirit."[35] Root coined the term *insidious trauma*, arguing that the impact of oppression "shapes a worldview rather than shatters assumptions about the world."[36] Insidious trauma reframes colonialism, racism, homophobia, trans-antagonism, and all such oppressions not as interruptions of an otherwise lithe and free subjectivity but as constitutive of the context and conditions that constrain our emergence as subjects in the first place—what kinds of subjects we can be and what kinds of interactions and relations we can enjoy.

Similarly, epidemiologist Ilan Meyer and social psychologist David Frost support the idea of a *minority stress model* among sexual minority populations, which "suggests that because of stigma, prejudice, and discrimination, lesbian, gay, and bisexual people experience more stress than do heterosexuals and that this stress can lead to mental and physical disorders."[37] Like insidious trauma, minority stress is a model for attending to the social stressors embedded in the context of a life, inquiring into the impact of both quotidian and explosive stressors such as prejudicial events, structural exclusions, expectations of rejection, pressures of concealment, internalized homophobia, and experiences of harassment and violence.[38] There is no doubt that this short list describes norms and instances of *harm* and *stress*. The question is how such minority stress impacts persons and communities in the short term and across a lifetime. Meyer and Frost contend that the assessment of minority stress thus necessitates inquiry into the ways that "health outcomes are determined by the balance of positive (coping and social support) and negative (stressors) effects."[39]

---

35 Maria P. P. Root, "Reconstructing the Impact of Trauma on Personality," in *Personality and Psychopathology: Feminist Reappraisals*, ed. Laura S. Brown and Mary Ballou (New York: Guilford Press, 1992), 240.

36 Root, "Reconstructing the Impact of Trauma," 240.

37 Ilan H. Meyer and David M. Frost, "Minority Stress and the Health of Sexual Minorities," in *Handbook of Psychology and Sexual Orientation*, ed. Charlotte J. Patterson and Anthony R. D'Augelli (Oxford: Oxford University Press, 2013), 252.

38 Ilan H. Meyer, "Prejudice, Social Stress, and Mental Health in Lesbian, Gay, and Bisexual Populations: Conceptual Issues and Research Evidence," *Psychological Bulletin* 129, no. 5 (2003): 674–697, https://doi.org/10.1037/0033-2909.129.5.674.

39 Meyer and Frost, "Minority Stress," 262.

Minority stress and insidious trauma become two ways of conceptualizing the impact of violence—structural, discursive, interpersonal, and intrapersonal—on LGBTQ+ personhood and community. LGBTQ+ people are disproportionately exposed to a range of potentially traumatic events, what many call *shock traumas*, but also to the buildup of chronic minority stress, the accumulation of which we can understand and assess as *queer allostatic load.*[40]

While, culturally, many of us think of stress and trauma as separate, "they share a neurobiological basis. Stress and trauma are not inherent in the event—they are internal mind-body responses on a continuum."[41] *Traumatic stress* then indexes one pole of that continuum, marking the most dysregulated of responses to cis-heteropatriarchal violence when our personal, relational, material, and structural resources for coping and connecting become overwhelmed or destroyed entirely. Whether gradual or sudden, traumatic stress is "the result of a complex interrelationship among psychological, biological, and social processes" and not "a unitary disorder consisting of separate clusters of symptoms."[42] Remembering that trauma is on a continuum with stress is crucial to help extract queerness from its historical conflation with trauma and relocate trauma in a range of defensive and adaptive survival responses to the stress of oppression.

The stress of oppression is chronic and insidious, like the pressure to conceal a relationship or repress a bodily knowing. It is also sudden and explosive, like physical abuse and family rejection. The ability of LGBTQ+ people to effectively manage and cope with that stress is directly connected to our past experiences (e.g., whether we found support outside and within to complete the stress-recovery cycle) and the ways those experiences live on in the mind-body-spirit and community. It is especially connected to our early social environments and parental attachments, which, to reiterate,

40 Elizabeth A. Stanley, *Widen the Window: Training Your Brain and Body to Thrive During Stress and Recover from Trauma* (New York: Penguin Random House, 2019), 31. Allostatic load is the cumulative burden of chronic stress on mental and physical health.

41 Stanley, *Widen the Window*, 32.

42 Bessel A. van der Kolk, Alexander C. McFarlane, and Lars Weisaeth, eds., *Traumatic Stress: The Effects of Overwhelming Experience on Mind, Body, and Society* (New York: The Guilford Press, 2007), ix.

are often the sources of LGBTQ+ stress and not its relief. As experts on childhood trauma Vincent J. Felitti and colleagues famously revealed, "the impact of . . . adverse childhood experiences on adult health status is strong and cumulative."[43] In other words, those who are already stressed and traumatized are more vulnerable to an ever-accumulating onslaught of stress, trauma, and adversity across a lifetime.

Pastorally, we might ask specific questions about, for example, how the constant neuroception of danger and threat along with the chronic pressures to identify and conceal all build up as stress in the mind-body-spirit of LGBTQ+ people. When such stress is repeated and unmetabolized, frequently due to a lack of social support, it changes the mind-body-spirit system of the person and impairs their capacity to cope, manage future stressors, and even imagine belonging to the future. The concern for us in spiritual care becomes about how we can lighten the queer allostatic load as well as increase the resources, resilience, and resistance of LGBTQ+ persons to stave off the chronic, insidious, and traumatic stress of interlocking systems of oppression.

The real challenge is how to respond with care to LGBTQ+ stressors and traumas while also confronting their sources. One of the most persistent issues with research into LGBTQ+ stress and trauma is that too often the agents of *perpetration* go uninterrogated—especially when those perpetrators are pastors, parents, and teachers. In *Epistemology of the Closet*, literary critic Eve Kosofsky Sedgwick argues that most discourses about sexuality tend to reproduce a *minoritizing* view of the subject, conceiving of, for example, same-sex attraction as the exclusive concern of particular people and thus reasserting a neoliberal, autonomous, stable subject.[44] In contrast, Sedgwick advances a *universalizing* view, one that understands any questions and conflicts of sexuality and subjectivity to be issues of "continuing, determinative

43 Vincent J. Felitti, Robert F. Anda, Dale Nordenberg, David F. Williamson, Alison M. Spitz, Valerie Edwards, Mary P. Koss, and James S. Marks, "Relationship of Childhood Abuse and Household Dysfunction to Many of the Leading Causes of Death in Adults: The Adverse Childhood Experiences (ACE) Study," *American Journal of Preventive Medicine* 14, no. 4 (1998): 251, https://doi.org/10.1016/s0749-3797(98)00017-8.

44 Eve Kosofsky Sedgwick, *Epistemology of the Closet* (Oakland: University of California Press, 2008).

importance in the lives of people across the spectrum of sexualities."[45] In this view, sexuality, like identity itself, is tenuous, contingent, and relational, and its effects are not isolated to one person or group but extend to the entire social order of relations. This is not to say that all people are the same but rather that all are connected. It is this connection we have forgotten when we attend to LGBTQ+ stress and trauma but not to holding accountable their abusers—which are both personal and intimate (pastors, parents, teachers) as well as social and cultural (discourses, institutions, structures).

When it comes to assessing LGBTQ+ experiences that fall along the stress-trauma continuum, then, everyone must be implicated, including and especially those who benefit from the preservation and reproduction of the white cis-heterosexual ideal—in the family, school, church, and society. This requires holistic attention to the web of relations and contexts in which identity and social formations occur as well as specific attention to LGBTQ+ stress and trauma as concerns for everyone.[46] Such a project is invested not merely in applying trauma theory to LGBTQ+ lives but also in letting the lived crises of queerness throw all our conceptual tools and subject positions into crisis, ultimately revealing a new starting place based in our interconnectedness and indebtedness to each other.

As philosopher Gillian Rose wrote, "I am abused and I abuse / I am the victim and I am the perpetrator."[47] To think of ourselves in both positions is to locate LGBTQ+ oppression in the discourses, systems, and structures that overdetermine who we can become, who we can connect with, and what those connections entail; it is also to locate the world's violence *in us*, not only in our emergence and formation as subjects but also in our quotidian and habitual perpetuation of oppressive norms and practices.

Responding to LGBTQ+ stress and trauma with care first requires attention to our own complicities and propensities to cause harm. Care also requires attention to the range of psychosocial effects and bodily materializations of anti-queer "soul violence,"[48] as well as to the resources and gifts

45 Sedgwick, *Epistemology of the Closet*, 1.

46 Bonnie J. Miller-McLemore, "The Living Human Web," in *Images of Pastoral Care: Classic Readings*, ed. Robert C. Dykstra (St. Louis: Chalice Press, 2005), 40–46.

47 Gillian Rose, *Judaism and Modernity: Philosophical Essays* (London: Verso, 2017), 31.

48 Sanders, *Christianity, LGBTQ Suicide.*

of the LGBTQ+ community for resisting and transforming a violent world order—both in the world and in us. A challenge will always be to respond with care to LGBTQ+ stress and trauma without collapsing queerness back into its conflation with unhealthiness and defect. After all, queerness may predispose a life to crisis, stress, and potential trauma, but only insofar as the world is *disordered* by white cis-heteropatriarchy. Queerness also mobilizes us toward previously foreclosed modes of desire, contact, embodiment, eroticism, community, and even futurity.

Temporality in Queering the Stress-Trauma Continuum

As psychiatrist Bessel van der Kolk described it, the experience of trauma involves the tyranny of the past over the present in the lives of traumatized people who "chronically feel unsafe inside their bodies" because "the past is alive in the form of gnawing interior discomfort."[49] The violence experienced in the past becomes so intolerable and overwhelming to the mind-body-spirit system that a series of splits and fractures occur that haunt victims of trauma and return in flashbacks, triggering experiences, and intrusive memories—creating unbearable pasts recapitulating in the present.

While much of what van der Kolk offered is also descriptive of the traumatic experience of some queer people, there are additional ways in which queer experience intersects a stress-trauma continuum along the axis of temporality.[50] For queer people—individuals and collectives—the tyranny of the present over the future and the absenting of collective pasts express two forms of chrono stress and traumatic temporality that should be considered within a pastoral theological assessment of stress and trauma for LGBTQ+ people. These experiences are not entirely unique to queer people, however, and attending to them in the temporalities of queer collectives can also benefit practical theologians and spiritual care practitioners in understanding experiences along the stress-trauma continuum for many others harmed by temporal possibilities conscripted by chrono hegemony.

49 Bessel A. van der Kolk, *The Body Keeps the Score: Brain, Mind, and Body in the Healing of Trauma* (New York: Penguin Books, 2014), 97.

50 Van der Kolk, *The Body Keeps the Score.*

Additionally, practical theologians and care practitioners exhibit a paucity of focus on temporality in our work to date. As pastoral theologian Andrew Lester pointed out nearly three decades ago, "pastoral theology . . . has ignored a significant aspect of the human condition, namely our temporality—the fact that we are constantly embedded in the context of time, which includes both past *and future,*" limiting our ability to adequately address the dimension of ultimacy bound up with the notion of "hope."[51] Thus, a queering of trauma frameworks through the lens of queer temporalities may benefit scholars and practitioners in the field more broadly.

Tyranny of the Present over the Future

The future is always already foreclosed to queer people in "straight time," that is, the linear time of neoliberal progress, the unending growth of extractive capitalism, and the future portended by heteronormative familial progeny (i.e., heterosexual biological reproduction).[52] This is a temporality in which the organization of time is tied to the organization of bodies in time and through time. In straight time, the present is a hegemonic construct, and any time to come is beholden to a form of presentism in which economic, political, and techno futures are only derivative versions of the present, always presumed to be getting "better" (but for whom?). Here, it is not the past that is continually revisiting the present but instead the present that is continually projected into the future.

However, as José Esteban Muñoz, scholar of performance studies and queer theory, states, "The present is not enough. It is impoverished and toxic for queers and other people who do not feel the privilege of majoritarian belonging, normative tastes, and 'rational' expectations."[53] It is not enough to survive the present if potential futures are projections, albeit slightly tweaked, of the current status quo. And it is the future that is at stake in many pervasive experiences of stress and trauma among queer people—not

51 Andrew D. Lester, *Hope in Pastoral Care and Counseling* (Louisville. KY: Westminster John Knox Press, 1995), 4.

52 José Esteban Muñoz, *Cruising Utopia: The Then and There of Queer Futurity* (New York: New York University Press, 2009), 25.

53 Muñoz, *Cruising Utopia*, 27.

simply the future of the individual but the possible futures for living lives of queerness against the grain of the cis-heteronormative regime.

Those who cannot (or who refuse to) reproduce the proper family, or embody the norms of ideal citizens, exist outside of time's straight flow from past to present to future. If trauma involves the experience of being stuck in an unending violent past in which there is no hope for escape or vision of a different future, it must also account for unending projections of violent futures in which there is no possibility for the flourishing of life.

Philosophers Matthew Ratcliffe, Mark Ruddell, and Benedict Smith argue that in traumatic aftermaths "the experience of time is itself affected. Rather than a change in what is anticipated, arising against a backdrop of intact temporal experience, there is an altered sense of temporal passage, of 'moving forward' in time, along with a change in how past, present, future, and the relationship between them are experienced."[54] What is eroded in the traumatic temporality resulting in a foreshortened future is a "*style of anticipation*." They explain,

> *Hence a sense of foreshortened future is not a judgment to the effect that the remainder of one's life will be short and that one has little or nothing to look forward to. It is a change in how time is experienced: an orientation toward the future that is inseparable from one's experience of past and present, and also from the short- and long-term "passage" of time, is altered.*[55]

While the discourse of trauma does not encapsulate the entirety of what needs to be addressed in our relationships to futurity, the concept of a foreshortened future is a helpful framework to explore the nature of care in or for the future with queer and trans people.

The type of traumatic response of a foreshortened future that Ratcliffe, Ruddell, and Smith described also seems especially pertinent to the work of spiritual care in larger collective futures of extreme loss and collapse caused

---

54 Matthew Ratcliffe, Mark Ruddell, and Benedict Smith, "What is a 'Sense of Foreshortened Future?' A Phenomenological Study of Trauma, Trust, and Time," *Frontiers in Psychology* 5 (2014): 1, https://doi.org/10.3389/fpsyg.2014.01026.

55 Ratcliffe, Ruddell, and Smith, "What is a 'Sense of Foreshortened Future?,'" 8.

by climate change (to name one among a variety of examples of disaster), which compounds chrono stress and traumatic temporalities of queer and trans collectives:

> *The longer-term sense of time is also very different. When the person looks ahead, the future lacks structure; it is not ordered in terms of meaningful projects, and so a coherent sense of long-term duration is absent. Hence the all-enveloping dread she feels before some inchoate threat is not situated in relation to a wider pattern of meaningful temporal events. There is nothing meaningful between now and its actualization, and so it seems imminent. A loss of interpersonal trust that is central to this form of experience is also what sets it in stone. Without the possibility of entering into trusting relations with others, the predicament seems unchangeable. There is no access to the process that might otherwise reveal its contingency and allow her to move beyond it. The person is isolated from others in a way that is incompatible with "moving forward in time"; her life story has been cut short.*[56]

This loss of trusting interpersonal relationships with others, as noted above, is often a hallmark of queer experience, starting with the family of origin and moving into experiences of school bullying and interpersonal violence. While this has long been noted as a feature of queer experience, its effect on an experience of time and imaginations of futures is lacking in the literature.

A sense of a foreshortened future is similar to what psychologist Mark Freeman describes as "narrative foreclosure," characterized by the conviction that one's story—the constitutive material of life's livability—is effectively over.[57] Freeman describes this as "the conviction that the story of one's life, or life work, has effectively ended. At an extreme, narrative foreclosure may lead to a kind of living death or even suicide, the presumption being that the future is a foregone conclusion, an inevitable reiteration of one's present suffering or paralysis."[58] This recapitulation of the present into

56 Ratcliffe, Ruddell, and Smith, "What is a 'Sense of Foreshortened Future?,'" 8.

57 Mark Freeman, *Hindsight: The Promise and Peril of Looking Backward* (Oxford: Oxford University Press, 2010).

58 Freeman, *Hindsight*, 125.

the future may have effects as damaging as the tyranny of the past over the present and should be considered as a factor in queer and trans trauma and suicidality.[59]

But the future is also queered in the lived experience of LGBTQ+ lives. Queer and trans people live into other futures in their very bodies with new names, new expressions, new community constellations, new bodily comportments, even transformed bodies through surgical and hormonal treatments. Whether these potential futures are cut off or not depends on a variety of factors, but even in their failed or curtailed "appearances," the queer community catches a glimpse of an otherwise world and future. The embodiments of queer futures can be seen in what Muñoz calls an "anticipatory illumination of a queer world, a sign of an actually existing queer reality, a kernel of political possibility within a stultifying heterosexual present."[60] These "otherwise possibilities" are a threat to powers that are invested in the present regime and are committed to a presentism that extends the status quo into the future.[61] We can observe the stress-trauma dimensions of the temporal in Alexis Lothian's words pointing to "the affective force that representations of unpleasant futures can carry when they invoke the impossible possibility that there might be no future at all."[62]

Queer and trans communities, through diverging from straight time and the inevitable future of presentism, are confronting the impossibility of that future with them in it—antagonizing futures that are unimaginable, intolerable, and ill-fitting for the flourishing of queer lives. A spiraling queer chronology is more shocking, random, and unpredictable than straight time. Queerness helpfully mobilizes a multiplicity of futures, keeping the question of the future always open to resignification and reimagination. As Muñoz says, "the present must be known in relation to the alternative temporal and spatial maps provided by a perception of past and future affective worlds. . . . the *then* that disrupts the tyranny of the *now* in both past and future."[63] Yet

59 Sanders, *Christianity, LGBTQ Suicide*.

60 Muñoz, *Cruising Utopia*, 49.

61 Ashon T. Crawley, *Blackpentecostal Breath: The Aesthetics of Possibility* (New York: Fordham University Press, 2017).

62 Alexis Lothian, *Old Futures: Speculative Fiction and Queer Possibility* (New York: New York University Press, 2018), 57.

63 Muñoz, *Cruising Utopia*, 27, 29.

pasts—and their seeming absence from queer consciousness—are another area of potential chrono stress and temporal trauma for queer and trans people.

Absenting of Collective Pasts

The production and reproduction of the dominant cis-heteropatriarchal capitalist status quo through the organization of bodies via "chrononormativity" visits its violence upon collective pasts as much as—or in service to—the foreclosing of myriad futures.[64] Cathy Caruth, scholar on the languages of trauma, argues, "The ability to recover the past is thus closely and paradoxically tied up, in trauma, with the inability to have access to it."[65] Queer and trans individuals often experience a dearth of past collective stories to integrate into current constructions of the self and future imaginings. From a constructionist standpoint, this might be viewed as a form of constitutive violence taking place at the level of narrative availability. There is no given "community" in the lives of queer and trans people in and through which these stories of collective pasts are kept alive and transmitted to the individual—neither the biological family, social institutions, nor churches. While now, more than ever, stories of queer collective pasts have been systemically uncovered, explored, written about, and archived digitally, how these narratives of queer collective pasts are *discovered* by LGBTQ+ people is much more haphazard. And very few institutions—LGBTQ+-affirming mainline liberal Christian churches included—have taken up the mantle of intentionally telling these stories in pulpits and public forums.[66] Thus, one important particularity of experiences that falls along the stress-trauma continuum for queer and trans people is the typical lack of a cohesive sense

---

64 Elizabeth Freeman, *Time Binds: Queer Temporalities, Queer Histories* (Durham, NC: Duke University Press, 2010), xiii.

65 Cathy Caruth, "Recapturing the Past: Introduction," in *Trauma: Explorations in Memory*, ed. Cathy Caruth (Baltimore: Johns Hopkins University Press, 1995), 152.

66 An anecdotal way to assess what we are arguing here might also be thinking back to times in the reader's own faith community when you've heard the history of LGBTQ+ religious organizing or faith practice iterated from the pulpit or within literature published by your denomination or religious organization. Even in LGBTQ+-affirming faith communities, these histories are not regularly made public or readily accessible to those who aren't actively looking for them and who may not even know that they exist to be discovered.

of belonging to a larger queer/trans collective through time—past and future as much as the present.

As sociologist Kai Erikson argues, "in order to serve as a generally useful concept, 'trauma' has to be understood as resulting from a *constellation of life experiences* as well as from a discrete happening, from a *persisting condition* as well as from an acute event," pointing to the possibilities of addressing "traumatized communities" rather than simply "assemblies of traumatized persons."[67] "Trauma can create community."[68] Yet, as Erikson also acknowledges, trauma typically has the effect of *damaging* the texture of community. In queer and trans collectives, we can observe both the creative and the damaging effects of trauma upon communal *possibility*, in addition to the lived present of community or the lack thereof.

In some sense, LGBTQ+ people can be considered a community because of the perpetuation of injustice and violence against us. We are not bound together by biology or nationality or race or religion. We have no necessary experience of queer kinship until kinship ties are created, and these have often been cultivated to provide affinity spaces within dominant cis-heteropatriarchal publics as well as activist spaces to counter institutional and societal discrimination and violence against queer and trans people. We are bound together by a collective experience of being targeted by our biological families, the legal structures of our nation-states, and our religious communities. We are often without a larger queer and trans collective to support us individually or provide us with a sense of a shared collective past.

As philosopher Susan J. Brison argues, "'personal' stories must be framed by longer historical accounts and by broader social and political ones."[69] But for queer and trans people who have little to no access to narrative sources of a collective past, even as they experience the foreclosure of futures, the chrono stress of absent pasts exacerbates present experiences of stress and trauma. While increasingly archived in the literature and in digital spaces, there may still exist few narrative resources of the broader

67 Kai Erikson, "Notes on Trauma and Community," in *Trauma: Explorations in memory*, ed. Cathy Caruth (Baltimore: Johns Hopkins University Press, 1995), 185. Emphasis added.

68 Erikson, "Notes on Trauma and Community," 185.

69 Susan J. Brison, *Aftermath: Violence and the Remaking of a Self* (Princeton, NJ: Princeton University Press, 2002), 34.

sociopolitical pasts of queer communal resilience and organizing that are readily available for queer and trans individuals to draw upon in forming personal stories that can serve as a bulwark against an encroaching violent present and its vanishing of futures.

Practical theologians and spiritual care practitioners must recognize the possibilities for hope and resilience in the collective past narratives for racial, ethnic, national, and religious minorities—among many others—in addressing the persistence of marginalization, injustice, and violence in the present. The words of Alexis Lothian, interdisciplinary scholar of queer and feminist media and cultural studies, are instructive here:

> *The lingering presences and possibilities of past futures open possibilities for thinking and living the present in different, deviant ways. If a forward-oriented narrative of historical development signifies the time of capitalism and colonialism, then the time of the colonized, excluded, and othered is most frequently to be found in the past.*[70]

For queer and trans people, caring praxis at the site of stress and trauma often lacks the buoying resources of resistance found in these "possibilities of past futures."

Indeed, as we can witness in the rise of conservative political organizing against teaching the history of race in the United States and in scrubbing public school curricula of any mention of LGBTQ+ people, intervening in the possibilities of collective memory is, itself, a form of violence. This is true not only in the context of the collective but also in the experience of the individual who is kept from knowledge of pasts to which they are connected. This is akin to what Kara Keeling, scholar of Black and queer cultural politics, calls the "micro-terrors . . . that we have habituated ourselves to accept" that sever us from "our roots and pasts and histories" through histories of white supremacy, coloniality, and cis-heteropatriarchal power.[71]

---

70 Lothian, *Old Futures*, 20.

71 Kara Keeling, *Queer Times, Black Futures* (New York: New York University Press, 2019), 78.

From a relational view of the self, violence that creates contexts of stress and trauma occurs not only at the level of present ruptures of relational life but in our ruptures with collective pasts as well. Philosopher Hilde Lindemann Nelson argues, "because group identities, like personal identities, are complex narrative structures of meaning . . . oppressive master narratives cause *doxastic* damage—the damage of distorting and poisoning people's self-conception and their beliefs about who other people are."[72] Recovery of these absented narratives of collective pasts serves the function of bolstering queer and trans lives against the continued perpetuation of injustice and violence.

In addition to the ways that queer communities have been forged through past experiences of collective trauma and the experience of marginalization and violence, we must also recover queer and trans collective narratives of pleasure, possibility, and flourishing. As Muñoz states, "past pleasures stave off the affective perils of the present while they enable a desire that is queer futurity's core."[73] Just as queer and trans lives should not be totalized by narratives of trauma and violence in the present—though these are part of queer experience in a dominant cis-heteropatriarchal society—neither should our collective pasts be totalized by these narratives. Queer and trans people have formed community at the margins of family, church, and society for generations, and these collectives of queer life and possibility were shaped by pleasure and relationality outside the restricting dictates of past status quos. These narratives, once recovered, hold the potential to serve as resources for resilience in the living of a queer present and constructing of queer futures.

Constructive Proposals for Care along a Queer Stress-Trauma Continuum

From our examination of queer individual and collective experience along a stress-trauma continuum, four constructive proposals emerge to guide practical theological engagement and spiritual care praxis. Each proposal is an

72 Hilde Lindemann Nelson, *Damaged Identities, Narrative Repair* (Ithaca, NY: Cornell University Press, 2001), 106.

73 Muñoz, *Cruising Utopia*, 26.

experiment with possibilities for how the notion of a stress-trauma continuum may serve theologians and practitioners well in addressing the myriad harms, injustices, and violences faced by LGBTQ+ people that create stress and trauma in the lives of queer and trans people.

First, a stress-trauma continuum would be helpful to practical theologians and spiritual care providers due to its ability to provide a framework for mapping dysregulation and responses to stressful contexts and traumatic circumstances. LGBTQ+ people encounter myriad occurrences of trauma, injustice, violence, and stress. Key to the usefulness of a stress-trauma continuum for queer and trans persons, however, is the ability to narrate this stress-trauma continuum and the map of dysregulation and response to stressful and traumatic circumstances from *queer perspectives*. Psychological discourses have long perpetuated violence against queer and trans people. A new language and framework for understanding LGBTQ+ stress and trauma should foreground the perspectives of queer and trans folks and not be beholden to diagnostic criteria, which, formulated without queer and trans people, have reinforced heteronormative and gender dichotomous assumptions in psychotherapy.[74] Relatedly, this framework must acknowledge that experiences that fall along the stress-trauma continuum are a part of queer and trans experience but that LGBTQ+ subjectivity is not totalized by trauma.

Second, in this vein, a stress-trauma continuum can also prompt the development of a resilience–growth–hope continuum, highlighting the myriad ways that queer and trans people behave agentially, with creativity and great resolve, to resist the violence that is perpetuated in relation to us. And this resistance is a part of the personal and communal response to trauma in our history and experience. Traumatic experience has, in part, helped to form us into a community because of our ability, demonstrated again and again, to resist the violences of a cis-heteropatriachal status quo. These resistance experiences (and absented pasts) must affect, inflict, and inflect the stress-trauma continuum for the framework to center care on

74 Catherine Butler and Angela Byrne, "Queer in Practice: Therapy and Queer Theory," in *Feeling Queer or Queer Feelings? Radical Approaches to Counselling Sex, Sexualities and Genders*, ed. Lyndsey Moon (London: Routledge, 2008), 89–105.

queer and trans people as well as beyond queer experiences. Our conviction is that queer and trans experience has much to teach us about stress and trauma more broadly, going beyond the specificity of LGBTQ+ experience, and that many of these lessons rest upon a resilience-growth-hope continuum of resistance.

Third, trauma discourse—and perhaps even a stress-trauma discourse—too easily focuses upon the experience of the traumatized while eliding focus on the perpetuation of the injustices and violence that create the stress-trauma experience in the first place. Of vital importance in our sense of this framework's usability is its ability to locate violence in discourses, systems, and structures that (over) determine who we can become, with whom we can connect across time and space, and what those connections entail. While it is essential to focus upon healing those who have been victimized by stress and trauma, it is also vital to name the locations from which the perpetuation of harm emanates. We too easily name these locales of injustice and violence on an individual level—also the level of the trauma upon which we typically focus—without noting the institutional and systemic levels at which they are perpetrated. With a focus on the sources of violence and trauma, we must also locate the ways that violence works to conscript something *in us* or *about us*, charting the introjection of those violences and examining how we become formed and deformed according to a discursive, political, material regime of white cis-heteropatriarchal normativity.

Finally, a stress-trauma continuum can allow for a more robust engagement with the ways that stress and trauma are experienced across temporalities as well as how they are experienced temporally. Interventions that develop in the wake of a queer stress-trauma continuum should be interventions that not only address the relational and material experiences of queer and trans people in the present—of critical importance, no doubt—but also lead practitioners and theologians into investigating ways of restoring absented pasts and reimagining vanishing futures for and with LGBTQ+ people. We need a collective history to survive and thrive in a present that continues to attack our bodies and assail our souls. And if we are to have a future, it will be a future of flourishing beyond the restricting dictates of a cis-heteropatriarchal persisting present that continually conscripts the possibilities for queer and trans life.

A queer stress-trauma continuum along with a queer resilience-growth-hope continuum must take shape as a spiraling temporality that continually draws upon past collective experience to meet the violence and injustices of the present, projecting queer imaginings of a future that is not conscripted by a projection of the present into a future overdetermined by the white cis-heteropatriarchal present. The past, the present, and the future must be open, fluid, undecided, and resilient—therein, they must be queer.

4

ONTOLOGICAL PSYCHOSPIRITUALITY

The Stress and Trauma of Other Species

Ryan LaMothe

JACK LONDON'S NOVEL *White Fang* is the story of a wolf-dog who was beaten into submission by a Native Alaskan, Gray Beaver.[1] One evening, "White Fang crawled straight toward Gray Beaver, every inch of his progress becoming slower and more painful. At last he lay at his master's feet, into whose possession he now surrendered himself, voluntarily, body and soul."[2] Eventually, White Fang was exchanged to a mendacious white man, Beauty Smith, who used White Fang to win money in dog fights, leading to even more instances of brutality.

We do not have to read a Jack London story to recognize that other species experience traumas.[3] Most caregivers of adopted pets know that past traumas are part of their pets' present anxieties and that care mitigates, but does not erase, traumatic memories. White Fang was eventually rescued by two men, one of whom realizes how painful White Fang's life has been and, with great patience, he tenderly cares for him, knowing the memories of the traumas will never be absent from this animal's life, but hoping White Fang will, to some degree, recover.

The trauma experienced by the fictional White Fang and other domesticated animals is only a fraction of the harm human beings inflict on other species. Decades ago, I ran every morning past a butcher factory in the

1 Jack London, *The Unabridged Jack London* (Philadelphia: Running Press, 1981).

2 London, *The Unabridged Jack London*, 462.

3 Anastassiya Andrianova, "Narrating Animal Trauma in Bulgakov and Tolstoy," *Humanities* 5, no. 4 (2016): 84, https://doi.org/10.3390/h5040084. Anastassiya Andrianova examines the works of Tolstoy and Bulgakov from the perspective of animal studies and trauma theory. These celebrated authors narrate the traumatic suffering of animals, much like Jack London did.

German city where I lived. The eerie painful screams of cows preparing to be slaughtered put me off eating meat and changed my morning route. Factory farms, the use of other species in scientific experiments, the degradation of habitats through real estate development are only some of the human actions that cause suffering and trauma to othered species.

For most of us, the sufferings and traumas of other species are unseen and unheard. The din of the cows awaiting slaughter becomes the background noise of civilization—simply the cost of doing business. It takes the empathy of an author like Jack London, a religious person like St. Francis of Assisi, a nineteenth-century scientist like Charles Darwin, and a nineteenth-century philosopher like Arthur Schopenhauer to recognize the suffering of othered species and to break the silence.[4] More recently, philosophers Peter Singer and Andrew Linzey have argued that the suffering of other species is a core ethical challenge for human beings, especially in the face of environmental degradation.[5]

Consider the notion of trauma in relation to more-than-human species in the context of the catastrophes of the Anthropocene Age,[6] wherein it is predicted that half of the known species will be extinct by the end of this

---

4 Charles Darwin, *The Expression of Emotions in Man and Animals* (London: Penguin Classics, 2009); Stephen Puryear, "Schopenhauer on the Rights of Animals," *European Journal of Philosophy* 25, no. 2 (2017): 250–269.

5 Peter Singer, *Animal Liberation* (New York: Harper Collins, 1975); Peter Singer, *Ethics in the Real World* (Princeton: Princeton University Press, 2016); Andrew Linzey, *Why Animal Suffering Matters: Philosophy, Theology, and Practical Ethics* (Oxford: Oxford University Press, 2009).

6 Paul Crutzen and Eugene Stoermer, "The 'Anthropocene,'" *IGB Global Change Newsletter* 41 (2000): 17–18; Elizabeth Kolbert, *The Sixth Extinction: An Unnatural History* (New York City: Henry Holt, 2014). "Scientists Paul Crutzen and Edward Stoermer coined the term "Anthropocene Age" to indicate that we are now out of the Holocene Age. Another reason for calling this age the Anthropocene Age is that, as Elizabeth Kolbert and Naomi Klein noted and provided evidence for, the Earth is in the midst of a sixth extinction event, which is being caused by human activity—human beings as a force of nature. Readers are likely familiar with some of the scientific data regarding global warming since it is in the news nearly every day. Nevertheless, for those interested in recent published research, I suggest: "Climate Change 2021: The Physical Science Basis;" IPPC Sixth Assessment Report, https://www.ipcc.ch/report/ar6/wg1/ and "Global Climate Change: Vital Signs of the Planet," NASA, https://climate.nasa.gov/. In addition, Pentagon and CIA reports indicate that there will be more political upheaval and violence within and between nations as resources become scarce as a result of climate change. While the reports do not take into consideration

century as a result of human beings.[7] More-than-human species have long experienced trauma at the hands of human beings, and this experience will only increase as the effects of climate change worsen. Even without the danger of climate change, the singularities of all species deserve respect.

Some may wonder about the relevance of attending to the traumas of other-than-human species when there is so much human misery, but the failure to consider the traumas of other species will result in more human traumatic sufferings.[8] We live on and depend on a biodiverse Earth, and mass extinctions associated with climate change will eventuate into a world not habitable for human beings and create varied human traumas associated with the process of being unhoused.[9] To care simply and solely about human traumas in the Anthropocene Age is myopic and counterproductive.

As we will see below, although meanings of trauma were first developed in the medical-psychological sciences in the late nineteenth century, the concept is relevant to more-than-human species. The Abrahamic scriptures, along with Western political philosophies and theologies, have served as apparatuses for producing and maintaining an ontological rift between human beings and other species. This ontological rift has led to the exclusion of other species from political questions of human dwelling. Moreover, this ontological rift provides the "ethical" legitimation of the instrumental exploitation of other species for human desires and needs, resulting in their sufferings and traumas. The ontological rift and its attributes produce disidentification with, and callous disregard for, the sufferings of other species. Inoperative pastoral care can bridge the ontological

---

the sufferings of other species, we can safely predict that other species will be negatively impacted by climate change and human violence.

7 Edward O. Wilson, *The Future of Life* (London: Abacus, 2005).

8 Kyle Keltz, *Thomism and the Problem of Animal Suffering* (Eugene, OR: Wipf & Stock, 2020); Matthew Scully, *Dominion: The Power of Man, the Suffering of Animals, and the Call to Mercy* (New York: St. Martin's Griffin, 2003); Bethany Sollereder, *God, Evolution, and Animal Suffering: Theodicy without a Fall* (Oxfordshire: Routledge, 2020). There is a distinction to be made between suffering and trauma. Suffering is not identical to trauma. That is, not all suffering is traumatic, but trauma is a particular type of suffering. This said, there are religious scholars who have explored the theological question of the suffering of other-than-human species (e.g., Keltz; Scully; Sollereder).

9 David Wallace-Wells, *The Uninhabitable Earth* (Spokane, WA: Dugan Books, 2020).

rift, inviting more empathic, compassionate, and inclusive relations with more-than-human species.

Before expanding on this argument, I should clarify that it is not my intention to suggest that Judeo-Christian scriptures and Western political theologies/philosophies are the only sources of trauma vis-à-vis other species (and othered human beings). The rapaciousness of global capitalism and the new imperialism of powerful nation-states (e.g., the United States, Russia, and China) leave a wide wake of human and other-species traumas, though I would contend that these, too, are rooted in the ontological rift. This chapter critiques Judeo-Christian scripture with the aim of confronting the beam in our eye with the hope of imagining other ways of compassionately respecting the singularities of other species. To argue that scripture produces and legitimates the ontological rift between humans and other species is not to overlook the seeds within scripture and Christian traditions that can bridge this rift. As Marxist philosopher Roland Boer noted, Ernst Bloch (and others; Walter Benjamin, Theodor Adorno, Louis Althusser, and Slavoj Žižek) was "enthusiastic about the revolutionary possibilities of certain types of biblical myth."[10] We can discover this emancipatory feature of myth only if we are clear-eyed about how scripture operates as an apparatus for producing the ontological rift. The concept of trauma as it applies to other-than-human species is, more often than not, associated with physical trauma, which is clearly seen in veterinary literature. I am using the concept as it pertains to types of situations that overwhelm animals' semiotic capacities. I recognize that it is a leap to take a clinical concept that was developed to understand a particular category of human suffering and apply it to other species, especially given that the discourse regarding human trauma is varied and contested. More directly, one can ask, Does the notion of trauma apply to ants or other insects? Do only sentient beings like dolphins, horses, pigs, dogs, cats, etc. experience trauma? And, if so, How would we seek to understand and respond to these traumas? I certainly do not know if insects undergo trauma, but I think there is plenty of anecdotal evidence of the traumatic sufferings of many species. Visit a factory farm and glimpse the misery of animals exploited

10 Roland Boer, *Criticism of Heaven: On Marxism and Theology* (Chicago: Haymarket Books, 2009), 27.

for human use. Consider the suffering of calves used in the production of veal. Listen to the stories of the cruelty done to animals (e.g., laboratory experimentation, puppy mills, and dogfighting). We know a lot about human trauma, but very little about the traumas of other species. Yet many species experience overwhelming suffering, and I consider this to fall under the category of trauma. Finally, while I think other species can traumatize other-than-human species (e.g., a lynx mauling a rabbit), the focus will be on human beings causing trauma to numerous species, including ourselves. The Anthropocene Age reveals that, in general, many human beings are gratuitously destructive.

Trauma and Other-than-Human Species

Decades ago, psychoanalyst Hanna Segal understood trauma to comprise the loss of symbolic function, which means that an experience associated with the traumatic event is organized semiotically, not semantically.[11] A child, for instance, who is traumatized is not able to organize the experience through symbolization, though the experience is organized semiotically.[12] When this occurs, the result is that trauma remains outside of symbolic meaning. Today we use the term *post-traumatic stress* (PTS) to refer, in part, to experiences that remain largely outside autobiographical or semantic memory systems, though they remain part of eidetic memory.[13]

Using different language, Cathy Caruth, scholar on the languages of trauma, has argued that trauma is identified as horrific events or crises in a person's life that are unassimilated vis-à-vis a person's consciousness and

11 Hanna Segal, "Notes of Symbol Formation," *International Journal of Psychoanalysis* 38 (1957): 391–397.

12 Ryan LaMothe, "The Absence of Cure: The Core of Malignant Trauma and Symbolization," *Journal of Interpersonal Violence* 14, no. 11 (1999): 1193–1210, https://doi.org/10.1177/088626099014011005.

13 Bessel A. van der Kolk, Lars Weisaeth, and Onno van der Hart, "History of Trauma in Psychiatry," in *Traumatic Stress*, ed. Bessel A. van der Kolk, Alexander McFarlane, and Lars Weisaeth (New York: Guilford, 1996), 57–76; Bessel A. van der Kolk, Onno van der Hart, and Charles R. Marmar, "Dissociation and Information Processing in Posttraumatic Stress Disorder," in *Traumatic Stress*, ed. Bessel A. van der Kolk, Alexander McFarlane, and Lars Weisaeth (New York: Guilford, 1996), 303–330.

narrative.[14] Caruth calls these "unclaimed experiences."[15] Unclaimed experiences is another way to conceptualize semiotically versus semantically organized experiences.

But it is not simply how trauma is organized that is important. Caruth added that the core of trauma is "the lack of support, of help, of comfort; being utterly left alone with the experience and having no one to listen."[16] Psychologist Sue Grand held a similar view, calling trauma an experience of catastrophic loneliness.[17] Connected to this catastrophic loneliness is the concomitant shattering of one's assumptive world, creating a sense of the non-reparability of relationships.[18] Like social psychologist Ronnie Janoff-Bulman, Fred Alford, professor emeritus of government and politics at University of Maryland, argued that "trauma takes away our confidence in the existence of a stable, ordered, and meaningful existence."[19] The shattering of one's assumptive world of trust and a corresponding belief in the non-reparability of relationships are attended by profound distrust and hopelessness, which undermines a person's capacity for intimate relationships.[20]

Developmentally, the capacities for, and use of, language and symbols to organize experience depend on relations of trust wherein persons can be vulnerable to adults. Attachment theorists have long observed that trauma disrupts children's capacities for relational trust, which, in turn, undermines their capacities for self-reflexivity and organizing coherent narratives.[21] Trauma shatters their assumptive world of trust, leaving experience

---

14 Cathy Caruth, *Unclaimed Experience: Trauma, Narrative, and History* (Baltimore: Johns Hopkins University Press, 1996); Cathy Caruth, *Listening to Trauma: Conversations with Leaders in the Theory and Treatment of Catastrophic Experience* (Baltimore: Johns Hopkins University Press, 2014).

15 Caruth, *Unclaimed Experience*, 4.

16 Caruth, *Unclaimed Experience*, 202.

17 Sue Grand, *The Reproduction of Evil* (Hillsdale, NJ: Analytic Press, 2000).

18 Ronnie Janoff-Bulman, *Shattered Assumptions: Towards a New Psychology of Trauma* (Washington, DC: Free Press, 1992); Philip Bromberg, "Treating Patients with Symptoms—and Symptoms with Patience," *Psychoanalytic Dialogues* 11, no. 6 (2001), 902.

19 Fred Alford, *Trauma and Forgiveness: Consequences and Community* (Cambridge: Cambridge University Press, 2013), 10.

20 Jennifer Freyd, *Betrayal Trauma* (Cambridge: Harvard University Press, 1996).

21 Peter Fonagy, *Attachment Theory and Psychoanalysis* (New York: Other Press, 2001); Peter Fonagy and Mary Target, "Attachment and Reflective Function: Their Role in Self-Organization," *Development and Psychopathology* 9, no. 4 (1997): 679–700, https://doi.org/10.1017/S0954579497001399; György Gergely and Zsolt Unoka,

unclaimed. Put differently, when trauma occurs at the point of extreme vulnerability, vulnerability becomes linked to distrust, intolerable anxiety, and catastrophic, existential loneliness. The experience is unclaimed because vulnerability is required to do the work of processing the trauma with another person, but any movement toward vulnerability heightens anxiety and distrust.

It is not that semiotic and symbolic capacities in organizing experience are two radically separate systems vis-à-vis one's assumptive world. Long before symbolization is taking place, infants are organizing experience semiotically. Relying on the work of philosopher Maurice Merleau-Ponty and psychiatrist Frantz Fanon, philosopher Athena Colman argued that infants first develop a corporeal schema that "can be understood as having to do with pre-representational [semiotic] mode of experience through which we continually, but without conscious effort, dynamically orient and restructure our body in the world according to our projects."[22] Similarly, philosopher Mark Johnson argued that embodied constitutional structures exist "preconceptually and nonpropositionally in our ongoing meaningful organization of our experience, understanding, and reasoning" (see also George Lakoff and Mark Johnson).[23] Semiotically organized, embodied schemas become intertwined with more complex symbolic organizations of our assumptive world, and both are contingent on consistent relations of care and trust. Trauma undermines embodied pre-representational and symbolic modes of organizing experience. Put another way, trauma is so disorienting and painful because it is in radical opposition to the foundations that make organizing experience possible, leaving victims struggling to find ways to make sense of what happened.

"Attachment and Mentalization in Infants," in *Mind to Mind: Infant Research, Neuroscience, and Psychoanalysis*, ed. Sharone Berger, Elliot Jurist, and Arietta Slade (New York: Other Press, 2008), 50–87; Jeremy Holmes, *Attachment, Intimacy, Autonomy* (New York: Jason Aronson, 1996).

22 Athena Colman, "Corporeal Schemas and Body Images: Fanon, Merleau-Ponty, and the Lived Experience of Race," in *Fanon, Phenomenology, and Psychology*, ed. Leswin Laubscher, Derek Hook, and Miraj U. Desai (Oxfordshire: Routledge, 2022), 128.

23 Mark Johnson, *The Body in the Mind: The Bodily Basis of Meaning, Imagination, and Reason* (Chicago: University of Chicago Press, 1987), 40; George Lakoff and Mark Johnson, *Philosophy in the Flesh: The Embodied Mind and Its Challenges to Western Thought* (New York: Basic Books, 1999).

An illustration is helpful here. Jean Amery, a French journalist and resistance fighter, was bound and beaten by the Gestapo during World War II. Some years later, he wrote of his experience of torture:

> *The first blow brings home to the prisoner that he is helpless. . . . Yet I am certain that with the very first blow that descends on him he loses something we will perhaps call "trust in the world." Trust in the world includes all sorts of things . . . the certainty that by reason of written or unwritten social contracts the other person will respect my physical, and with it also my metaphysical being. The boundaries of my body are also the boundaries of my self. My skin surface shields me against the external world. If I am to have trust, I must feel on it only what I want to feel. . . . The expectation of help, the certainty of help, is indeed one of the fundamental experiences of human beings. . . . The expectation of help is as much a constitutional psychic element as is the struggle for existence. . . . But with the first blow of the policeman's fist, against which there can be no defense and which no helping hand will ward off, a part of our life ends and it can never again be revived. . . . Whoever has succumbed to torture can no longer feel at home in the world.*[24]

The first blow of the police officer occurs at the point where Jean Amery was at his most vulnerable, shattering his assumptive world—a world of self-body integrity, of trust vis-à-vis the expectation of help/care, of ownership of his body, and of caring repair. Put differently, Amery's assumptive world was grounded in early life, wherein he could trust and be vulnerable to caring parents, which grounded his ability to make use of cultural symbols to organize and relationally process experience—to make sense of the world. In being tortured, this assumptive world no longer made sense, leaving these unbearable experiences unassimilable, unclaimed.

One may immediately question this, noting that Jean Amery later wrote about his experience, suggesting that he was able to assimilate the

24 Jean Amery, "Torture," in *Art from the Ashes*, ed. Lawrence Langer (Oxford: Oxford University Press, 1995), 126, 127, 136.

experience into symbols and autobiographical memory. This is true, but only to an extent. Many people who have been traumatized can, in time, talk about their experiences, but this does not mean that these unbearable experiences are entirely claimed. In one sense, they cannot be claimed because the trauma, especially trauma at the hands of other human beings, is completely at odds with the assumptive embodied, pre-representational world of trust and vulnerability. Put another way, experiences associated with severe trauma essentially lie outside human capacity for symbolization because the very capacity for symbolization is existentially dependent on care, trust, and vulnerability—the openness to receive care.[25] Trauma is antithetical to care and trust. Jean Amery never fully recovered from his experiences of being tortured. He survived, for a time, and narrated his experience, but he lived in a world where he was alienated and isolated from routine meanings, purposes, and intimacies. As anthropologist and sociologist Didier Fassin and psychiatrist Richard Rechtman note, "Trauma . . . is not simply the consequence of unbearable experiences, but [is] also in itself a testimony."[26] And the testimony of Jean Amery "is both the product of an experience of inhumanity and the proof of the humanity of those who have endured it."[27]

There is also trauma experienced by groups or communities. Primo Levi, a Holocaust survivor, poignantly narrated his traumatic experiences and their close connection between personal and cultural objects and a sense of self. He writes,

> *But consider what value, what meaning is enclosed even in the smallest of our daily habits, in the hundred possessions which even the poorest beggar owns: a handkerchief, an old letter, the photo of a cherished person. These things are part of us, almost like* limbs of our body *[emphasis added]. . . . Imagine now a man who is deprived of everyone he loves, and at the same time of his house,*

25 Ryan LaMothe, "The Absence of Cure: The Core of Malignant Trauma and Symbolization," *Journal of Interpersonal Violence* 14, no. 11 (1999): 1193–1210, https://doi.org/10.1177/088626099014011005.

26 Didier Fassin and Richard Rechtman, *The Empire of Trauma: An Inquiry into the Condition of Victimhood* (Princeton, NJ: Princeton University Press, 2009), 20.

27 Fassin and Rechtman, *The Empire of Trauma*, 20.

> *his habits, his clothes, in short everything he possesses: he will be a* hollow *man . . . for he who loses all often easily loses himself.*[28]

Levi is obviously talking about himself as an individual, but the backdrop of this experience is the brutal deprivation of Jewish cultural symbols and practices that provided shared meanings and purposes necessary for mutual intimacies. Stripping these away symbols is to deprive individuals and a people of their sense of self and their making sense of the world.

Another illustration of this communal trauma is the treatment of native peoples by white European colonizers. Philosopher and psychoanalyst Jonathan Lear describes how Plenty Coup, the Crow chief, led his people through a period of cultural devastation.[29] For Lear, cultural devastation involves the traumatic loss of narratives and rituals that a group of people uses to interpret current and past events, thus providing intersubjective meaning and purpose. These narratives and rituals make it possible to assimilate experiences, and when these narratives and rituals are stripped away, making sense of the world and experience is undermined. For the Crow community, cultural devastation involved the violent and traumatic incursion of white Europeans, the dominance of white European narratives, and the corresponding loss of Crow cultural rituals and narratives that had provided meaning, a sense of hope, purpose, and direction vis-à-vis a Crow future. As writer and Holocaust scholar Terrence Des Pres writes, "gone were the myths and institutions, the symbols and technologies which in normal times allow the self to transcend and lose sight of its actual situation."[30]

This brief dive into the notion of trauma highlights its key features as it relates to human beings, namely unbearable and unclaimed experiences, de-symbolization, shattering of a person's assumptive world, initiation of psychological defenses for survival, and isolation/alienation—resulting from profound fear of vulnerability. When using the notion of trauma in relation to more-than-human species, a few questions immediately come to the fore. Other species do have complex semiotic capacities for communicating and,

---

28 Primo Levi, *Survival in Auschwitz* (New York City: Collier, 1960), 27.

29 Jonathan Lear, *Radical Hope: Ethics in the Face of Cultural Devastation* (Cambridge: Harvard University Press, 2006).

30 Terrence Des Pres, *The Survivor* (Oxford: Oxford University Press, 1976), 188.

no doubt, for organizing their experiences, but it is not clear whether these species are capable of symbolization. Do other species have an assumptive world that can be shattered? Do they have a culture, which can be destroyed? When it comes to trauma, we know a great deal about how it affects human beings but little about how it pertains to other species—assuming we can apply this concept to the suffering of more-than-human species.[31] Acknowledging this limitation means any inquiry is speculative, though necessary if we are to acknowledge and begin to learn more about the suffering of more-than-human species so that we can begin to become more empathic and compassionate toward other species.

Charles Sanders Peirce, scientist, mathematician, and philosopher, argued that all living beings, from the "lowly" amoeba to apes and human beings, have varying semiotic capacities that are necessary to move about and engage their world.[32] It is, of course, easier for us to take note of the communications of mammals like dolphins, whales, and chimpanzees, though we are a long way from understanding them. Given this, it is not a stretch to consider that other species have assumptive worlds linked to their semiotic capacities, which we largely do not comprehend. And if they have assumptive semiotic worlds, these worlds can be shattered. Jack London's imaginative stories offer an unscientific illustration.[33]

Buck was a large dog who "lived at a big house in the sun-kissed Santa Clara Valley. . . . And over this great demesne, here he was born and here

---

31 Hope Ferdowsian and Debra Merskin, "Parallels in Sources of Trauma, Pain, Distress, and Suffering in Humans and Non-human Animals," *Journal of Trauma and Dissociation* 12, no. 4 (2012): 448–468, https://doi.org/10.1080/15299732.2011.652346.

32 Charles Peirce, *Peirce on Signs: Writings on Semiotic by Charles Sanders Peirce*, ed. James Hoopes (Chapel Hill, NC: North Carolina University Press, 1991); Barry Stampfl, "Theorizing Canine PTSD," *Semiotics* (2012): 159–168, https://doi.org/10.5840/cpsem201216. Barry Stampfl also uses Peirce and semiotics to argue for PTS in referring to canine suffering. I am extending the use of semiotics to living beings, because Peirce does as well.

33 I recognize that literary writers like Jack London can easily slip into projecting human attributes onto other animals like Buck. This is especially true when we encounter the silence of other-species and we fill this silence with our imaginations. Nevertheless, it is clear that there is a motivation to empathically understand the experiences of other-than-human species. This empathy is an attempt to bridge the ontological rift, discussed below, as well as eschew psychological defenses implicated in legitimating the instrumental use of other-than-human species.

he had lived the four years of his life."[34] London depictes Buck's assumptive world, which was disrupted. One day, the gardener took Buck for a walk with the aim of selling Buck to a stranger who tied a rope to Buck's collar. "Buck had accepted the rope with quiet dignity. To be sure, it was an unwonted performance: but he had learned to trust in men he knew."[35] This was the beginning of a series of traumas that would lead him to being sold in Alaska. London writes, "Buck's first day on the Dyea beach was like a nightmare. Every hour was filled with shock and surprise. He had been suddenly jerked from the heart of civilization and flung into the heart of things primordial."[36] London's empathic imagination gives voice to the shattering of Buck's assumptive world.

The Ontological Rift: A Source of Other-Species Trauma and the Anthropocene Age

In Genesis, one of the creation myths has God commanding human beings to "have dominion over the fish of the sea, and over the birds of the air, and over the cattle, and over all the wild things of the earth, and over every creeping thing that crawls upon the earth."[37] This commandment is repeated in the next verse. The other creation story has Adam naming every creature. These are familiar stories for many Jews, Christians, and Muslims, becoming a part of our assumptive world. Many of us believe that not only are we distinct from other animals, but that we are given dominion over them.[38] The basis of this assumptive world is a kind of recognition wherein human beings are differentiated from all other animals, possessing the putative, God-given privilege of naming and having authority over them.

---

34 London, *The Unabridged Jack London*, 761–762.

35 London, *The Unabridged Jack London*, 763.

36 London, *The Unabridged Jack London*, 770.

37 Genesis 1:26 (NRSV)

38 Paul Tyson, *Theology and Climate Change* (Oxfordshire: Routledge, 2021). While I am focusing on the relation between the theological notion of sovereignty/dominion and the ontological rift between human beings and other species, theologian Paul Tyson similarly identifies Western progressive dominion theologies as foundational for the destructive relations many Christians have in relation to other species and the Earth.

In addition, human beings are at the center of the creation stories, which privileges human beings and makes other species secondary—at best, supporting actors in the drama of creation. While the creation myths do not say this directly, there are attending beliefs that God is superior to human beings and human beings are superior to other species. When distinctions and accompanying beliefs are combined with authority and power over "them," a rift forms between those who have power and those who are subordinate, inferior, and different. In this case, the rift is ontological, because it is situated in ontological myths of creation.

The assumptive world of these and other religious stories is part of Western political theologies and philosophies. As German jurist Carl Schmitt argued, "all significant concepts of the modern theory of the state are secularized theological concepts," which are rooted in these ancient myths.[39] The biblical narratives that undergird Western political theologies and philosophies reproduce the chasm between human beings and other species. Put differently, for philosopher Giorgio Agamben, Western political theologies and philosophies function as apparatuses[40] that produce and maintain a "deep ontological rift . . . between animal and human,"[41] which is a part of the assumptive world of most Western persons. Agamben writes:

39 Wendy Brown, *Walled States, Waning Sovereignty* (New York: Zone Books, 2010), 59.

40 Giorgio Agamben, *What is an Apparatus? And Other Essays* (Redwood City, CA: Stanford University Press, 2009), 13, 19. For Giorgi Agamben, the term "apparatus" refers to "a set of practices, bodies of knowledge, measures and institutions that aim to manage, govern, control, and orient—in a way that purports to be useful—the behaviors, gestures, and thoughts of human beings." Referencing Foucault, Agamben wrote that "in a disciplinary society, apparatuses aim to create—through a series of practices, discourses, and bodies of knowledge—docile, yet free, bodies that assume their identity and their 'freedom' as subjects."

41 Colby Dickinson, "The Absence of Gender," in *Agamben's Coming Philosophy: Finding a New Use for Theology*, ed. Colby Dickinson and Adam Kotsko (Washington, DC: Rowman & Littlefield, 2015), 173; Charles Mills, *The Racial Contract* (Ithaca, NY: Cornell University Press, 1997); Charles Mills, *Black Rights/White Wrongs* (Oxford: Oxford University Press, 2017); Orlando Patterson, *Slavery and Social Death* (Cambridge: Harvard University Press, 1982). This ontological rift also applies to those human beings who are constructed as absolutely other and inferior, which we observe in varied forms of racism (and other types of oppression and marginalization) and attending traumas. My focus in this paper is, however, the source of the traumas to other species.

> *It is as if determining the border between human and animal were not just one question among many discussed by philosophers and theologians, scientists and politicians, but rather a fundamental metaphysico-political operation in which alone something like 'man' can be decided upon and produced. If animal life and human life could be superimposed perfectly, then neither man nor animal—and, perhaps, not even the divine—would any longer be thinkable.*[42]

The ongoing drive in the West to differentiate between human beings and animals, which is a project of philosophy, theology, and some of the sciences, leads to "a radical and total discontinuity between human and nonhuman" and, consequently, privileging human beings over all other species—anthropocentrism.[43]

Agamben also points out this rift is evident in the fact that Western political theologies and philosophies exclude other species in political theorizing. At best, a political system, like democracy, offers the idea of representation and participation of citizens. Questions of care and justice are framed in terms of citizens' needs for survival and flourishing. Yet, when it comes to other species, they are excluded from the public-political realm and notions of care and justice.[44] Indeed, it would, for many people, seem ludicrous to include other species in our political deliberations because other species are not capable of political agency and thus cannot participate. While

---

42 Giorgio Agamben, *The Open: Man and Animal*, trans. Kevin Attell (Redwood City, CA: Stanford University Press, 2004), 92.

43 Nikolas Kompridis, "Nonhuman Agency and Human Normativity," in *Nature and Value*, ed. Akeel Bilgrami (New York: Columbia University Press, 2020), 252.

44 Bryant Rousseau, "In New Zealand Lands and Rivers Can Be People Too (Legally Speaking)," *New York Times*, July 13, 2016, https://www.nytimes.com/2016/07/14/world/what-in-the-world/in-new-zealand-lands-and-rivers-can-be-people-legally-speaking.html; There are exceptions. Bryant Rousseau discusses New Zealand's parliament that has two political representatives who represent the land and species of two geographical areas. New Zealand's inclusion of land and other species in politics is not the result of Western political imaginations or myths, but rather the indigenous myths of that country. See also Eva Meijer, *When Animals Speak: Toward an Interspecies Democracy* (New York: New York University Press, 2019); Eva Meijer, *Animal Languages* (Cambridge, MA: MIT Press, 2020).

it is true that other species lack political agency, it is also true that many human beings, for various reasons (age, illness, etc.) cannot exercise their political agency, yet they are considered to be members of the polis and thus due justice and care, at least ideally. It might also be that people would believe it is silly to consider other species vis-à-vis the political because other species are not due the same consideration as human beings. Other species are constructed as less than, as inferior.

Scripture illustrates further how this ontological rift is evident in Christian political imaginations. The kingdom of God is a political metaphor that has come to have varied meanings ascribed by scripture scholars, theologians, and philosophers over the centuries. It is fair to say that this metaphor replicates the ontological rift. There is no reference that the kingdom includes other species. Apparently only human beings need salvation and get to enjoy the kingdom—if they qualify. While it may make sense that human beings are the center of the cosmic story, it does not necessarily follow that other species are subordinate, inferior and, therefore, to be excluded from political life. Nevertheless, Western political theologies, which are based on the mythoi of Abrahamic scripture, function as apparatuses to produce and maintain the ontological rift between human beings and other species.

There are consequences to this ontological rift. This rift attends instrumental epistemologies that are implicated in the use and brutal exploitation of other species to meet human needs and desires. These instrumental epistemologies provide the logic, legitimation, and ethical justifications for the use of other species, whether to meet fundamental human needs (e.g., food) or for frivolous pleasures.

There are several attending features of these epistemologies. First, they include objectification and disidentification. As noted above, other species are constructed as inferior animals, while human beings are superior and have authority and power over other species. Second and relatedly, the singularities and dignity, which are central for personal recognition and identification, are not ascribed to other species (and othered human beings). Other animals simply fall into a generalized category, which, along with the logic of inferiority, objectifies other species and legitimates human exploitation of other species (e.g., factory farms, mass slaughter of other species for human consumption, experimentation, hunting, trafficking of rare and endangered species). Third, instrumental epistemologies, in relation to other species, accompany the attitude that they are not due care, except in the cases where care is required for their being used for some human need or desire (e.g., tending to cattle for sale and slaughter). In addition to not being due care, they are also not due justice.[45]

This ontological rift can be further understood in terms of its psychological "benefits" for human animals. Existential philosophers discuss the anxiety human animals have regarding their existential impermanence and insignificance, as well as their vulnerability and dependence. Religious myths, like creation stories and notions of the kingdom of God, function psychologically to mitigate this existential anxiety by providing a belief in one's (and one's group's) ontological permanence and significance. Many Christians believe they are special in the eyes of God and possess the potential for eternal life. On these occasions, our existential vulnerability and dependency are placed in the background, while in the foreground is our belief in our permanent significance. In terms of the ontological rift, the existential realities of impermanence and insignificance are projected onto other species. They are ascribed as insignificant. They are vulnerable to and dependent on the seemingly indifferent whims of nature. So, too, are human beings, but we are relieved of our existential anxiety by anchoring our significance in a God that ranks above nature, which mitigates our existential vulnerability.

Coming from a different angle, the ontological rift can be further understood in terms of historical unconscious and normative unconscious.[46] These concepts can help explain the persistence of epistemic apparatuses that produce the ontological rift as well as the inclination to objectify and disidentify with the sufferings of more-than-human species. The historical unconscious refers to the use of narratives in constructing experience such

---

45 I recognize that many people care deeply about their pets or other animals, and animal rights advocates seek to provide safeguards for other species. The focus here is on what attends the ontological rift.

46 Timothy Zeddies, "Behind, Beneath, Above, and Beyond: The historical unconscious," *Journal of the American Academy of Psychoanalysis* 30, no. 2 (2002): 211–222; Lynne Layton, *Toward a Social Psychoanalysis: Culture, Character, and Normative Unconscious Processes* (Oxfordshire: Routledge, 2020).

that the lives and (past and present) experiences of oppressed and marginalized peoples are overlooked or denied. Examples of this are the absence of the past life experiences of Native peoples and African Americans from the collective memories of dominant white European groups in the United States. Normative unconscious refers to experiences that fall outside the hegemonic, synchronic collective stories of a group by splitting off what is considered to be non-normative. An example of this is the exclusion of queer persons. In terms of other-than-human species, both the normative and historical unconscious applies. Other species are not remembered in our collective stories, signifying a kind of weak dissociation when it comes to the singularities and dignity of other species, all of which is connected to the ontological rift. That which is constructed as insignificant is excluded from our collective consciousness.

Put differently, the notions of normative and historical unconscious represent ongoing disidentification with othered species, leading to their exclusion from collective memory. This accompanies an absence of empathy and compassion for the suffering of other species—past and present—as well as a lack of accountability for the traumas caused by human beings.

In brief, the ontological rift, which has roots in the stories of the Abrahamic traditions and their accompanying political theologies and philosophies, is a foundation of our assumptive world. This rift attends instrumental epistemologies that objectify other species and legitimate their exploitation, which attends human indifference (disidentification and objectification) and lack of remorse to the sufferings and traumas of other species. Stated differently, the ontological rift occludes our capacities for empathy and compassion in relation to the singular existences of other species, which is attended by an absence of accountability. This rift provides a buffer against the harsh existential realities of human animals' impermanence and insignificance, which are projected onto other species. This projection further explicates our indifference to their sufferings and traumas.

Anthropocentrism or narcissism lies at the basis of the ontological rift and the concomitant exclusion of other species from Western political theorizing. More specifically, anthropocentrism is an illusion, perhaps a delusion—a delusion that leaves a wake of destruction vis-à-vis other species and, in the long run, has tragic consequences for human beings. Given the stark realities of the climate emergency, it becomes increasingly clear that anthropocentrism is a delusion because the very existence of human life, community, and political belonging, rests on a biodiverse Earth. Other species are necessarily part of the polis—not to be instrumentally used, traumatized, or ignored.

Bridging the Ontological Rift: Inoperative Pastoral Care

Facing the dire realities of the climate emergency, Clayton Crockett, scholar of continental philosophy of religion and postmodern theology, suggests that "we need to experiment radically with new ways of thinking and living, because the current paradigm is in a state of exhaustion, depletion, and death."[47] The current paradigm refers to political theologies that produce and maintain the ontological rift between human animals and other species. Philosopher Giorgio Agamben offers ways that we might work to bridge this rift so that we realize that other species are integral to the polis and empathically recognize and care for the singularities and potentialities of other species.

Rasmus Ugilt, scholar of political theory and contemporary philosophy, argues that Agamben's philosophical anthropology is, "centered on the notion of potentiality."[48] The concept of potentiality is important if we are to understand inoperativity and impotentiality and bridge the ontological rift. The notion of potentiality stems from Aristotle's work regarding the relation between potentiality (*dynamis*) and actualization (*energeia*). For Agamben, Western philosophical traditions have largely "subordinated potentiality to actuality: so we begin with the actual, speaking humans and their political and artistic productions, and we see potentiality at present as a capacity or skill that is defined by the final action. We see potentiality as secondary or accidental."[49] This is derived, in part, from Aristotle's notion that "actuality

47 Clayton Crockett, *Radical Political Theology* (New York: Columbia University Press, 2012), 165.

48 Rasmus Ugilt, *Giorgio Agamben: Political Philosophy* (London: Humanities-E-books, 2014), 22.

49 Claire Colebrook and Jason Maxwell, *Agamben* (Cambridge, MA: Polity Press, 2016), 188.

is prior to potentiality,"[50] though this does not mean that Aristotle believed that "potentiality exists only in actuality."[51] From Agamben's perspective, there are two features of Aristotle's views. First is that "the very essence of humanity lies in a potentiality that is expressed when it does not unfold into actuality."[52] Agamben illustrates potentiality in terms of impotentiality.

> Other living beings are capable only of their specific potentiality; they can only do this or that. But human beings are the animals who are capable of their own impotentiality. The greatness of human potentiality is measured by the abyss of human impotentiality. *Here it is possible to see how the root of freedom is to be found in the abyss of potentiality. To be free is not simply to have the power to do this or that thing, nor is it simply to have the power to refuse to do this or that thing. To be free is . . .* to be capable of one's own impotentiality.[53]

Agamben illustrates this by relying on Herman Melville's *Bartleby, the Scrivener: A Story of Wall Street*, wherein Bartleby is asked by his boss to do something and Bartleby replies, "I prefer not to."[54] For Agamben, Bartleby was exercising the freedom of not actualizing his potentiality, which means, in part, that Bartleby was not determined and cannot be determined (in the sense of being commanded by others) to actualize his potentiality. Cultural theorists Claire Colebrook and Jason Maxwell add that "to have potentiality is to be capable of not becoming what one has the capacity to be."[55] A

---

50 Ugilt, *Giorgio Agamben*, 26.

51 Giorgio Agamben, *Potentialities: Collected Essays in Philosophy*, trans. Daniel Heller-Roazen (Redwood City, CA: Stanford University Press, 1999), 180.

52 Colebrook and Maxwell, *Agamben*, 289.

53 Agamben, *Potentialities*, 182–183. I wish to stress that Agamben's differentiating between human animals and other species does not imply a hierarchy or belief in the superiority of human beings. Coming from a different, but related angle, philosopher John Gray wrote, "The distance between human and animal silence is a consequence of the use of language. . . . But if animals lack this interior dialogue, it is not clear why this should put humans on a higher plane." John Gray, *The Silence of Animals* (New York: Farrar, Straus, and Giroux, 2013), 163–164.

54 Herman Melville, *The Piazza Tales*, ed. Egbert S. Oliver (New York: Hendricks House, Farrar Straus, 1948), 26.

55 Colebrook and Maxwell, *Agamben*, 38.

concert pianist, for instance, can prefer not to actualize her capacity to perform. Human beings, then, are not (and cannot be completely) compelled to actualize their potentiality because they possess the freedom to prefer not to. For Agamben, this confirms that potentiality precedes actuality.

The notions of potentiality and impotentiality are closely associated with Agamben's depiction of "inoperativity," which means deactivating the function of the apparatuses. Inoperativity, for Agamben, is not passive.[56] That is, inoperativity does not "affirm inertia, inactivity or apraxia . . . but [is] a form of praxis."[57] Bartleby's impotentiality, for instance, renders inoperative the apparatuses associated with his job. This said, the exercise of impotentiality does not mean that these apparatuses cease to operate or have effects.[58] Rather, inoperativity in relation to individuals means that they are not captive to the grammar of the apparatuses, even if these apparatuses continue to have their effects. Bartleby, for example, exercises his impotentiality by preferring not to fulfill his boss's demands, thereby rendering inoperative the apparatuses of, in this case, capitalism. Of course, Bartleby's act of impotentiality does not diminish the power of capitalistic apparatuses to impact him.

An illustration from Christian scriptures can further illuminate the notion of inoperativity and move us toward its applicability in caring as a response to the ontological rift. Impotentiality and inoperativity is evident in Jesus's care-full decision to forgive his tormentors. The apparatuses of the Roman Empire included torture and crucifixion to terrorize colonized people, keeping them subjugated. Jesus preferred not to operate out of the grammar of these apparatuses of terror when he forgave the soldiers. His act of forgiveness rendered these apparatuses inoperative in that they did not determine or end Jesus's ability to actualize his impotentiality toward terror. Put another way, actualizing his capacity to forgive meant that he was not subject to, or subjugated by, these apparatuses of terror that traumatize individuals. Of course, as Agamben points out, making apparatuses inoperative does not mean these apparatuses do not continue to have impacts, which is

56 Sergei Prozorov, *Agamben and Politics* (Edinburgh: Edinburgh University Press, 2014), 134.

57 Prozorov, *Agamben and Politics*, 33.

58 Prozorov, *Agamben and Politics*, 31–34.

evident in Jesus having been tortured and put to death. The Roman Empire's apparatuses of terror continued for centuries.

This illustration is apropos for moving to bridge ontological rifts. The Roman Empire's apparatuses or disciplinary regimes produced a rift between Roman citizens and colonized peoples. We might consider imperialisms to be exemplars of instrumental epistemologies based on an ontological rift between colonizers and colonized (i.e., inferior, subordinate). Imperial apparatuses legitimate the exploitation, torture, and execution of colonized peoples, which necessarily includes objectification, disidentification, lack of accountability, and the absence of empathy and care for traumatized victims. Jesus's impotentiality and inoperativity, then, was an act of care that did not operate out of the grammar of Roman apparatuses. Jesus's forgiveness of others was inoperative, bridging the rift created by Roman apparatuses.

In London's story, White Fang eventually was rescued by two men who cared for him. These numerous acts of care can be understood as these two men rendering inoperative the apparatuses of the ontological rift implicated in White Fang's traumas. In so doing, their inoperative care provided a space and relation wherein White Fang's potentiality could become actualized. This actualization would not have erased memories of trauma, but would have made possible White Fang's ability to render inoperative, in time, these traumatic memories in his relations with these caretakers.

Likewise, pastoral care in the Anthropocene Age can be understood, in part, in terms of inoperativity and impotentiality that aims to bridge the ontological rift between humans and other species. Considering inoperativity, religious communities, and more-than-human species, we need to recognize and be accountable for the ontological rift that has led to the inordinate suffering and trauma to more-than-human species. To care for the potentialities and needs of other species means we need to make inoperative the apparatuses that create and maintain the ontological rift. By making these apparatuses inoperative, we also make inoperative the beliefs (illusions) in human superiority and other species' inferiority, as well as instrumental epistemologies that legitimate exploitation of other species.

Positively stated, inoperativity entails accepting that human beings are like all other animals, which includes accepting collective existential vulnerability and dependence on the Earth and other species, accepting insignificance and impermanence, accepting the singularities of other species, and acknowledging that other species are necessarily part of the polis. In other words, acts of impotentiality vis-à-vis the ontological rift entail the categorical demand to care for othered human beings,[59] other species, and the Earth. Acts of inoperative care also create spaces for the actualization of our potential for empathic and compassionate recognition in relation to other species.

Because pastoral care is rooted in a community of faith, then impotentiality or inoperativity must be cultivated. Some religious communities are intentional about caring for a biodiverse Earth and seek to make inoperative previous ways of being in the world that contribute to climate change.[60] Robert Shore-Goss, for instance, has been the senior pastor of MCC United Church of Christ in California since 2004.[61] During his pastoral leadership, he and other pastoral leaders have listened to congregants and facilitated the congregation's discernment about climate change and how to respond.[62] Similarly, Rev. Brooks Berndt, United Church of Christ environmental justice minister, has argued that "the role of churches at this time is not simply to raise awareness and alter our consumer habits. We can and should do these things. But at the same time, the role most needed from us is the

---

59 Knud Løgstrup, *The Ethical Demand* (Notre Dame, IN: Notre Dame University Press, 1997), 290. Danish philosopher and theologian K. E. Løgstrup argues that the "ethical demand takes its content from the unshakable fact that the existence of human beings is intertwined with each other in a way that demands human beings protect the lives of others who have been placed in their trust." Løgstrup was not considering the fact that the polis depends on a biodiverse Earth and therefore the ethical demand to care applies here as well.

60 My focus is on our relations to other species and the Earth. This said, one could find other instances of inoperative communities of care dealing with oppression and marginalization stemming from political, economic, and cultural apparatuses that undermine their well-being. The nonviolent political and economic actions evident in the civil rights movement can be understood as inoperative forms of care vis-à-vis racist apparatuses that produce an ontological rift between white and Black persons. Another example, is South Africa's Truth and Reconciliation Commission.

61 Robert Shore-Goss, *God is Green: An Eco-spirituality of Incarnate Compassion* (Eugene, OR: Cascade Books, 2016).

62 Shore-Goss, *God is Green*; Jim Antal, *Climate Church, Climate World: How People of Faith Must Work for Change* (Washington, DC: Rowman & Littlefield, 2018); Nick Spencer and Robert White, *Christianity, Climate Change, and Sustainable Living* (London: SPCK, 2007).

prophetic role," which requires "public action in confronting those in power."[63] The World Council of Churches and the Catholic Church also advocate for climate action—caring for the planet. Some of this discourse entails advocating changes in how we consume (especially those of us in market societies), which can be understood as making inoperative the rubrics of neoliberal capitalism. Climate discourses emanating from religious circles include critiques of states that seek to dominate markets and other states, because these superpowers impede global cooperation toward climate action. This, too, can be understood as advocating inoperativity in relation to global powers that contribute to the sufferings and traumas of other species.

All this action is welcome, but it reminds me of the passage about a splinter in a person's eye and a beam in our own. Christian communities largely do not confront how our scriptures and theological traditions (e.g., political theologies and concomitant rituals) function as apparatuses that produce and maintain the ontological rift. Our theologies and rituals privilege human beings (and usually a segment of humanity), making other species tangential, secondary, or simply ignored. Our theologies and rituals portray a vision of the future or hope that elides more-than-human beings. Pastoral care, then, becomes reserved for human beings, caring for their suffering and traumas. By facing how our theologies and rituals produce and maintain the ontological rift that overlooks the suffering and traumas of other species, we can take steps to opt out of operating out of these theologies and rituals. We can exercise our impotentiality—a praxis that creates a space for empathy and compassion for more-than-human species.

To render inoperative apparatuses that produce the ontological rift is an ethical demand and act of care, whether we understand this to be individual or communal action. Given this, it is important to recall that to make apparatuses inoperative, to exercise one's impotentiality, does not mean that these apparatuses no longer have effects. It simply means we are choosing to care such that the rubrics of these apparatuses of the ontological rift are not in play. Will our acts of impotentiality have any significant effect on the sufferings and traumas of other species? This question, while understandable,

63 Hans Holznagel, "Dire Climate Report Prompts Call for Church Action; UCC Offers Ways to Respond," last modified March 7, 2022, https://www.ucc.org/dire-climate-report-prompts-call-for-church-action-ucc-offers-ways-to-respond/.

is secondary and not foundational to the imperative to care for other species and exercising our capacity for impotentiality. What is primary is that acts of impotentiality, acts of care, are synchronic. They occur in the present and are not contingent on any future outcome, though this does not mean we do not possess a hope or desire for a particular outcome.[64] Simply stated, we care for other species and the Earth not because our lives and communities depend on it but because it is our vocation.

Conclusion: Creating a New Story

Philosopher Jonathan Gray wrote that "in [Martin] Heidegger's neo-Christian view rats and tigers, gorillas and hyenas simply exist, reacting passively to the world around them. Lacking any perception of the mysterious 'Being' from whence they came, other animals are no more than objects. Humans, on the other hand, are not objects, since they shape the world in which they live. This dreary old story is best forgotten."[65] This is the story of the ontological rift between humans and other species. It is a dreary story that is rooted in the Abrahamic traditions and Western political theologies and philosophies, producing instrumental epistemologies that legitimate the exploitation of other species and the disavowal of their suffering and traumas.

In this Anthropocene Age, I am not sure we can or should forget this story. However, we can make this story inoperative and create a space to tell a new story—a story that includes the singularities of more-than-human species and gives rise to epistemologies that demand and legitimate empathic and compassionate care that bridges the ontological gap.

64 Ryan LaMothe, *A Radical Political Theology for the Anthropocene Age* (Eugene, OR: Cascade, 2021).

65 Johnathan Gray, *The Silence of Animals* (New York: Farrar, Straus, and Giroux, 2013), 163.

5

PSYCHOSPIRITUAL STRESS, TRAUMA, AND MIGRATION

Understandings for Displaced Communities

Eunil David Cho

VIET THANH NGUYEN, a Vietnamese-American Pulitzer Prize–winning novelist and literary scholar, writes in his collection of short essays *The Displaced*: "To become a refugee is to know, inevitably, that the past is not only marked by the passage of time, but by loss—the loss of loved ones, of countries, of identities, or selves."[1] Since his arrival in America as a refugee in 1975, Nguyen has been endlessly trying to make sense of his "loss of loved ones, of countries, of identities, or selves."[2] This lifelong battle is the reason why he writes about his journey of fleeing his war-torn country, surviving a refugee camp, and fighting to belong in America. Nguyen says that refugees and immigrants tell their stories because they want to remember people whom they have lost and "to give voice to all those losses that would otherwise remain unheard."[3] Yet according to Nguyen, because of the traumatic nature of being displaced, he cannot remember everyone. He cannot remember the voice of his sister nor "the voices of all the refugees who shared the exodus with [him] and did not make it, or did not survive."[4]

According to the United Nations' definition of a *refugee*, Nguyen no longer is a refugee because he found a new and permanent home in the United States. He is no longer "someone who has been forced to flee his or

1 Viet Thanh Nguyen, ed., *The Displaced: Refugee Writers on Refugee Lives* (New York: Abrams Press, 2018), 22.

2 Nguyen, *The Displaced*, 22.

3 Nguyen, *The Displaced*, 22.

4 Nguyen, *The Displaced*, 23.

her country because of persecution, war, or violence."[5] However, Nguyen insists on calling himself a refugee even today because he does not feel "completely at home" even after many years.[6]

Nguyen's family left their relatives and friends behind in a country that was being torn apart by global war, a colonial legacy, and extreme poverty. After leaving Vietnam, for several years they had to survive the subhuman conditions of refugee camps with no clear end to their stay. Finally, they found themselves a permanent home in the United States. Yet, what Nguyen and his family experienced in their new country included social discrimination and systemic injustice that told them, "You don't belong here." In other words, for many displaced persons and communities, especially those living in the United States, they were "unwanted where they fled from," "unwanted where they are," and "unwanted where they want to go."[7]

Being displaced can compel refugees and immigrants to make sense of their losses of countries, properties, loved ones, and personal identities through the lens of trauma. Psychospiritual wisdom on displaced communities requires understanding the traumatic experience of refugees and immigrants who repeatedly re-experience the horrifying process of leaving their home countries, surviving the arduous process of migration, and adjusting to new places. Care, recovery, and healing are necessarily distinctive for these endlessly "unwanted" individuals and communities.

Trauma is often defined as "an emotional response to a terrible event like an accident, rape, or natural disaster" or "having experienced, witnessed or been confronted with an event that involved actual or threatened death or serious injury, or threat to the physical integrity of oneself or others."[8] In Western Europe and North America, when we talk about psychological trauma, we generally focus on examining how individuals become

---

5 Nguyen, *The Displaced*, 17.

6 Nguyen, *The Displaced*, 17.

7 Nguyen, *The Displaced*, 17.

8 American Psychological Association, "Psychology Topics: Trauma," *American Psychological Association*, last modified August 2022, https://www.apa.org/topics/trauma; Krista M. Perreira and India Ornelas, "Painful Passages: Traumatic Experiences and Post-Traumatic Stress Among Immigrant Latino Adolescents and their Primary Caregivers," *International Migration Review* 47, no. 4 (2013): 1, https://doi.org/10.1111/imre.12050.

traumatized by an experience, an event, or an act of violence and the individual responses to these experiences framed as symptoms of post-traumatic stress disorder (PTSD) such as re-experiencing the event, avoiding thoughts, anxious feelings, insomnia, and hypervigilance.[9] Whether about an event or a response, Western discourses of psychological trauma focus on understanding one individual's trauma as a "moment-of-injury," which has an identifiable structure of "pretrauma" and "posttrauma."[10]

The research on the traumatic impact of transnational migration, however, reveals that migration trauma does not happen in one specific event for a single individual. Rather, it normally happens to historically marginalized individuals and communities within lengthy and sustained processes, especially for those who must make transnational journeys for the sake of survival. Thus, to understand the full scope of migration trauma, our understanding of trauma needs to be expanded to include people's ongoing and collective lived experience that is deeply rooted in the sociocultural and political realities of systemic injustice, oppression, violence, and the continuing legacies of colonialism.

Because Western psychological discourses on trauma are insufficient to address the intercultural, collective, systemic, and political dimensions of migration trauma, pastoral theologians, pastoral psychologists, and spiritual caregivers must expand and reexamine our understanding of trauma to comprehensively recognize the traumatic impact of transnational migration, and to think about contextually appropriate ways of promoting recovery and healing. The current model of trauma needs to be reexamined (1) as an ongoing lived experience, (2) as an inherently collective experience, (3) as a spiritual experience, and (4) through local wisdom and cultural expressions.

An Ongoing and Cumulative Lived Experience

In Western societies, prevailing psychological and psychiatric models of trauma are linear and fixed and view trauma primarily as "something that

9 Perreira and Ornelas, "Painful Passages," 2.

10 Rebecca Lester, "Back from the Edge of Existence: A Critical Anthropology of Trauma," *Transcultural Psychiatry* 50, no. 5 (2013): 755, https://doi.org/10.1177/1363461513504520.

happens to an individual that fragments his or her experience into 'pre-trauma' and 'posttrauma' life."[11] There is a clear distinction between the two phases of "pretrauma" and "posttrauma" that need to be examined separately in realizing one's traumatic experience. What makes one's specific experience "traumatic" is how this event suddenly causes one to experience "a radical loss of agency, a sense of powerlessness, vulnerability and fear for one's very existence, in the face of a person or a force much greater than oneself," such as a perpetrator or a political regime.[12] Nguyen writes about this kind of "traumatic" experience by describing how he lost his personal agency and identity in a manner that powerfully damaged his own bodily integrity and psychological existence.[13]

However, psychological anthropologist Rebecca Lester argues that in many cases trauma can never be easily perceived as an act, an event, or "a moment of injury" with the clear temporal structure of a beginning and an end.[14] Likewise, it is challenging to accurately identify and separate between victim and perpetrator status, especially in incidents where multiple traumatic events take place for a group of individuals in a prolonged and sustained progression.[15]

Difficulty Differentiating between Perpetrators and Victims

Immigrants and refugees may be both victim-survivors and perpetrators of trauma. A qualitative study on undocumented immigrant families who crossed the US-Mexico border examined how they encounter a series of traumatic experiences such as hostile encounters with the US Border Patrol, heat and cold injury, dehydration, the danger from wild animals, and most importantly, the loss of family members as they attempt to enter the United

---

11 Lester, "Back from the Edge of Existence," 756.

12 Lester, "Back from the Edge of Existence," 756.

13 Nguyen, *The Displaced*; Bessel van der Kolk, *Psychological Trauma* (Washington, DC: American Psychiatric Publishing, 2003).

14 Lester, "Back from the Edge of Existence," 758.

15 Ibrahim Kira, "Etiology and Treatment of Post-Cumulative Traumatic Stress Disorders in Different Cultures," *Traumatology* 16, no. 4 (2010): 128–141, https://doi.org/10.1177/1534765610365914; Lester, "Back from the Edge of Existence"; Irene Visser, "Decolonizing Trauma Theory: Retrospect and Prospects," *Humanities* 4, no. 2 (2015): 250–265, https://doi.org/10.3390/h4020250.

States.[16] In-depth interviews with several adult male undocumented immigrants have revealed that they crossed the border with the willingness to "put themselves and their families at substantial perceived risk in order to seek economic opportunity."[17] Reflecting on the harshness of the desert crossing, a man named Javier shared: "I thought I was going to die there without seeing my family, and so I felt very afraid." Another man named Antonio explained that "we were doing it for our families and that is what gave us courage, really, that is what inspired us to keep on walking . . . we spent about two hours under a tree. We were very cold and had to hug each other to stay warm."[18] These undocumented immigrants used their agency to cross the border, knowing that they were putting themselves and their spouses and children at great risk of victimization. In another study on Latinx immigrants' traumatic experiences in the United States, health economist Krista M. Perreira and scholar of public health India Ornelas suggest, not surprisingly, that children immigrating at younger ages are more intensely vulnerable to victimization during the traumatic journey of migration.[19] In the traumatic experience of border crossing, if migrant children are likely to be victims, their parents may be cast as the perpetrators. Yet, if migrating parents are perpetrators because they decided to cross the border for economic opportunities, they are also victims to the systemic oppression of economic inequality and poverty in rural Mexico.

The Ongoing Legacy of Colonialism

These case studies strongly suggest that people's relationships to trauma are often quite complex, making it difficult to draw an absolute distinction between victims and perpetrators. This complexity also highlights the significance of understanding the historical, sociocultural, and political dimensions of the contexts where trauma continues to be experienced by displaced individuals and communities.

---

16 Lawrence A. DeLuca, Marylyn M. McEwen, and Samuel M. Keim, "United States-Mexico Border Crossing: Experiences and Risk Perceptions of Undocumented Male Immigrants," *Journal of Immigrant and Minority Health* 12, no. 1 (2010): 113–123, https://doi.org/10.1007/s10903-008-9197-4.

17 DeLuca, McEwen, and Keim, "United States-Mexico Border Crossing," 113.

18 DeLuca, McEwen, and Keim, "United States-Mexico Border Crossing," 119.

19 Perreira and Ornelas, "Painful Passages," 4.

A group of scholars in literary studies and comparative literature who specialize in Holocaust and postcolonial literature began a scholarly movement to decolonize or reconfigure conventional trauma theory.[20] In his influential article "Decolonizing Trauma Studies: A Response," Michael Rothberg, who specializes in Holocaust studies, cultural memory, and critical theory, claims that the Euro-American and Freudian psychoanalytic foundation of trauma theory as originally conceptualized by Cathy Caruth, scholar on the languages of trauma, "distorts the histories it addresses (such as the Holocaust) and threatens to reproduce the very Eurocentrism that lies behind those histories."[21] For Rothberg, the original trauma theory's Eurocentrism is found in its exclusive focus on "the event-based model of trauma" with "a more clearly definable period of history, and a clearer historical sense of victims, perpetrators, and responsibilities."[22] Mentioning the ongoing violence and colonization suffered by Indigenous individuals and communities in North America, Rothberg discusses how the Eurocentric model of trauma presupposes "the completed past of a singular event—while colonial and postcolonial trauma persist into the present" for those whose lives have been displaced throughout the world.[23]

Because European commercial and colonial expansion created the initial demand for intercontinental and transnational migrations in the eighteenth century, Rothberg's account of the ongoing, sustained, and cumulative processes of the trauma of colonialism is critical to understanding the complex and ongoing traumatic experience of refugees and immigrants across the globe. Moreover, because the Eurocentric and event-based framework of trauma cannot fully capture non-Western or intercultural trauma, Rothberg argues that scholars must rethink trauma

20 Michael Rothberg, "Decolonizing Trauma Studies: A Response," *Studies in the Novel* 40, no. 1 (2008): 224–234, https://doi.org/10.1353/sdn.0.0005; Irene Visser, "Decolonizing Trauma Theory: Retrospect and Prospects," *Humanities* 4, no. 2 (2015): 250–265, https://doi.org/10.3390/h4020250.

21 Rothberg, "Decolonizing Trauma Studies: A Response," 227; Cathy Caruth, *Unclaimed Experience: Trauma, Narrative, and History* (Baltimore, MD: John Hopkins University Press, 1996).

22 As cited in Irene Visser, "Decolonizing Trauma Theory," 252.

23 Rothberg, "Decolonizing Trauma Studies," 230.

as "collective, spatial, and material (instead of individual, temporal, and linguistic)."[24]

In psychological studies, to address the limitation of this Eurocentric, event-based model of understanding trauma, a group of mental health professionals working in apartheid-era South Africa developed the concept of *continuous traumatic stress* in the 1980s.[25] Gill Straker and her team, who worked with the victims of political violence within the South African context of ongoing state violence, claim that the existing framework or PTSD fails to describe the "enduring traumatic stress symptoms" and "realistic expectations of ongoing threat and danger, often combined with an absence of safe spaces in which to find protection and experience 'recovery'."[26] Particularly, in order to measure the impact of violence, conflict, and trauma on the millions of refugees, asylum seekers, and displaced persons living in the context of war, endemic civil and political conflict, or pervasive community violence, the notion of continuous traumatic stress offers an alternative way of understanding "the psychological impact of living in conditions in which there is a realistic threat of present and future danger, rather than only experiences of past traumatic events."[27] Since then, researchers and practitioners have engaged the framework of continuous traumatic stress to further examine many cases of people experiencing *continuous* and *ongoing* trauma exposure in many parts of the world.[28]

---

24 Rothberg, "Decolonizing Trauma Studies," 228.

25 Gillian Straker and The Sanctuaries Counselling Team, "The Continuous Traumatic Stress Syndrome: The Single Therapeutic Interview," *Psychology in Society* 8 (1987), 48–78.

26 As cited in Garth Stevens, Gillian Eagle, and Debra Kaminer, "Continuous Traumatic Stress: Conceptual Conversations in Contexts of Global Conflict, Violence and Trauma," *Peace and Conflict: Journal of Peace Psychology* 19, no. 2 (2013): 76, https://doi.org/10.1037/a0032484.

27 Stevens, Eagle, and Kaminer, "Continuous Traumatic Stress," 76.

28 Judith A. Cohen, Anthony P. Mannarino, and Laura K. Murray, "Trauma-Focused CBT for Youth Who Experience Ongoing Traumas," *Child Abuse and Neglect* 35, no. 8 (2011): 637–646, https://doi.org/10.1016/j.chiabu.2011.05.002; Gary M. Diamond, et al., "Ongoing Traumatic Stress Response (OTSR) in Sderot Israel," *Professional Psychology: Research and Practice* 41, no. 1 (2010): 19–25, http://doi.org/10.1037/a0017098; Stevens, Eagle, and Kaminer, "Continuous Traumatic Stress"; Mooli Lahad and Dmitry Leykin, "Ongoing Exposure Versus Intense Periodic Exposure to Military Conflict and Terror Attacks in Israel," *Journal of Traumatic Stress* 23, no. 6 (2010): 691–698, https://doi.org/10.1002/jts.20583.

Displacement and Trauma as a Collective Experience

Migration trauma is often expressed not simply as an individual experience but as a community enterprise, particularly in the face of war, colonialism, poverty, natural disaster, systemic racism, and political oppression, which are primary reasons for people to leave their homes and migrate to safer places as refugees, asylum seekers, exiles, and immigrants.[29] For example, since Russia's invasion of Ukraine in late February 2022, over 7.6 million refugees fleeing Ukraine have been recorded crossing into Europe while an estimated eight million people have been displaced within the country as of late May 2022.[30]

Moreover, due to the devastating effects of extreme weather events and disasters within communities in vulnerable situations across the world, of the approximate 59.1 million people who were internally displaced across the world in 2021, most were displaced by climate-related disasters in 2021.[31] Disasters, whether natural or human-caused, not only harm an individual's personal sense of agency but also destroy the fabrics of local systems that protect and respond to the needs of individuals and communities. Oftentimes, disasters bring "an array of stressors to populations—from direct threat to life, physical injury, exposure to the dead and dying, bereavement, loss, societal and community disruption, and ongoing hardship."[32] These disasters tend to have the greatest impact on those who are situated in more

---

29 Lester, "Back from the Edge of Existence," 756; Ria Reis, "Children Enacting Idioms of Witchcraft and Spirit Possession as a Response to Trauma: Therapeutically Beneficial, and for Whom?," *Transcultural Psychiatry* 50, no. 5 (2013): 622–643, https://doi.org/10.1177/1363461513503880.

30 United Nations High Commissioner for Refugees, "Refugees from Ukraine Recorded Across Europe," *United Nations, Office of the High Commissioner for Refugees*, October 11, 2022, https://data.unhcr.org/en/situations/ukraine.

31 Office of the High Commissioner for Human Rights, "'Intolerable' Tide of People Displaced by Climate Change: UN Expert," *United Nations, Office of the High Commissioner for Human Rights*, https://www.ohchr.org/en/press-releases/2022/06/intolerable-tide-people-displaced-climate-change-un.

32 Jack Saul, *Collective Trauma, Collective Healing: Promoting Community Resilience in the Aftermath of Disaster* (Oxfordshire: Routledge, 2014), 1. See also Fran H. Norris, et al., "60,000 Disaster Victims Speak: Part I. An Empirical Review of the Empirical Literature, 1981–2001," *Psychiatry* 65, no. 3 (2002): 207–239, https://doi.org/10.1521/psyc.65.3.207.20173.

historically marginalized areas of society, such as children, youths, women, elders, LGBTQ+ individuals, racial and ethnic minorities, and people with disabilities.

This inevitable consequence of natural and human-caused disasters is called *collective trauma*,[33] the "shared injuries to a population's social, cultural, and physical ecologies" as well as "the cumulative effects of poverty, oppression, illness and displacement" that harm relationships in families, communities, and societies at large.[34] In such situations, trauma cannot be fully explained by intrapsychic, individual terms alone nor collapsed into the simplistic perpetrator-victim dichotomy.[35] This is true of migration trauma as well. Both Rothberg and Lester contend that trauma in the context of transnational and intercultural migration is primarily a community enterprise.[36] Lester urges those who study trauma and desire to care for traumatized individuals and communities to recognize "the complex relationship of the individual person to the traumatic event itself and the community within which s/he is located as well as local responses to trauma that specifically center on accommodating these multiples forms of agency."[37]

American sociologist Kai Erikson was the first scholar to make the distinction between *individual trauma* and *collective trauma* following the Buffalo Creek disaster that destroyed a hollow in Appalachia. Erikson writes,

> *By individual trauma I mean a blow to the psyche that breaks through one's defense so suddenly and with such brutal force that one cannot react to it effectively. This is what clinicians normally mean when they use the term, and the Buffalo Creek survivors experienced precisely that. . . . By collective trauma, on the other*

33 There are two types of disasters: natural and human-caused. But recently the distinction between the two types has been much more difficult to determine because some disasters are caused by both natural and human actions. To describe these kinds of disasters, the World Health Organization has begun using the term "complex humanitarian disaster." Joseph Zibulewsky, "Defining Disaster: The Emergency Department Perspective," *Baylor University Medical Center Proceedings* 14, no. 2 (2001): 144, https://doi.org/10.1080/08998280.2001.11927751.

34 Saul, *Collective Trauma, Collective Healing*, 1, 3.

35 Lester, "Back from the Edge of Existence."

36 Lester, "Back from the Edge of Existence," 757.

37 Lester, "Back from the Edge of Existence," 757.

> *hand, I mean a blow to the basic tissues of social life that damages the bonds attaching people together and impairs the prevailing sense of communality. The collective trauma works its way slowly and even insidiously into the awareness of those who suffer from it, so it does not have the quality of suddenness normally associated with "trauma." But it is a form of shock all the same, a gradual realization that the community no longer exists as an effect source of support and that an important part of the self has disappeared.*[38]

Based on his study of the Buffalo Creek disaster, Erikson argues that it is common after a catastrophic event for people to experience both individual and communal trauma. People who suffer from individual trauma encounter difficulty in recovery if the community they belong to remains shattered. In the same way, individual therapy becomes more effective when it is done in a nurturing and supportive community or environment. Erikson stresses the importance of understanding both the individual and collective dimensions of trauma when helping traumatized individuals and communities. After many recent disasters in North America such as the September 11 terrorist attacks, Hurricane Katrina, Columbine mass school shooting, and other catastrophic events, individual-oriented ideologies and institutional practices embedded in trauma work "posed tremendous obstacles to addressing the collective consequences of massive trauma."[39]

Responding to Collective Trauma

Jack Saul, a clinical trauma expert and public health scholar who established a clinic in New York City, worked closely with many refugee individuals who had survived torture in their home countries as well as migration trauma. Saul writes that "by the time many asylees or refugees reach a host country like the United States, they may have endured multiple traumas, often living through years of violence inflicted upon their family and community."[40]

---

38 Kai Erikson, *Everything in Its Path: Destruction of Community in the Buffalo Creek Flood* (New York: Simon & Schuster, 1976), 153–154.

39 Saul, *Collective Trauma, Collective Healing*, 6.

40 Saul, *Collective Trauma, Collective Healing*, 32.

Saul eventually learned that while the process of fleeing their homes and surviving imprisonment was traumatic, the trauma continued even after the refugees and asylum seekers had finally arrived in the United States. They faced "problems of residency status, racial prejudice, and numerous other types of obstacles—socioeconomic, educational, occupational, and linguistic."[41] For these newly arrived refugees, the trauma from the past was still ongoing—"concern about family and friends back home, ambivalence and grief about fleeing their country, and additional physical and psychological sequelae of torture and related traumas."[42] Saul and his clinical team also observed that many political asylees became socially isolated because they were not able to join their ethnic community in America due to factionalism and political conflicts that related to repressive regimes back in their home countries.[43] In providing clinical services to refugees and asylum seekers, Saul and his team finally learned that what these newly arrived migrants in New York needed most was social support due to their experience of profound isolation in their exile.[44]

One significant challenge Saul found in providing mental health care was the fact that, for many refugees and asylum seekers, psychotherapy or mental health counseling was a foreign concept. Although individual counseling and therapy would be tremendously helpful for these torture survivors who were still experiencing trauma, "speaking about one's experience as a means to healing" was not a culturally appropriate form of care and healing for many newly arrived refugees.[45] Most of the migrants who came to Saul's clinic were not necessarily there to receive trauma-informed mental health counseling; they came seeking social services in various areas, such as housing, finance, employment, and English language competency.[46]

---

41 Saul, *Collective Trauma, Collective Healing*, 33.

42 Saul, *Collective Trauma, Collective Healing*, 33.

43 For instance, refugees and asylum seekers from North Korea who settle in the United States struggle with intense social isolation because they are not able to join Korean American communities, most of whose members are South Koreans. Due to the historical and ongoing political tensions in the Korean Peninsula, North Korean migrants in America experience great difficulty joining ethnic communities that are predominantly South Korean. Saul, *Collective Trauma, Collective Healing*, 32–33.

44 Saul, *Collective Trauma, Collective Healing*, 33.

45 Saul, *Collective Trauma, Collective Healing*, 34.

46 Saul, *Collective Trauma, Collective Healing*, 34–35.

Psychologists Matthew Porter and Nick Haslam, who conducted in-depth research on the mental health of refugees and internally displaced persons, argue that what best promotes the positive mental health of these transnational migrants is providing them with various forms of social support, including employment, housing, education, help raising families, political stability, health care, and cultural access.[47] Psychologists Kenneth Miller and Lisa Rasco also conducted similar research on the mental health of refugee communities in North America and recommend an ecologically oriented and community-based model of recovery and healing rather than clinic-based services such as psychotherapy and psychiatric medication.[48] According to Saul, when working with traumatized individuals and communities who are displaced, clinicians and caregivers must address "problems in the ecological settings in which refugees live and work; reflect the concerns and priorities of the community; and, when possible, prioritize prevention over treatment."[49]

Based on Erikson's earlier work on collective trauma, Saul argues that one of the most important symptoms of collective trauma is the "betrayal of social trust."[50] This betrayal of social trust "leaves one feeling devalued and humiliated, with a sense that previously established communal trust and decency is no longer present."[51] This is especially true for migrants who come from non-Western, collectivistic societies where one's personal identity is defined by one's community. In collective trauma, restoring social trust then becomes one of the most fundamental challenges for traumatized individuals and communities who have survived multiple forms of trauma in their displacement. In New York City, in order to meet the psychological as well as social needs of these newly arrived refugees and asylees, Saul and his clinical team decided to act as a "transitional family" (rather than a

47 Matthew Porter and Nick Haslam, "Predisplacement and Postdisplacement Factors Associated with Mental Health of Refugees and Internally Displaced Persons: A Meta-Analysis," *JAMA* 294, no. 5 (2005): 602–612, https://doi:10.1001/jama.294.5.602. See also Saul, *Collective Trauma, Collective Healing*, 33–35.

48 Kenneth E. Miller and Lisa M. Rasco, eds., *The Mental Health of Refugees: Ecological Approaches to Healing and Adaptation* (Mahwah, NJ: Lawrence Erlbaum Associates, 2004).

49 Saul, *Collective Trauma, Collective Healing*, 35.

50 Saul, *Collective Trauma, Collective Healing*, 4.

51 Saul, *Collective Trauma, Collective Healing*, 4.

mental health clinic) for these individuals and communities who were in the uncertain process of seeking or forming a support network of their own.[52] In this "transitional family," these displaced individuals were able to take the very first step toward gradually restoring social trust by interacting and cultivating meaningful relationships with staff members and fellow refugees and asylum seekers who visited the clinic.

Migrant Trauma as a Spiritual Experience

In 1978, American historian Timothy Smith, in his influential study on religion and ethnicity in North America, presented the compelling argument that migration itself is a "theologizing experience." According to Smith, when migrants struggle with the disorienting experiences of loss, separation, and adjustment, faith or religion provides its own language for them to cope with their sense of existential uncertainty and to make sense of their experiences of being displaced.

Moreover, religious communities offer places of resources, support, and intimacy for migrant individuals and communities. American sociologist Charles Hirschman explains that there are three psychological and sociocultural functions of religious communities in North America for migrant individuals and communities: refuge, respectability, and resources.[53] First, immigrants attend and join religious communities to seek refuge and to fill the psychological void and attain a sense of belonging. "The search for refuge by immigrants has been for physical safety as well as psychological comfort."[54] Second, faith communities are rare places that acknowledge the respectability of immigrant individuals and communities. Churches, mosques, temples, and synagogues often "provide respectability or opportunities for status recognition and social mobility that is denied in the broader [host] society."[55] Third, religious communities often respond to the needs for

52 Saul, *Collective Trauma, Collective Healing*, 33.

53 Charles Hirschman, "The Role of Religion in the Origins and Adaptation of Immigrant Groups in the United States," *Interntional Migration Review* 38, no. 3 (2004): 1206–1233.

54 Hirschman, "The Role of Religion," 1228.

55 Hirschman, "The Role of Religion," 1229.

the lives of immigrants through the provision of various resources. In North America, immigrants often turn to religious communities for information and practical assistance related to social services, families and children, legal issues, health care, educational programs, and language training. Both Smith and Hirschman contend that religion accompanies the process of migration as a means of alleviating the traumas of departure and early settlement, providing a haven against external discrimination, and facilitating migrants' smooth acculturation within the new context.

Sociologists and anthropologists often validate the theologizing hypothesis of religion or spirituality when studying human trauma and pay particular attention to the role of spirituality in fostering resilience in traumatized individuals and communities.[56] Traumatized individuals may raise existential and spiritual questions about their identities, beliefs, and worldviews. Belief in the existence of God or a divine being, as well as religion and spirituality in general, provide helpful concepts, worldviews, languages, and rituals that help them cope with their experiences of trauma and facilitate new meanings in retelling of their narratives as an important step toward recovery and healing.[57]

Despite the significance of religion and spirituality in fostering human adaptation to trauma, Roger Luckhurst, scholar of literature, film, and cultural history claims that the conventional trauma theory informed by Eurocentric, individualistic, and psychoanalytic approaches has not embraced religion and spirituality as important conversation partners because religion

---

56 Eunil David Cho, "Coping with a Double Pandemic of Health Crisis and Anti-Asian Racism in America: The Role of Immigrant Churches," in *Between Pandemonium and Pandemethics: Responses to Covid-19 from Theology and Religions*, ed. Volker Küster and Dorothea Erbele-Küster (Berlin: Evangelische Verlagsanstalt, 2022), 57–86; Helen Rose Ebaugh and Janet Saltzman Chafetz, *Religion and the New Immigrants: Continuities and Adaptations in Immigrant Congregations* (Lanham, MD: AltaMira Press, 2000); R. Stephen Warner and Judith G. Wittner, eds., *Gatherings in Diaspora: Religious Communities and New Immigration* (Philadelphia: Temple University Press, 1998).

57 Judith Herman, "Recovery from Psychological Trauma," *Psychiatry and Clinical Neurosciences* 52, no. S1 (2002): S98–S103, https://doi.org/10.1046/j.1440-1819.1998.0520s5S145.x; Kenneth Pargament, *Spiritually Integrated Psychotherapy: Understanding and Addressing the Sacred* (New York: Guilford Press, 2007); Kenneth Pargament and Julie J. Exline, *Working with Spiritual Struggles in Psychotherapy* (New York: Guilford Press, 2021).

has been long seen as pathological.[58] Moreover, the lack of attention to the conversation between spirituality and trauma may also be due to the fact that in North America psychologists and psychoanalysts tend to be far less religious than Americans as a whole.[59]

For example, many psychologists and psychotherapists have noted that forgiveness is not a psychoanalytic concept and should not be used in understanding and helping traumatized people.[60] In her compelling article in *Psychology Today*, trauma therapist Amanda Ann Gregory argues that forgiveness is "potentially problematic when incorporated into trauma treatment."[61] While many claim that forgiveness can help survivors move on or let go of the pain of their past, Gregory suggests that forgiveness has the potential to create serious challenges in trauma treatment, saying that forgiveness (1) diminishes harms and wrongs, which ultimately inhibits safety; (2) focuses on the perpetrator instead of the survivors; (3) blames survivors, which intensifies and perpetuates shame and guilt; (4) encourages and prolongs silence; and, finally, (5) can be used as a means to avoid recovery and healing. Gregory's critical analysis of forgiveness in trauma treatment is crucial in pointing out that religion can be a source of trauma and that post-traumatic symptoms can emerge from people's extremely stressful religious experiences.

However, for many refugees and immigrants, religion carries particular significance. Precisely because of their ongoing experience of migration, they continue to grapple with existential questions about their identities, purpose

---

58 Roger Luckhurst, *The Trauma Question* (Oxfordshire: Routledge, 2008); Visser, "Decolonizing Trauma Theory," 261.

59 Harold D. Delaney, William R. Miller, and Ana M. Bisono, "Religiosity and Spirituality Among Psychologists: A Survey of Clinician Members of the American Psychological Association," *Professional Psychology: Research and Practice* 38, no. 5 (2007): 538–546, https://doi.org/10.1037/0735-7028.38.5.538; Crystal L. Park, Jospeh M Currier, J. Irene Harris, and Jeanne M. Slattery, *Trauma, Meaning, and Spirituality: Translating Research into Clinical Practice* (Washington, DC: American Psychological Association, 2017), 6.

60 Julia Kristeva, *Intimate Revolt: The Powers and Limits of Psychoanalysis* (New York: Columbia University Press, 2002); Irene Visser, "Decolonizing Trauma Theory."

61 Amanda Ann Gregory, "Why Forgiveness Isn't Required in Trauma Recovery," *Psychology Today*, February 20, 2022, https://www.psychologytoday.com/us/blog/simplifying-complex-trauma/202202/why-forgiveness-isn-t-required-in-trauma-recovery.

of life, divine intervention, and uncertain future and seek to make sense of their constant feelings of confusion, uncertainty, and loss. A recent qualitative study on the internally displaced people of Puerto Rico in the wake of the devastation and loss following hurricanes Irma and Maria demonstrated that Christian religious affiliation and the participants' propensity toward the Christian belief in forgiveness played a crucial role in mitigating PTSD symptoms.[62] For these Christians in Puerto Rico, forgiveness was a helpful religious concept that enabled them to find a sense of hope in the aftermath of the two consecutive hurricanes.

Furthermore, Witi Ihimaera's novel *The Whale Rider*, a historical narrative that depicts the lives of the Indigenous Māori community on the eastern edge of New Zealand's North Island, presents forgiveness as a spiritual and cultural resource for recovery and healing in both individual and collective trauma in the larger Māori community.[63] Kahu, the protagonist, engages in a formal ritual of forgiveness that marks the turn to healing from the trauma of rejection and exclusion.[64] At the end of the story, when Kahu begins this ritual by respectfully asking for forgiveness in Māori and repeats it multiple times, he finally experiences "a very powerful psychological force, reconciling differences and healing the wounding of the past."[65]

Renowned anthropologist Tanya Luhrmann has called out academics and practitioners in human sciences and mental health for overlooking the significance of religion and spirituality. On the intersection of trauma and spirituality, she challenges health care clinicians to "consider the possibility that [people's] relationship with God may be a response to their trauma, and that it is sometimes quite effective."[66] Of course, when examining trauma in intercultural contexts, this study of the "human

---

62 Loren Toussaint, Sowmya Kshtriya, Ani Kalayjian, Erinn Cameron, and Daria Diakonova Curtis, "Christian Religious Affiliation is Associated with less Posttraumatic Stress Symptoms through Forgiveness but Not Search for Meaning after Hurricane Irma and Maria," *Psychology of Religion and Spirituality* 15, no. 1 (2022): 79–82, https://doi.org/10.1037/rel0000454.

63 Witi Ihimaera, *The Whale Rider* (London: Penguin Books, 1987).

64 Ihimaera, *The Whale Rider*, 149.

65 Visser, "Decolonizing Trauma Theory," 262.

66 Tanya Marie Luhrmann, "Making God Real and Making God Good: Some Mechanisms Through Which Prayer May Contribute to Healing," *Transcultural Psychiatry* 50, no. 5 (2013): 708, https://doi.org/10.1177/1363461513487670.

relationship with God" must go beyond the framework of Western Christian theology and practices. Trauma scholars need to be open to converse with non-Western religions and indigenous belief systems and rituals in order to examine the local perceptions of trauma, healing, and recovery in various cultural contexts. The case studies of internally displaced persons in Puerto Rico and New Zealand demonstrate that understanding the full complexity of the experience of migration trauma and their healing modalities often required the perspectives of religion and spirituality. While many migrants do encounter migration as a theologizing or spiritual experience, those who find migration to be a traumatizing experience can engage religion and spirituality in generative ways as potential resources for coping, meaning making, and healing.

Local Wisdom and Cultural Expressions

Intercultural Perspectives on Migrants' Experience of Trauma

Culture affects how individuals and communities understand and perceive trauma.[67] Culture also affects how people make sense of their traumatic experience and how they imagine what healing and recovery mean and look like in their lives. As the cases of the Māori community in New Zealand and the refugees and asylum seekers at Saul's clinic in New York City indicate, to understand the full scope and complexity of migration trauma, scholars and practitioners must pay close attention to how each individual or community experiences and perceives what trauma is, and observe local ways of coping and healing.[68] Mary-Jo DelVecchio Good, a leading expert in social medicine and public health, argues that in studying individual and collective trauma within intercultural and international settings, scholars and clinicians need to focus on observing and examining how people express

67 Sofie Bäärnhielm and Mike Mösko, "Cross-Cultural Communication with Traumatised Immigrants," in *Truama and Migration: Cultural Factors in the Diagnosis and Treatment of Traumatised Immigrants*, ed. Meryam Schouler-Ocak (New York: Springer International, 2015), 39–55.

68 Mary-Jo DelVecchio Good, "Perspectives on Trauma and Healing from Anthropology and Social and Affective Neuroscience," *Transcultural Psychiatry* 50, no. 5 (2013): 744–752, https://doi.org/10.1177/1363461513508174.

emotions and engage in "bodily and daily life experiences" in the midst of ongoing trauma, rather than making categorical and clinical diagnoses.[69]

In her book *Longing for Home*, pastoral theologian Jan Holton explores the psychological, sociological, and theological impact of losing one's home by studying several communities in North America and Africa who suffered forced displacement.[70] One of the displaced communities Holton looks at is an Indigenous tribe named the Batwa in the Ugandan mountains. Holton examines the traumatic experience of losing home for the Batwa, who were forced out of their mountain forest homes. Based on her fieldwork, Holton draws on several key stories that leaders of the Batwa community used to make sense of their experiences of being displaced or having no place to call home. In her interpretation, Holton explains that the Batwa people's understanding of their forest home is significantly different from how people in Western cultures understand and perceive home. Holton argues that for people in Western cultures, home or space is "something to be owned, shaped, molded, or designed to fit our tastes and desires. Even pseudo-natural spaces, such as yards, gardens, playing fields, and the like, exist for our pleasure and enjoyment."[71] However, for the Batwa, home is the entire natural environment. They are "people with a culture whose perception of the natural world is not that of something to be conquered but a gift to be respected and lived with cooperatively."[72] The stories of the Batwa people reveal that "they lived in a *partnership* with the natural environment" and "the forest provided shelter, sustenance, and healing."[73]

It is significantly challenging to fully understand and measure the level of the collective trauma or continuous traumatic stress of Batwa individuals. What would healing and recovery look like for the different generations of the Batwa, including grandparents, parents, and children? What does restoring social trust look like in the context of the Batwa? Holton does not provide clear answers but describes how losing the forest home meant multiple

69 DelVecchio Good, "Perspectives on Trauma and Healing," 744.

70 Jan Holton, *Longing for Home* (New Haven, CT: Yale University Press, 2016).

71 Holton, *Longing for Home*, 68.

72 Holton, *Longing for Home*, 68.

73 Holton, *Longing for Home*, 68–69.

losses of many generations of life, including their memories from the past as well as their hopes and dreams for the future:

> *For the Batwa, the forest home cannot be approximately replicated. All of the ways that everyday life was enfolded and enriched by the forest were lost. All referents to interpreting their experience in the world changed. What is the cultural, spiritual, and psychological impact of living with this irreplaceable loss of home? Dwellings made in or under the forest canopy, the thin air in the mountain forest, the rituals of death and burial in the forest floor, the freedom to move the community to fresh forest spaces when custom or nature demands—all became memories. How does one recover from such profound, irreplaceable loss? How does the culture absorb the disintegration of its source of meaning making? And, at what cost do they survive thereafter?*[74]

Holton's work emphasizes that the notion of trauma must be redefined and reexamined according to each place's historical, social, cultural, and ecological context. Joseph Gone, who studies the historical trauma of Native American communities in North America, claims that when examining the complex lives of Indigenous communities, scholars and practitioners must listen to and observe how members of these Indigenous communities express and live out their cultural and spiritual ways in order to deal with trauma and how they participate in their own communities as a therapeutic mechanism to pursue healing and recovery on their own terms.[75]

Cultivating Social Support and Networks

In Saul's clinic for refugee health services in New York City, Saul and his team observed that the refugees did not come to the clinic just to receive support from the clinicians. They also consistently came to the clinic to help other recently arrived refugees and asylum seekers navigate the

---

74 Holton, *Longing for Home*, 77–78.

75 Joseph P. Gone, "Redressing First Nations Historical Trauma: Theorizing Mechanisms for Indigenous Culture and Mental Health Treatment," *Transcultural Psychiatry* 50, no. 5 (2013): 683–706, https://doi.org/10.1177/1363461513487669.

bureaucracies of New York City.[76] Saul wrote that "these refugees valued helping others as an adaptive way of dealing with the trauma and loss they had experienced as a result of torture and migration, and separation from their families."[77] In this particular transitional family setting, refugees and asylum seekers actively take various roles of leading, guiding, and helping other fellow refugees to become adjusted to a new home, teaching English and cultural competency, listening to their concerns in their own native languages, and also working closely with the staff at the clinic to provide both psychological and social support. By working to support fellow refugees and asylum seekers, these migrants not only cope with their own ongoing experience of trauma but also regain their sense of personal and communal agency through serving the larger refugee communities in New York City. For these refugees at the clinic, work becomes a meaning-making platform that enables them to find a new sense of purpose and demonstrate generativity.

In similar ways, a group of medical anthropologists have found that work is a significant act of self-care in coping with chronic pain.[78] For many people who have experienced chronic illness or the loss of family members, work becomes a means to revisit and remake their own worlds in life and to work through personal sources of suffering. Mary-Jo DelVecchio Good and colleagues mention that people who suffer from depression see "work as a haven from pain and loss, . . . an arena for self-realization and effective performance, and . . . as a vehicle for control over the intrusiveness and daily disruptiveness of pain."[79] For migrant individuals and communities who are already in their host countries, work, especially work to help and serve fellow migrants who are actively experiencing migration trauma, becomes a ritualized way of healing and treatment. Specifically, as Hirschman points out, religious communities often become communal sites where immigrants are committed to working together and helping to provide a place

76 Saul, *Collective Trauma, Collective Healing.*

77 Saul, *Collective Trauma, Collective Healing*, 34.

78 Mary-Jo DelVecchio Good, Paul Brodwin, Byron J. Good, and Arthur Kleinman, eds., *Pain as Human Experience: An Anthropological Perspective* (Oakland, CA: University of California Press, 1992).

79 DelVecchio Good, et al., *Pain as Human Experience*, 50.

of refuge, a sense of respectability, and many kinds of social and cultural resources during the confusing and uncertain times of resettlement and adjustment.[80] In the context of collective trauma in North America and many other places in the world, working to serve others with a spirit of care and hospitality can be seen as a generative way to build a sense of community and restore social trust, not only for themselves but also for those who receive their help.

Further Research on Displacement and Healing

Because the traumatic impact of migration on individuals and communities is inherently ongoing, cumulative, and collective in nature rather than individualistic, linear, and event-based, the prevailing trauma theory based on Eurocentric and biomedical perspectives fails to understand the full scope and complexity of migration trauma. Likewise, Western psychology and psychiatry alone are insufficient to examine the trauma of non-Western refugees, asylum seekers, immigrants, and internally displaced individuals for whom migration is intercultural and profoundly rooted in the historical and ongoing realities of systemic injustice, oppression, violence, and the continuing legacy of colonialism. For the critical task of reexamining and redefining trauma, pastoral theologians, religious scholars, and spiritual caregivers are uniquely positioned to engage a wide range of perspectives in sociology, anthropology, theology, and religious studies to examine the deeply intercultural, collective, and even spiritual nature of migration trauma.

Pastoral theologians, pastoral psychologists, and spiritual caregivers need to produce scholarship on religion and spirituality concerning the intercultural nature of trauma and the treatment of traumatized individuals and communities across the globe. One significant way to do this is to make a sociocultural turn in studying trauma and spirituality by going beyond the conventional framework of psychology and psychiatry in current trauma studies. As the work of practical theologian Joyce Ann Mercer and pastoral

80 Hirschman, "The Role of Religion."

theologian M. Jan Holton demonstrate, social scientific approaches, including ethnographic research on the intersection of trauma, spirituality, and migration, are invaluable ways to understand how various socially marginalized communities perceive trauma and healing in their own cultural terms and subsequently consider how they engage local resources, such as Indigenous spirituality, religious rituals, cultural symbols, and natural environments, to imagine culturally appropriate and socially just coping strategies and healing works in the midst of displacement.[81]

81 Joyce Ann Mercer, "Pastoral Care with Children of War: A Community-Based Model of Trauma Healing in the Aftermath of Indonesia's Religious Conflicts," *Pastoral Psychology* 64, no. 6 (2015): 847–860, https://doi.org/10.1007/s11089-015-0654-4; Holton, *Longing for Home*.

6

PSYCHOSPIRITUALITY AND GENOCIDAL RAPE

Stress, Trauma, and Post-Traumatic Growth in Victim-Survivors

Nazila Isgandarova

"The cure for the pain is in the pain. Good and bad are mixed."[1]

—Jalāl al-Dīn Rūmī

IN THE CONTEXT of trauma, the Sufi poet Rumi's quote about the cure for pain might sound a bit odd. It suggests that healing can be found even in the painful experiences of genocidal rape as a tool of war. What Rumi posited is that resilience and strength are embedded within every painful experience and these pains might promise the seed of great transformation and healing.

Genocidal rape is a heinous crime that goes against the core values of humanity. Movies such as *The Death and the Maiden*, *Rob Roy*, *Immortal Beloved*, and *Braveheart* depict the impact of genocidal rape. The works of classical Russian writers and even the ancient *Gilgamesh* also describe the vulnerability of women, not only during times of war but also during "peaceful" times. According to human rights scholars Daniela de Vito, Aisha Gill, and Damiel Short, genocidal rape is not only "the violation of an individual's sexual autonomy," but a "group violation."[2] Although this chapter focuses mainly on genocidal rape against women as a tool of war, it is also important to acknowledge that men are also victims.

---

1 Jalāl al-Dīn Rūmī, *The Essential Rumi*, trans. Coleman Barks with John Moyne (New York: HarperCollins, 1996), 205.

2 Daniela de Vito, Aisha Gill, and Damiel Short, "Rape Characterised as Genocide," *Sur: International Journal on Human Rights* 6, no. 10 (2009), 28.

Journalist and feminist activist Susan Brownmiller rightfully observes that rape is "one of the most important discoveries of prehistoric time, along with the use of fire and the first crude stone axe."[3] However, what is important is that in genocidal rape the "victor" tends to normalize rape against the "other," who is viewed by the former as low, subordinate, and the "enemy." As journalist Alexandra Stiglmayer states, "because [women] are women," these "victors" "are using against them their most effective weapon: rape."[4]

The Prevalence of Genocidal Rape

On February 25 to 26, 1992, when the Armenian military forces along with the Soviet army committed the Khojali genocide in Azerbaijan, I was in high school in Azerbaijan. A teenage girl, who became a refugee as a result of the forced evacuation, painfully described to the girls in the classroom her relatives' experience, including the rape of women and girls in her small town. I did not know much about vicarious trauma at that time. However, I remember being terrified of her pain. Probably for the first time in my life, I realized the danger of being attacked and taken hostage as a female. I also remember that the international community did not immediately react to the crimes, including rape, against women in the Karabagh region of Azerbaijan. However, I am glad that these crimes garnered the attention of the international community after Serbian soldiers and men used rape as a pervasive, gross tool against women in Bosnia-Herzegovina in 1994, Hutu soldiers against Tutsi women in Rwanda in 1994, Russian soldiers against Chechen women in 1999, Burmese soldiers against Rohingya women in 2016, Chinese military forces against Uyghur women in 2020, and, most recently, the Russian army against Ukrainian women and Hamas militants' rape of hostages taken from Israel.

Although there are no reliable data on the number of people raped during recent wars, some authors draw attention to the massive scale of rape as a war tool against women and girls. From the lens of contemporary psychology, the mass rapes in the twentieth and twenty-first centuries, and the

3 Susan Brownmiller, *Against Our Will: Men, Women and Rape* (New York: Simon and Schuster, 1975), 14.

4 Alexandra Stiglmayer, *Mass Rape: The War Against Women in Bosnia-Herzegovina* (Lincoln, NB: University of Nebraska Press, 1994), 84.

use of infectious diseases such as HIV as weapons of war against hundreds of thousands of women, have been devastating. The impact of the aforementioned genocidal rapes as a tool against particular nations has been lasting and has spread to neighboring countries. For example, according to the 2022 *Independent International Commission of Inquiry on Ukraine*, authored by the United Nations (UN):

> *The Commission has been investigating cases of rape committed by some Russian armed forces soldiers in localities that came under their control, which are war crimes. Victims range from four to over 80 years old. Perpetrators raped the women and girls in their homes or took them and raped them in unoccupied dwellings. In most cases, these acts also amount to torture and cruel or inhumane treatment for the victims and for relatives who were forced to watch. Other incidents of sexual violence were also documented against women, men, and girls. The Commission continues to investigate the extent to which sexual and gender-based violence constituted a widespread pattern.*[5]

Another report provides shocking statistics regarding the Rwandan genocide. It is estimated that up to half a million women were subject to rape and that 60 to 70 percent of the Tutsi population was killed.[6] In the Democratic Republic of Congo, forty-eight women were raped every hour.[7]

In 1992, the purpose of the ethnic cleansing by Armenians against Azerbaijani women in Khojali city was to incite fear and force them to abandon their homes. This genocide involved extreme forms of violence because

---

5 United Nations, *Report of the Independent International Commission of Inquiry on Ukraine* (A/77/533) (Ukraine: United Nations, 2022), 16, https://documents-dds-ny.un.org/doc/UNDOC/GEN/N22/637/72/PDF/N2263772.pdf?OpenElement.

6 Megan Bastick, Karin Grimm, and Rahel Kunz, *Sexual Violence in Armed Conflict: Global Overview and Implications for the Security Sector* (Geneva: Geneva Centre for the Democratic Control of Armed Forces, 2008). https://www.dcaf.ch/sites/default/files/publications/documents/sexualviolence_conflict_full.pdf.

7 Amber Peterman, Tia Palermo, and Caryn Bredenkamp, "Estimates and Determinants of Sexual Violence against Women in the Democratic Republic of Congo," *American Journal of Public Health* 101, no. 6 (2011): 1060–1067, https://doi.org/10.2105/AJPH.2010.300070.

Azerbaijanis did not want to leave their homeland. They were therefore subjected to brutal physical and emotional torture, cultural cleansing, burning, and rape. In wars, men usually take up arms to defend the land while the women and children stay behind. This makes them more vulnerable to attack by the enemy. In the case of the Khojali genocide, many Azerbaijani men:

> *are usually the first to take up arms, go to the hills, resist, if possible. Once again, the women and children stay behind and are in harm's way. In Karabagh, Azerbaijani men went to the army to defend their lands against the occupation by Armenian and Soviet troops; many of them died, leaving mostly women, children, and old people behind who then became the main victims of Armenian soldiers.*[8]

In Bosnia-Herzegovina, at the end of the war multiple sources reported that the number of deaths was more than 250 thousand. It was also reported that by 1995, "more than 250,000 people died, 200,000 were wounded, and nearly three million people were forced to leave their homes and become refugees or internally displaced persons. An estimated 1.3 million were internally displaced, and some 500,000 became refugees."[9] In addition, hundreds of thousands of women were subjected to genocidal rape as an instrument of terror and ethnic cleansing.[10] A very recent example of using rape as a genocidal tool against an "other" nation or ethnic/religious group is the rape of Muslim Rohingya women by Burmese armed forces, which began in 2013 and continues into 2025. Taking into consideration the scale

---

8 Nazila Isgandarova, "Rape as a Tool against Women in War: The Role of Spiritual Caregivers to Support the Survivors of an Ethnic Violence," *CrossCurrents* 63, no. 2 (2013): 176–177, https://doi.org/10.1111/cros.12022.

9 Marie-Antoinette Sossou, Carlton D. Craig, Heather Ogren, and Michelle Schnak, "A Qualitative Study of Resilience Factors of Bosnian Refugee Women Resettled in the Southern United States," *Journal of Ethnic & Cultural Diversity in Social Work* 17, no. 4 (2008): 366, https://doi.org/10.1080/15313200802467908. See also Daniel F. Becker, Stevan M. Weine, Dolores Vojvoda, and Thomas H. Mcglashan, "Case Series: PTSD Symptoms in Adolescent Survivors of 'Ethnic Cleansing.' Results from a 1-Year Follow-up Study," *Journal of the American Academy of Child and Adolescent Psychiatry* 38, no. 6 (1999): 775–781, https://doi.org/10.1097/00004583-199906000-00027.

10 David M. Crowe, *War Crimes, Genocide, and Justice: A Global History* (London: Palgrave Macmillan, 2013).

and impact of the trauma on women who were subjected to genocidal rapes, this chapter explores the process of the transformative power of resilience in women who are victims of war as well as the psycho-spiritual counseling practices to support this process.

The Definition of Genocidal Rape

Case studies 1 and 2 provide insight into the nature of genocidal rape.

Case Study 1

At the beginning of March 2022, two Russian armed forces servicemen repeatedly raped a thirty-three-year-old woman after killing her husband. One of the alleged perpetrators has been identified and criminal proceedings have been initiated in absentia against him. The Commission is investigating another incident which occurred later that month in the same village. A fifty-six-year-old woman explained how two of the three Russian armed forces servicemen who broke into her home gang-raped her as the third one watched while masturbating. They stole food and money from her. She learned a couple of weeks later that, in a separate incident, her husband had been tortured and executed.[11]

Rape is an act of crime that occurs under physical force or threat against the will of the person. There are various definitions of rape. By its nature, rape is coercive and involves penetration by specified body parts.[12] In the case of ethnic cleansing committed by the Serbian army against Bosnian residents from 1992 to 1994 in the town of Foca, the United Nations' policy defined rape as "the sexual penetration, however slight: (a) of the vagina or anus of the victim by the penis of the perpetrator or any other object used by the perpetrator; or (b) [of] the mouth of the victim by the penis of the

11 United Nations, *Report of the Independent International Commission of Inquiry on Ukraine.*

12 United Nations, *International Tribunal for the Prosecution of Persons Responsible for Serious Violations of International Humanitarian Law Committed in the Territory of the Former Yugoslavia since 1991* (United Nations, 1993), https://www.icty.org/x/cases/kunarac/tjug/en/kun-tj010222e.pdf.

perpetrator; where such sexual penetration occurs without the consent of the victim."[13]

Case Study 2 also highlights the nature of genocidal rape, illustrating the rape of massive numbers of people during war. Most often, these kinds of genocidal rape are carried out by organized groups—usually police, military, and paramilitary—who specifically target women, girls, men, and boys of the "other" ethnic and religious groups.[14] As a carefully planned and carried-out act, genocidal rape is a weapon that has many goals. The 1948 Convention on the Prevention and Punishment of the Crime of Genocide states that "causing serious bodily or mental harm to members of the group" or "deliberately inflicting on the group conditions of life calculated to bring about its physical destruction in whole or in part" is a crime of genocide.[15]

Case Study 2

M. H., 33, mother of four children, whose daughters were taken hostage, said "in Karabagh women learnt not to be afraid of death. They were afraid of only one thing—to be taken hostage. Since those wild bandits, who did not have fear of God cruelly scoffed at girls, young girls and women." When Azerbaijanis tried to save the lives of seven girls of Khojali who were Armenian hostages, they answered through a portable radio set: "You had better exchange corpses or for the stolen cattle." After those mockeries, we have suffered here, we cannot live in any case." G. H., born in 1940, said that when he was in hostage in a cellar, there were four women and two children, and in a corner, the corpse of the woman laid. It was visible that she was pregnant, and her stomach had been cut and scratched. Armenians adhered a live cat to her stomach, and while she was alive, Armenians stood and laughed. M. H., 33, mother of four children, whose daughters and husband were

13 United Nations, *International Tribunal*, 149.

14 Samuel Totten and Paul R. Bartrop, *Dictionary of Genocide* (Westport, CT: Greenwood, 2007).

15 United Nations, *Convention on the Prevention and Punishment of the Crime of Genocide* (Paris: United Nations, 1951), 1, https://www.un.org/en/genocideprevention/documents/atrocity-crimes/Doc.1_Convention%20on%20the%20Prevention%20and%20Punishment%20of%20the%20Crime%20of%20Genocide.pdf.

> *taken hostages, said that hope made her survive. She reported "we anyway hoped that we would not be forgotten." M. A. tried to run hundreds of kilometers from the Armenian soldiers to save her toddler daughter Aghdam. Hope was the main reason how she survived from the bitter February cold and fear of being taken hostage.*[16]

Case Study 2 presents genocidal rape as a strategy of war that aims to terrorize rival groups, communities, and nations. Genocidal rape tends to:

- penalize the other due to ethnic hatred;[17]
- create gender inequality;[18]
- claim "a cross-cultural language of male domination;"[19]
- "impurify" progeny or simply serve as a prologue to mass murder;[20]
- cause fear because "his genitalia could serve as a weapon to generate fear;"[21] and
- create fear and change the balance in the war and claim the racial, ethnic, and religious superiority of one group over another.[22]

In almost all historical and contemporary wars, including in Yugoslavia, Azerbaijan, Rwanda, and Myanmar, these were the lethal aims of the genocidal rape: to procreate, impurify, breakdown, mortify, domineer, scare, and torture people on multiple levels. Such crimes against women of other ethnic and religious groups revealed deep feelings of hatred for and revenge against the other party. Unfortunately, as the UN report on Ukraine states:

---

16 Isgandarova, "Rape as a Tool against Women in War," 180.

17 Donald L. Horowitz, *Ethnic Groups in Conflict* (Berkeley, CA: University of California Press, 1985).

18 Anne Llewellyn Barstow, ed. *War's Dirty Secret: Rape, Prostitution, and Other Crimes against Women* (Cleveland, OH: Pilgrim Press, 2000); Brownmiller, *Against Our Will.*

19 Claudia Card, "Rape as a Weapon of War," *Hypatia* 11, no. 4 (1996): 7, https://doi.org/10.1111/j.1527-2001.1996.tb01031.x.

20 Christopher W. Mullins, "'He Would Kill Me with His Penis': Genocidal Rape in Rwanda as a State Crime," *Critical Criminology* 17, no. 1 (2009): 21, https://doi.org/10.1007/s10612-008-9067-3.

21 Brownmiller, *Against Our Will*, 14.

22 Barstow, *War's Dirty Secret*.

> *Cases relating to sexual and gender-based violence are challenging to investigate. Victims face obstacles in reporting such violations. Because of the current security situation and forced displacement, victims have difficulties accessing appropriate healthcare, psychological support services, and law enforcement offices in a timely fashion. It is also not always possible to document the existence of rape and the full extent of the victims' trauma forensically. Autopsy reports often focus on the immediate cause of death rather than the entirety of the trauma sustained by the victims because of a lack of resources, of families' requests that the post-mortem examination not be carried out, or of the condition of the remains.*[23]

Even though most perpetrators of this kind of crime remain unpunished, genocidal rape is a crime under Article 28 of the Rome Statute of the International Criminal Court, which holds commanders, soldiers, and other people responsible for sexual violence during armed conflict.

The Consequences of Genocidal Rape

Case studies 3 and 4 provide insight into the consequences of genocidal rape.

Case Study 3

> *A witness testifying in the trial against Alfred Musema, experienced many of these factors simultaneously. She stated, "I have some trauma in my stomach because I continue to bleed and I cannot be treated. . . . I cannot get married any longer. . . . To be able to get married, you have to be physically fit. You have to be able and capable, I am no longer fit. . . . I was sent to Kigali for treatment. But then, when I didn't have enough money, I went back to my area and because I am poor I cannot get adequate treatment."*[24]

---

23 United Nations, *Report of the Independent International Commission of Inquiry on Ukraine*, 16.

24 Mullins, "'He Would Kill Me With His Penis,'" 26.

The consequences of genocidal rape against women can be devastating. Those who have been subjected to this crime report multiple mental health problems, including anxiety disorders such as social phobia, panic attacks, panic disorder and agoraphobia, specific phobias, social phobias, separation anxiety disorder, selective mutism, depression, and, of course, post-traumatic stress disorder.[25] For example, in case study 2 the women and girls do not explicitly talk about mass rape in captivity. They use the term "mockeries" to refer to rapes that affected their future. In case study 3, the survivor lost hope of getting married due to her physical and emotional problems.

Case studies 1, 2, and 3 also highlight the impacts of genocidal rape that go beyond the women who were subjected to these crimes. There is often deep and profound communal and multigenerational suffering. Genocidal rape can contribute to an existential crisis, thus causing the community and individuals to search for new meaning and hope. In some cases, there is a process of questioning God or a higher being or the universe for the suffering caused by genocidal rape. The survivors as well as the community might feel betrayed or abandoned by God, or they might question their faith, thus intensifying their mental and emotional suffering.[26]

Case Study 4

Tursunay Ziawudun was held in a camp for nine months in 2018. She reported that masked men gang-raped her on three occasions, that these same men used electroshock on and inside her genitals, and that camp authorities took women in her cell to be raped "every night."[27]

Many survivors suffer long-lasting effects of genocidal rape. It is extremely difficult to overcome the feeling of being penalized by the perpetrators. The United Nations report on Ukraine states, "Survivors and their families

25 American Psychiatric Association, *Diagnostic and Statistical Manual of Mental Disorders*, 5th ed., Text Revision (Washington, DC: American Psychiatric Association, 2022), https://doi.org/10.1176/appi.books.9780890425787.

26 Isgandarova, "Rape as a Tool against Women in War."

27 Matthew Hill, David Campanale, and Joel Gunter, "'Their Goal is to Destroy Everyone': Uighur Camp Detainees Allege Systematic Rape," *BBC News*, February 2, 2021, https://www.bbc.com/news/world-asia-china-55794071.

remain deeply traumatized by the ordeal they endured. One victim told the Commission: 'this experience is very shameful for me and I am extremely scared and intimidated.'"[28]

In addition, the stigma that continues to surround sexual violence requires patience until victims feel safe enough and adequately cared for to speak out about what happened. As a result, some victims refuse to speak. Some have considered suicide. One psychologist working with survivors said: "All victims with whom I am working are blaming themselves for being spotted by perpetrators and being raped."[29]

Unfortunately, children are also the victims of genocidal rape. For example, the same UN report highlights that, as the victims of war crimes and violations, "including indiscriminate attacks, torture, and rape,"[30] children also suffer from the psychological consequences of war crimes and rape.

The literature on the impact of genocidal rape tends to focus on post-traumatic stress disorder (PTSD). Previous versions of the American Psychiatric Association's *Diagnostic and Statistical Manual of Mental Disorders* described PTSD as an anxiety disorder. However, since 2013 PTSD has been reclassified as a trauma-and-stressor-related disorder. Under this reclassification, the criterion of fear, helplessness, or horror as a response to a traumatic event was removed and new symptoms were added.[31] PTSD is redefined as "an abnormal reaction to an abnormal event" due to "the intense experience of threat to life" that causes intense "emotions other than fear, helplessness, or horror" that "occur in traumatic situations."[32] As psychologist Chris R. Brewin and psychiatrists Ruth A. Lanius, Andrei Novac, Ulrich Schnyder, and Sandro Galea outline,

> *Individual differences in sensitization and vulnerability clearly suggest that specifying triggering events is not just difficult, but*

---

28 United Nations, *Report of the Independent International Commission of Inquiry on Ukraine*, 17.

29 United Nations, *Report of the Independent International Commission of Inquiry on Ukraine*, 18.

30 United Nations, *Report of the Independent International Commission of Inquiry on Ukraine*, 2.

31 American Psychiatric Association, *Diagnostic and Statistical Manual.*

32 John Marzillier, *The Trauma Therapies* (Oxford: Oxford University Press, 2014), 25.

> *undesirable. An individual's symptomatic profile will often be shaped by their genetics, by their environmental history, and by the interaction of the two. To imagine that a single triggering event will always outweigh these runs contrary to contemporary thinking.*[33]

PTSD is one of the most common mental health problems among women who have been subject to genocidal rape, experienced or witnessed death, survived torture, witnessed the rape of their loved ones, or survived the intense fear, helplessness, or horror of war. Not all women who experience these tragic situations develop PTSD as people respond to life stressors differently. Moreover, it is important to consider that, depending on their cultural background, women subjected to genocidal rape might describe and experience their symptoms differently. This is also true for other populations, including refugees who suffer from PTSD.[34]

Women subjected to genocidal rape tend to reprocess and respond to trauma in one of three possible ways: they assimilate, accommodate, or over-accommodate. These terms are defined as follows:

> ***Assimilation***. *The information is changed in order to be assimilated into existing beliefs or schemas. For example, emotional problems may be denied to preserve a schema that the rape victim is strong and competent. Or she may blame herself because of an existing schema that she is always in control of her life. Dual processing theory also suggests that part of the information is kept from being assimilated into existing schemas through states like dissociation.*

> ***Accommodation***. *The existing beliefs or schemas are changed in order to accommodate the discrepant information. Following the trauma of rape, a patient's belief in the fundamental safety of the world and her willingness to trust others, men in particular, is changed.*

---

33 Chris R. Brewin, Ruth A. Lanius, Andrei Novac, Ulrich Schnyder, and Sandro Galea, "Reformulating PTSD for DSM-V: Life after Criterion A," *Journal of Traumatic Stress* 22, no. 5 (2009): 369, https://doi.org/10.1002/jts.20443.

34 Marzillier, *The Trauma Therapies*; Francine Shapiro, *Eye Movement Desensitization and Reprocessing (EMDR) Therapy: Basic Principles, Protocols and Procedures*, 3rd ed. (New York: Guilford Press, 2017).

> ***Overaccommodation***. *This is when existing beliefs or schemas are changed into extreme forms. It leads to the sorts of dysfunctional thinking that (Aaron) Beck's CT [cognitive therapy] has focused on such as absolutist thinking (e.g., there is no way I can ever trust anyone again) and overgeneralization (e.g., nowhere is safe).*[35]

Similar to case studies 2 and 3, survivors subjected to genocidal rape often demonstrate avoidance behavior. Most survivors also may have trouble remembering the traumatic event as an attempt to avoid intrusive images and strong emotions such as fear, anger, sadness, guilt, and horror.[36] In respect to memories related to the rape, psychologist Chris Brewin suggests that victims may develop problems with verbally accessible memories and situationally accessible memories, which contain nonconscious and nonverbal information about the rape.[37] These women have difficulty remembering information prior to, during, and after the traumatic event, and conscious processing usually gets transferred to long-term memory. Their primary memory is usually associated with their conditioned response during the traumatic event (i.e., fear, helplessness, horror). The secondary emotions are post hoc considerations from the traumatic event (i.e., anger, shame, sadness). Emotional processing of a traumatic event involves the activation of both verbally and situationally accessible memories.[38] Furthermore, women might also respond to their trauma by somatizing PTSD symptoms (i.e., headaches, stomachaches, or back pain) instead of emotional complaints. This is especially true in cultures wherein mental health issues are stigmatized.

Resilience and Genocidal Rape

Resilience is one of the best human capacities in the context of trauma and adverse life events. It is different from post-traumatic growth (PTG) and mainly focuses on "a return to baseline or resistance to trauma, and

35 Marzillier, *The Trauma Therapies*, 123.

36 Marzillier, *The Trauma Therapies*.

37 Chris R. Brewin, "The Nature and Significance of Memory Disturbance in Post-Traumatic Stress Disorder," *Annual Review of Clinical Psychology* 7 (2011): 203–227, https://doi.org/10.1146/annurev-clinpsy-032210-104544.

38 Marzillier, *The Trauma Therapies*.

'recovery,' which has similar connotations."[39] The main focus of PTG is to achieve change, which is hoped to be "transformative" and "profound" and targets "cognitive and emotional life that are likely to have behavioral implications."[40] Humans have the capacity to survive and live despite horrible events in life. Resiliency contributes to this capacity as it enables us to survive in a positive way. The ability to be resilient then helps us as it enables us to view everyday life with its challenges and adversities in a positive way.

The literature in psychology, psychiatry, and other social sciences mainly focuses on trauma and explores its harmful consequences for women's health. However, resilience associated with trauma has benefits. For example, resilience might help women with trauma transcend their experience and find a new meaning in life. Women and girls who survive genocidal rape demonstrate resilience in many ways. Resilience is their ability to cope, maintain equilibrium, adapt, and develop effective strategies to handle overwhelming emotions and memories despite serious threats, difficulties, and stress related to adaptation or development following life-changing adversities.[41]

There is a strong relationship between resilience and determinants of mental health in terms of risk factors and protective factors. Risk factors such as imprisonment, death of a family member, poverty or economic insecurity, and isolation affect people's ability to bounce back. Conversely, these

---

39 Richard G. Tedeschi, Jane Shakespeare-Finch, Kanako Taku, and Lawrence G. Calhoun, *Posttraumatic Growth: Theory, Research, and Applications* (New York: Routledge, 2018), 5, https://doi.org/10.4324/9781315527451.

40 Tedeschi, Shakespeare-Finch, Taku, and Calhoun, *Posttraumatic Growth*, 5.

41 Barstow, *War's Dirty Secret*; Debra B. Bergoffen, *Contesting the Politics of Genocidal Rape: Affirming the Dignity of the Vulnerable Body* (New York: Routledge, 2012); Natalia Suarez Bonilla, "Rape, Blaming the Victim and Social Control in Paramilitary Enclaves: An Approach to the Case of Colombia," in *Rape in Wartime: Genders and Sexualities in History*, ed. Raphaelle Branche and Fabrice Virgili, 79–89 (London: Palgrave Macmillan, 2012); Anns-Karin Evaldsson, "Grass-roots Reconciliation in South Africa" (PhD diss., University of Gothenburg, 2007); Suniya S. Luthar, Dante Cicchetti, and Bronwyn Becker, "The Construct of Resilience: A Critical Evaluation and Guidelines for Future Work," *Child Development* 71, no. 3 (2000): 543–562, https://doi.org/10.1111/1467-8624.00164; Leah Woolner, Myriam Denov, and Sarilee Kahn, "'I Asked Myself If I Would Ever Love My Baby': Mothering children born of genocidal rape in Rwanda," *Violence Against Women* 25, no. 6 (2019): 703–720, https://doi.org/10.1177/1077801218801110.

risk factors make people more vulnerable to developing a mental disorder and can trigger preexisting mental health problems.

Resilience following genocidal rape can be fostered by increasing protective factors such as "extended family, employment, human rights organizations, self-help groups, small scale communities and settlements, cultural practices, and situational transcendence (i.e., the ability to frame an adverse situation differently and give them meaning, e.g. as part of cultural identity or history)."[42] Clinical psychologist and family therapist Froma Walsh developed a family/community resilience framework,[43] which addresses three key processes that foster resilience: belief systems, organizational patterns, and communication processes. According to Walsh, "family resilience is fostered by shared beliefs that help members make meaning of crisis situations; facilitate a positive, hopeful outlook; and provide transcendent or spiritual values and purpose."[44] Resilience is also fostered by organizational patterns that feature flexibility, connectedness, shared leadership, and the leveraging of social and economic resources.[45] "Communication processes that clarify ambiguous situations, encourage open emotional expression and empathetic response, and foster collaborative problem solving" also aid in facilitating resilience. Scholar of religious studies Maria Ericson presents reconciliation as a process but with a focus on diverse "moral landscapes" such as "experiences of the conflicts; views of the conflict, oneself and 'the other'; identifications and loyalties; certain norms for interaction and interpretations of values such as 'peace' and 'reconciliation.'"[46]

---

42 Anthony J. Marsella, Thomas Bornemann, Solvig Ekblad, and John Orley, eds., *Amidst Peril and Pain: The Mental Health and Well-Being of the World's Refugees* (Washington, DC: American Psychological Association, 1994), https://doi.org/10.1037/10147-000, quoted in Laura Simich, Brenda Roche, and Leigh Ayton, "Defining Resiliency, Constructing Equity" (Toronto: Wellesley Institute, 2012), 7, http://wellesleyinstitute.com/wp-content/uploads/2012/03/Defining-Resiliency-Constructing-Equity1.pdf.

43 Froma Walsh, "A Family Resilience Framework: Innovative Practice Applications," *Family Relations: Interdisciplinary Journal of Applied Family Science* 51, no. 2 (2002): 130–137, https://doi.org/10.1111/j.1741-3729.2002.00130.x.

44 Walsh, "A Family Resilience Framework," 132.

45 Walsh, "A Family Resilience Framework," 132.

46 Maria Ericson, "Reconciliation and the Search for a Shared Moral Landscape: Insights and Challenges from Northern Ireland and South Africa," *Journal of Theology for Southern Africa* 115 (2003): 19.

What is promising in these studies is that, regardless of cultural origin, many people who have been subjected to multiple traumas, including rape, are resilient and can survive traumatic events without developing lasting psychiatric disorders.[47] These factors helped many women in Bosnia, for example, to be strong, face challenges with courage, and meet social obligations such as raising their children and overcoming their trauma. In addition, collective grieving also helps women to gain resilience.

Trauma, Mental Health Care, and Resilience

Case studies 1, 2, and 3 highlight different responses to genocidal trauma and the need of victim-survivors to address the consequences of their experiences. Care providers need to remember that the consequences of genocidal rape might still be apparent and that PTSD symptoms might arise months or even years later. According to social work scholars Leah Woolner, Myriam Denov, and Sarilee Kahn, it is important to address the perceived stressfulness of the events, which is the most important determinant of psychological outcomes.[48]

Treatment of victim-survivors of genocidal rape starts with mental health promotion, counseling, community and social support, and spirituality. Counseling is one of the most important treatment options to help women to achieve PTG and resilience. Trauma-focused cognitive behavioral therapy, narrative exposure therapy, narrative therapy, and eye movement desensitization and reprocessing (EMDR) are among the most effective forms of treatment for women and girls who were subjected to genocidal rape.[49] Counseling helps survivor-victims build resilience by managing their feelings, developing plans to stay safe, learning healthy coping skills, and connecting with other resources and support. During counseling, therapy provides a safe space for the women to tell and rewrite their stories.

47 Rita Rosner, Steve Powell, and Willi Butollo, "Posttraumatic Stress Disorder Three Years After the Siege of Sarajevo," *Journal of Clinical Psychology* 59, no. 1 (2003): 41–55, https://doi.org/10.1002/jclp.10116.

48 Woolner, Denov, and Kahn, "'I Asked Myself If I Would Ever Love My Baby.'"

49 Marzillier, *The Trauma Therapies*.

A safe space implies physical safety, psychological safety, confidentiality, and other aspects of safety. The women need to tell the stories "without being interrupted, ridiculed or disputed." Such a safe space provides an "opportunity to work through one's own trauma and achieve a sense of security in one's own identity."[50] For example, it would be helpful to ask: "'What would help you feel confident about talking about difficult things?' The rules tend to include confidentiality, mutuality and asking questions in a way that enabled others to speak."[51] In trauma work with clients, the therapeutic process allows survivor-victims to rewrite their history and accept their vulnerability, which is paramount to their recovery.[52]

EMDR was introduced in 1987 by Dr. Francine Shapiro first as EMD and then as EMDR in 1990.[53] The working mechanisms of EMDR are based on adaptive information processing and associative networks. In general, EMDR is "an interactive, intrapsychic, cognitive, behavioral, body-oriented therapy" that aims "to rapidly metabolize the dysfunctional residue from the past and transform it into something useful."[54] With its use of eye movements, EMDR is "structured to facilitate a rapid integration of the new information, coping skills, and behaviors offered by the clinician . . . [it] is unique, including the specific use of bilateral dual attention stimuli such as eye movements, taps, or tones."[55] EMDR is an eclectic treatment that incorporates elements or techniques of CBT (such as cognitive reappraisal), exposure techniques, mindfulness practices, clinical hypnotherapy, somatic therapies, and so forth. As one of the golden treatment modalities to treat trauma, EMDR is more effective than drugs such as fluoxetine.[56]

EMDR therapists speculate that the nature of the problem of PTSD is the presence of unprocessed and blocked memories or information of trauma,

---

50 Ericson, "Reconciliation and the Search for a Shared Moral Landscape," 26.

51 Ericson, "Reconciliation and the Search for a Shared Moral Landscape," 26–27.

52 Judith M. Siegel, Susan B. Sorenson, Jacqueline M. Golding, M. Audrey Burnham, and Judith A. Stein, "The Prevalence of Childhood Sexual Assault: The Los Angeles Epidemiologic Catchment Area Project," *American Journal of Epidemiology* 126, no. 6 (1987): 1141–1153, https://doi.org/10.1093/oxfordjournals.aje.a114752.

53 Shapiro, *Eye Movement Desensitization and Reprocessing (EMDR) Therapy.*

54 Shapiro, *Eye Movement Desensitization and Reprocessing (EMDR) Therapy*, xii.

55 Shapiro, *Eye Movement Desensitization and Reprocessing (EMDR) Therapy*, 23.

56 Marzillier, *The Trauma Therapies.*

which leads to the development of pathologies. For example, trauma affects the brain's physiological structure that allows us to process information and use that information later. However, this system does not function properly in someone who is suffering from trauma. For example, in cases of genocidal trauma, images, sounds, affects, and physical sensations associated with rape are stored in disturbing ways. Therefore, the goal of EMDR is to overcome blocked neural patterns, mimicking REM sleep and reciprocal inhibition.[57] This process is also called accelerated information processing.[58]

However, women's responses to genocidal rape and their abilities to become resilient depend on multiple factors. These factors include but are not limited to personal and sociocultural factors such as age, sex, personality, length and number of traumatic events (exposure to more than one traumatic event or to continuous trauma correlates with a greater negative impact on mental health), and the presence of support (the presence of extended family, involvement in religious activities, and traditional cultural practices may have a protective effect).[59]

Transitional Justice

According to the United Nations, transitional justice entails "the full range of processes and mechanisms associated with a society's attempts to come to terms with a legacy of large-scale past abuses, in order to ensure accountability, serve justice and achieve reconciliation."[60] Transitional justice, which often includes truth-telling and forgiveness, is important in fostering resilience within women subjected to genocidal rape. Yet many women report that what hurts them most is that the crime was committed by people they know and that the perpetrators did not get punished. For example, the ethnic cleansing in Konjic was an intimate act of violence performed by

57 Greenwald, "Eye Movement Desensitization and Reprocessing."

58 Shapiro, *Eye Movement Desensitization and Reprocessing (EMDR) Therapy.*

59 R. Srinivasa Murthy and Rashmi Lakshminarayana, "Mental Health Consequences of War: A Brief Review of Research Findings," *World Psychiatry* 5, no. 1 (2006): 25–30.

60 United Nations, *The Rule of Law and Transitional Justice in Conflict and Post-Conflict Societies: Report of the Secretary-General* (United Nations, 2004), https://www.unhcr.org/us/media/rule-law-and-transitional-justice-conflict-and-post-conflict-societies-report-secretary.

a collective of neighbors. Johanna Mannergren Selimovic, scholar of peace processes, highlighted the daily pain survivors experienced seeing the killers in the streets.[61] Survivors need healing based on hearing their enemies take responsibility for their atrocities.[62] Perpetrators' failures to acknowledge the injuries they inflicted might cause a "second wound of silence,"[63] and denial of the consequences of their actions can cause deep wounds. Human rights scholar Julie Mertus states, "Without such acknowledgement, survivors feel invisible, erased, forgotten."[64] Survivors in Konjic also struggled because justice came only after the siege had lasted for eight months—after the city was destroyed and fifty-six children were killed.[65]

International criminal tribunals have failed to establish a central formula for a transitional justice paradigm. When survivors seek transitional justice, they often feel that an international criminal trial singles out individual offenders and shatters efforts that aim to hold entire groups accountable. This is problematic as genocidal rape is both an individual crime and a group offence. For the survivors of genocidal rape, it is important that criminal trials bring to justice the individuals who took part in the atrocities. Survivors are often suspicious of the honesty, sincerity, and transparency of these trials. Furthermore, although transitional justice intends to foster reconciliation, this is not the case in all communities. Depending on the context, people perceive the relationship among truth, forgiveness, and reconciliation differently. In Sierra Leone, local understandings of the relationship between truth-telling and reconciliation differ markedly from how they are conceived in theories and practices of transitional justice.[66] Human

---

61 Johanna Mannergren Selimovic, "Perpetrators and Victims: Local Responses to the International Criminal Tribunal for the Former Yugoslavia," *Focaal* 57 (2010): 50–61, https://doi.org/10.3167/fcl.2010.570104.

62 Selimovic, "Perpetrators and Victims."

63 Trudy Govier, "What is Acknowledgement and Why is it Important?," paper presented at *OSSA Conference, University of Windsor, May 15, 1999*, 17, https://scholar.uwindsor.ca/cgi/viewcontent.cgi?article=1845&context=ossaarchive.

64 Julie Mertus, "Truth in a Box: The Limits of Justice through Judicial Mechanisms," in *The Politics of Memory, Truth, Healing and Social Justice*, eds. Ifi Amadiume and Abdullahi An-Na'im (New York: Bloomsbury, 2000), 149.

65 Selimovic, "Perpetrators and Victims."

66 Rosalind Shaw, "Memory Frictions: Localizing the Truth and Reconciliation Commission in Sierra Leone," International Journal of Transitional Justice 1, no. 2 (2007): 183–207, https://doi.org/10.1093/ijtj/ijm008.

rights scholar Richard A. Wilson notes the importance of taking revenge as a local tool for closure in post-Apartheid South Africa.[67] For survivors in Bosnia, transitional justice is still limited because the citizens of Bosnia did not trust the international justice system and had negative perceptions of the international criminal tribunals.[68]

Although imperfect, and not always adequately tailored to the local context, transitional justice intends to open venues for negotiation and reconciliation in divided societies.[69] Transitional justice takes time but is necessary to rebuild society. It is an important factor in the renewal of the relationships between the groups. Moreover, transitional justice can facilitate the transformation of social relationships in ways that foster healing, PTG, and resilience.[70] Transitional justice is also a problem-solving mechanism following a genocide that should address the tragedy's technical and political aspects.

In the Christian context, truth-telling might occur in the context of seeking redemption. In the Muslim context, truth-telling might relate to people's belief in the reward after life. Researchers in the psychological sciences argue that even following severe trauma, people and societies can heal through telling and retelling their stories.[71] Therefore, truth-telling in the form of acknowledgment eases the healing process: "the telling of Truths turns the survivors from objects to subjects."[72]

Mental Health Promotion

Mental health promotion is "the process of enhancing the capacity of individuals and communities to take control over their lives and improve their mental health."[73] Mental health promotion includes the development of

---

67 Richard A. Wilson, *The Politics of Truth and Reconciliation in South Africa: Legitimizing the Post-Apartheid State* (Cambridge: Cambridge University Press, 2001).

68 Selimovic, "Perpetrators and Victims."

69 Selimovic, "Perpetrators and Victims."

70 Selimovic, "Perpetrators and Victims."

71 Duncan Bell, "Introduction: Memory, Trauma and World Politics," in *Memory, Trauma and World Politics: Reflections on the Relationship between the Past and the Present,* ed. Duncan Bell, 1–29 (London: Palgrave Macmillan, 2006).

72 Mertus, "Truth in a Box," 149.

73 Natacha Joubert and John Raeburn, "Mental Health Promotion: People, Power and Passion," *International Journal of Mental Health Promotion* 1, no. 1 (1998): 16.

cognitive, social, and emotional skills, like "problem-solving, social skills, and social support," while also addressing lifestyle factors such as "physical activity and healthy eating and reduction of smoking and drinking behaviors."[74] In the context of genocidal rape, mental health promotion should involve the enhancement of victims' well-being rather than treating illness only, assessment for risk factors and conditions in the context of their everyday life, the promotion of protective factors and elimination of risk factors and conditions, assessment of community support, and valuing the strength of the women.

The Crucial Role of Social Support

Genocidal rape disrupts the social support networks of victim-survivors. For example, they are often subject to chaos, forced displacement, physical separations, and breakdowns in family functioning. Given that many of these women belong to collectivistic societies, their families and communities play an important role in their lives. Social isolation increases the suffering of women and girls, especially women bearing children due to rape, and delays PTG through resilience.[75]

Therefore, treatment should consider social support crucial in mitigating the symptoms and enhancing resilience, moderating the impact of stressors, enhancing coping skills, promoting health, and enabling help-seeking.[76] In the context of treatment, social support includes interactions with family members, friends, peers, and professionals where the women and girls find practical aid or emotional help. Counseling should include a discussion of traumatic experiences, positive early experiences, family support, religious or spiritual beliefs, and political commitment or ideology in order to assess the patient's support network.[77] The therapist should consider the quality

74 Ana Fernandez, Patricia Moreno-Peral, Edurne Zabaleta-del-Olmo, Juan Angel Bellon, Jose Manuel Aranda-Regules, Juan Vicente Luciano, Antoni Serrano-Blanco, and Maria Rubio-Valera, "Is There a Case for Mental Health Promotion in the Primary Care Setting? A Systematic Review," *Preventive Medicine* 76 (2015): S6, https://doi.org/10.1016/j.ypmed.2014.11.019.

75 Woolner, Denov, and Kahn, "'I Asked Myself If I Would Ever Love My Baby.'"

76 Marzillier, *The Trauma Therapies*.

77 Simich, Roche, and Ayton, "Defining Resiliency, Constructing Equity."

of social support. For example, if social support is perceived as supportive, it may enhance coping, moderate the impact of stressors, and promote health.[78]

The Role of Spirituality

Religion and spirituality can be a source of hope for the survivors of rape in war as they deal with adversity.[79] For example, spirituality and belief in God can be a source of strength or comfort, help victims to overcome the burden of tragedy, and support effective coping with emotional problems or mental illness by fostering resilience, hope, and the ability to deal with challenges. Victim-survivors might use sacred texts or spirituality to seek answers to their concerns within the context of death, dying, life's meaning, loss of self-esteem, powerlessness, and emptiness. However, religious and spiritual resources must be used with extra caution as these women might perceive that they are being pushed to forgive their perpetrators or not seek justice.

During therapy, when a therapist uses spirituality as a resilience factor, the task should not be to find answers to the victim's questions about suffering. In the plight of women raped in war, spirituality should focus on sharing their vulnerability. For example, when victims ask existential questions such as, Where was God when I was raped? the therapist should admit their own powerlessness. In my professional experience, when I hear the suffering of my clients, I also wonder "whether God is just a 'watcher' over us, or a 'victim' like us, or both."[80] Nevertheless, whether we have answers to these questions or not, spirituality encourages reflecting on the meaning of life and values that extend beyond material goals.

---

78 Miriam J. Stewart and Lynn Langille, "A Framework for Social Support Assessment and Intervention in the Context of Chronic Conditions and Caregiving," in *Chronic Conditions and Caregiving in Canada*, ed. Miriam J. Stewart, 3–28 (Toronto: University of Toronto Press, 2000).

79 Sossou, Craig, Ogren, and Schnak, "A Qualitative Study of Resilience Factors of Bosnian Refugee Women."

80 Nazila Isgandarova, "Effective Islamic Spiritual Care: Foundations and Practices of Imams and Other Muslim Spiritual Caregivers, Imams and Other Muslim Spiritual Caregivers" (DMin thesis, Wilfrid Laurier University, 2011), 4.

Fostering Resilience and Post-Traumatic Growth

Despite the harmful impact of genocidal rape, women and girls carry resilience that helps them and can foster PTG. Their resilience should be supported by mental health promotions, including various counseling techniques, facilitating social support, and using spirituality as a resource. However, various factors also prevent PTG among survivors of genocidal rape. For example, survivors might need to overcome barriers such as the stigma against rape and the lack of culturally appropriate mental health services. Therefore, PTG and resilience are best fostered using a comprehensive approach to the care of survivors.

7

THE PSYCHOSPIRITUALITY OF HISTORICAL TRAUMA IN SOUTH KOREA

Mapping the Colonial Legacy

Hee-Kyu Heidi Park

MY FAMILY LIVES with the historical trauma of my homeland's past. It took me a long journey to name the monstrous dynamics within my family as such. Once identified, there develops an intimate knowledge of historical trauma of the legacy of colonialism in South Korea, understanding of its vicissitudes and ambiguous complexity, with the passage of time revealing yet again deeper, newer layers of its history and trauma.

The impact of historical traumas such as colonization and war haunts the lives of individuals, families, and communities across the generations. There have been multiple efforts to define such trauma experiences apart from the medical model. However, the particularity of historical trauma sometimes creates dissonance in such understandings, calling for further articulation.

This chapter maps out the dissonance in the conceptualization of collective trauma and the communal experiences in South Korea to suggest a relational and communal understanding of collective trauma experiences and possible healing trajectories. The term "trauma" is examined from several angles that generate a sense of dissonance with the lived experience to build a thicker understanding of the term. The notion of spectrality, as a repeatedly articulated element in many trauma studies, then becomes useful for conceptualizing intergenerational historical trauma. Special attention is given to Korean trauma scholarship to analyze the points of tension in understanding the collective, cultural, and historical trauma present in South Korea today.

Tensions in Understandings of Trauma

Intimate knowledge of historical trauma creates a dissonance with the prevailing notion of psychological trauma. The general sense of trauma as a deeply disturbing psychological wound seems to generate persuasive emotional language that motivates many to adopt the term to describe a difficult past that constantly evades other forms of language. *Han*, a Korean term that denotes a deep-seated, accumulated pain, is being replaced by the term *trauma* in more recent Korean scholarly and theological literature, possibly because the public has acclimated to the language of psychology. Simultaneously, there is a sense that the term trauma, with its psychiatric underpinnings, somehow betrays what those of us living with historical trauma know intimately.

Psychiatric Trauma and Post-Traumatic Stress Disorder

The first point of dissonance lies in the psychiatric notion of trauma. To distinguish it from the older definition of trauma that denoted the event itself, trauma is now defined as the experience of a traumatic event. The most recent definition articulated in the *Diagnostic and Statistical Manual of Mental Disorders* (DSM-5-TR; see also ICD-10-CM code F43.10) requires the experience of "actual or threatened death, serious injury, or sexual violence" for it to be defined as trauma, distinguishing it from other psychological stressors or stressful events that do not involve a threat to life or physical injury.[1] While a deadly traumatic event may happen simultaneously to multiple individuals, the trauma as an injury afflicts an individual's psyche. However, the collective experience of trauma does not seem to be captured in this DSM-5-TR definition, leaving some crucial experiential knowledge unacknowledged.

The dissonance named here is not unique to Koreans, nor is it limited to the sense of collective trauma. Attaching the psychiatric notion of trauma to the diagnosis of post-traumatic stress disorder (PTSD) has been contested

---

1 American Psychiatric Association, *Diagnostic and Statistical Manual of Mental Disorders*, 5th ed., Text Revision (Washington, DC: American Psychiatric Association, 2022), https://doi.org/10.1176/appi.books.9780890425787.

even in the realm of psychiatry. In the *British Medical Journal* article "The Invention of Post-Traumatic Stress Disorder and the Social Usefulness of a Psychiatric Category," psychiatrist Derek Summerfield notes that the diagnosis of PTSD is a legacy of the Vietnam War that allowed the veterans of this war to be viewed "not as perpetrators or offenders but as people traumatized by roles thrust on them by the US military,"[2] giving them moral exculpation by naming their victimhood. Global humanitarian programs describing the "impact of events like war in terms of the trauma, regardless of the background culture, current situation, and subjective meaning brought to the experience by survivors,"[3] thus also contributed to simplifying the complex experience of the misery and horror of war by confining it within a Western medical construct.

This reveals several layers of dissonance. The psychiatric notion of trauma, which defines an experience within an individual psyche, is, in fact, an intricately produced notion that masks (1) the political structure that generates the pain; (2) the distinction between the perpetrator and offended, thus erasing the complexity of moral questions about the violation when the perpetrator also experiences stress; and (3) the collective phenomenon by locating the burden of pain on the individual.

Anthropologist and sociologist Didier Fassin and psychiatrist Richard Rechtman traced the development of the political dynamics around the concept of trauma in their book *The Empire of Trauma* and excavated the complex history surrounding the term.[4] One fact that drove their research was the dramatic shift in the understanding of trauma and its victims. The disturbing impact of traumatic events, such as war and industrial disasters, was regarded with suspicion even thirty-five years ago. Trauma victimhood, however, has gained legitimate recognition that warrants sympathy, psychiatric care, and compensation. On the global scene, such a shift in understanding has also shaped the responses to international violence and ensuing humanitarian efforts, with a strong impact on the finances and politics behind such

---

2 Derek Summerfield, "The Invention of Post-Traumatic Stress Disorder and the Social Usefulness of a Psychiatric Category," *British Medical Journal* 322, no. 7278 (2001), 95, https://doi.org/10.1136/bmj.322.7278.95.

3 Summerfield, "The Invention of Post-Traumatic Stress Disorder," 95.

4 Didier Fassin and Richard Rechtman, *The Empire of Trauma: An Inquiry into the Condition of Victimhood* (Princeton, NJ: Princeton University Press, 2009).

efforts. In this process, the ethical responsibility has been reassigned to the helpers of the victims, rearranging the politics of compensation and giving victimhood and victimology a new status.

Psychiatric conceptions of trauma were also investigated by psychologists who were driven to construct a different understanding of trauma response following the terrorist attacks of September 11, 2001, in the United States. The curiously small percentage of PTSD patients found in New York after the seemingly traumatic attack in 2001 turned out to be not too dramatically different from that of the general population not affected by the attack,[5] and this difference diminished to almost zero after four months.[6] This made many psychologists wonder about the prevailing notion of the human psyche's vulnerability to extraordinarily difficult events. This dissonance motivated the research on different trajectories of trauma responses.[7] Such findings were in line with the age-old wisdom that suffering leads to transformation and strength, which is articulated through the concepts of post-traumatic growth (PTG) and of resilience.[8]

---

5 Fassin and Rechtman, *The Empire of Trauma*; Sandro Galea, Heidi Resnick, Jennifer Ahern, Joel Gold, Michael Bucuvalas, Dean Kilpatrick, Jennifer Stuber, and David Vlahov, "Posttraumatic Stress Disorder in Manhattan, New York City, after the September 11th Terrorist Attacks," *Journal of Urban Health: Bulletin of the New York Academy of Medicine* 79, no. 3 (2002): 340–353. https://doi.org/10.1093/jurban/79.3.340.

6 George A. Bonanno, *The Other Side of Sadness: What the New Science of Bereavement Tells Us About Life After Loss* (New York: Basic Books, 2009); Sandro Galea, David Vlahov, Heidi Resnick, Jennifer Ahern, Ezra Susser, Joel Gold, Michael Bucuvalas, and Dean Kilpatrick, "Trends of Probable Post-Traumatic Stress Disorder in New York City after the September 11 Terrorist Attacks," *American Journal of Epidemiology* 158, no. 6 (2003): 514–524, https://doi.org/10.1093/aje/kwg187.

7 George A. Bonanno and Anthony D. Mancini, "Beyond Resilience and PTSD: Mapping the Heterogeneity of Responses to Potential Trauma," *Psychological Trauma: Theory, Research, Practice, and Policy* 4, no. 1 (2012): 74–83, https://doi.org/10.1037/a0017829; George A. Bonanno, Courtney Rennicke, and Sharon Dekel, "Self-Enhancement Among High-Exposure Survivors of the September 11th Terrorist Attack: Resilience or Social Maladjustment?" *Journal of Personality and Social Psychology* 88, no. 6 (2005): 984–998, https://doi.org/10.1037/0022-3514.88.6.984.

8 Richard G. Tedeschi and Lawrence G. Calhoun, "Posttraumatic Growth: Conceptual Foundations and Empirical Evidence," *Psychological Inquiry* 15, no. 1 (2004): 1–18, https://doi.org/10.1207/s15327965pli1501_01.

Moral injury

In an investigation of conceptions of trauma, the naturalistic understanding of trauma—that the traumatic event naturally results in destructive damage to the human psyche—breaks down. Along with the revision of the naturalistic assumption, the question about the morality of the unwilling perpetrator begins to surface through the concept of moral injury. The concept of moral injury addresses the ethical dimension—and, extending from it, the spiritual dimension—of traumatic experiences that are foreclosed when a person's experience is only conceptualized in terms of victimhood without accounting for the possibility of violating ethical values.[9] Calling for restoration of consideration of the ethical dimension of a destructive traumatic experience, the concept of moral injury focuses on the experience of damage to individual moral subjectivity in the context of an immoral structure.

Morality and Collective Trauma

In the eyes of sociologists, the ethical dimensions of trauma are examined in the social processes of formulating trauma. When the concept of trauma is scrutinized from a collective point of view, the medical notion is significantly revised. Sociologist Jeffrey C. Alexander notes, "When social groups do construe events as gravely endangering, suffering becomes a matter of collective concern, cultural worry, social panic, gut-wrenching fear, catastrophic anxiety;"[10] unlike in the individual experience of "denial, repression, and 'working through,' it is a matter of symbolic construction and framing, of creating stories and characters and moving along from there."[11] Even in events in which thousands of people lose their lives, "the lives lost and pains experienced are individual facts; shared trauma depends on collective processes of cultural interpretation."[12] Thus, such loss and suffering are individual experiences. In this understanding, "Trauma is not the result of a group

9 Rita Nakashima Brock and Gabriella Lettini, *Soul Repair: Recovering from Moral Injury After War* (Boston: Beacon Press, 2012); Larry Kent Graham, *Moral Injury: Restoring Wounded Souls* (Nashville, TN: Abingdon Press, 2017).

10 Jeffrey Alexander, *Trauma: A Social Theory* (Medford, MA: Polity Press, 2012), 3.

11 Alexander, *Trauma: A Social Theory*, 3.

12 Alexander, *Trauma: A Social Theory*, 3.

experiencing pain. It is the result of this acute discomfort entering into the core of the collectivity's sense of its own identity."[13]

In other words, collective trauma is necessarily a cultural trauma. As sociologist Ron Eyerman puts it, such cultural traumas are "not things, but processes of meaning-making and attribution, a contentious contest in which various individuals and groups struggle to define a situation and to manage and control it."[14] Sociologist Neil Smelser argues that "cultural traumas are for the most part historically made, not born."[15] When the collectives are examined, the naturalistic fallacy of seeing an extremely distressing event as necessarily traumatic breaks down and the connection between the difficult event and traumatic experience collapses.

The work of sociologist Tong Ch'un Kim and of the Republic of Korea's Truth and Reconciliation Commission for the victims of violence in Korea's past reveal a dynamic generated from traumatic historical experiences. Kim's works on the Korean War—*War and Society* (전쟁과 사회),[16] *The Engine of the USA: War and Market* (미국의 엔진, 전쟁과 시장),[17] *This Is a War Against Memories* (이것은 기억과의 전쟁이다),[18] *War Politics* (전쟁정치),[19] *The History of Cruelty in the Republic of Korea* (대한민국 잔혹사),[20] *Anticommunist Liberalism: The Stigma That Makes Us Dysfunctional* (반공자유주의- 우리를 병들게 하는 낙인)[21]—are focused on revealing the massacres and other state violence committed during, before,

---

13 Alexander, *Trauma: A Social Theory*, 15.

14 Ron Eyerman, "Cultural Trauma: Emotion and Narration," in *The Oxford Handbook of Cultural Sociology*, ed. Jeffrey C. Alexander, Ronald N. Jacobs, and Philip Smith (Oxford: Oxford University Press, 2012), 570.

15 Neil J. Smelser, "Psychological and Cultural Trauma," in *Cultural Trauma and Collective Identity*, ed. Jeffrey C. Alexander, Ron Eyerman, Bernhard Giesen, Neil J. Smelser, and Piotr Sztompka (Oakland, CA: University of California Press, 2004), 37.

16 Tong Ch'un Kim, 전쟁과 사회 [*War and Society*] (Seoul: Tolbegae, 2000).

17 Tong Ch'un Kim, 미국의 엔진, 전쟁과 시장 [*The Engine of the USA: War and Market*] (Paju: Changbi, 2004).

18 Tong Ch'un Kim, 이것은 기억과의 전쟁이다 [*This is a War Against Memories*] (Paju: Sagyejeol, 2013).

19 Tong Ch'un Kim, 전쟁정치 [*War Politics*] (Seoul: Gil, 2013).

20 Tong Ch'un Kim, 대한민국 잔혹사 [*The History of Cruelty in the Republic of Korea*] (Seoul: Hangyure, 2013).

21 Tong Ch'un Kim, 반공자유주의- 우리를 병들게 하는 낙인 [*Anticommunist Liberalism: The Stigma That Makes Us Dysfunctional*] (Seoul: Pilyohanchaek, 2021).

and after the Korean War with a sharp analysis of the social processes surrounding the work of Truth and Reconciliation Commission. The events that can be interpreted as collective, cultural trauma are mostly framed as state violence.

The language of trauma began to appear in *This Is a War Against Memories*, where the struggles of the descendants of the victims of the war are described.[22] When Kim interviewed descendants of the victims of violence, he found that those with more social, educational, or political status tended to argue that their parents (victims) were well-intended ordinary citizens with no trace of contamination by communism, aligning themselves with the state's narrative. In Eyerman's terms, their cultural trauma was already formed.[23] The narrative of cultural trauma regards anything that is not in total alliance to the collective identity of the anti-Communist, liberal state of South Korea as a communal threat. Noting that the state was the perpetrator of the violence that caused such a significant loss of life, Kim called out the irony of the claims by these intergenerational victims.[24]

In Kim's understanding, the problem with this narrative arises with those who cannot make such claims because their family members' involvement with communism is rather difficult to deny. Wherever they lie in the spectrum of the degree of involvement with the left, any small association makes them impure in terms of their ideological tendencies. The first group, which views their parents (victims) as well-intended ordinary citizens with no trace of contamination of communism, actively avoids the latter. Whether aligning with the left or right, they all are descendants of victims of the state-led massacres, but the latter group's descendants were excluded from labor-sharing in the rice-field work because they were labeled "red." Their children systematically became social outcasts, prevented from holding public service positions, working for private companies, or attending military academies. A strong in-group identity developed among the left-leaning factions of society against the right-leaning victims. However,

22 Kim, 이것은 기억과의 전쟁이다 [*This is a War Against Memories*].
23 Eyerman, "Cultural Trauma: Emotion and Narration."
24 Kim, 이것은 기억과의 전쟁이다 [*This is a War Against Memories*], 82.

for the socially excluded to be included, a new terminology that could contain both factions was needed. In another ironic turn, Kim used the term *trauma* to achieve this.

Tong Ch'un Kim edited with Myeong Hee Kim an anthology titled *Reading Korea Through Trauma* (트라우마로 읽는 대한민국), which is composed of two parts: "Control: War, State Violence and Trauma" and "Discrimination Social System and Trauma."[25] The authors specifically aimed to go beyond the dichotomy of perpetrator/victim: "The chapters included in this book intend to go beyond the dualistic structures of suffering/politics, victim/perpetrator, and reconciliation/punishment to achieve social justice and social healing."[26] They are keenly aware that human suffering arises within social and political contexts, and they try to distance themselves from the medical model of trauma, which they argue is the first step toward relational restoration and the establishment of social justice.[27] To do this, they define their understanding of trauma as historical trauma, which helps them to transcend the dichotomies of historical events/daily happenings, individual/social history, and past/present by focusing on trauma as "a past alive in the present."[28] Thus, the concept of historical trauma overcomes the dichotomy between the perpetrators and victims that the medical term trauma and the identity-forming notion of cultural trauma tend to solidify.

Nonetheless, their narrative constantly points toward the state that perpetrated the violence. Thus, rather than overcoming the dichotomy, we see the narratives oscillate between violence and trauma. A narrative of trauma, whether individual, daily, inherited, or collective, exposes the violence that was done and brings back the question of the perpetrator's moral responsibility. Thus, trauma's ironic circular turns around the dichotomy that Tong Ch'un Kim attempted to ameliorate in his work and takes us back to the frustrating dualistic starting point.

25 Tong Ch'un Kim and Myeong Hee Kim, 트라우마로 읽는 대한민국 [*Reading Korea Through Trauma*] (Seoul: Yeoksabipyeongsa, 2014).

26 Kim and Kim, 트라우마로 읽는 대한민국 [*Reading Korea Through Trauma*], 9. Translated by the author.

27 Kim and Kim, 트라우마로 읽는 대한민국 [*Reading Korea Through Trauma*], 10. Translated by the author.

28 Kim and Kim, 트라우마로 읽는 대한민국 [*Reading Korea Through Trauma*], 8–9. Translated by the author.

Historical Trauma and the Limits of the Dichotomy

The concept of historical trauma addresses the intergenerational impact of trauma. Oddly enough, examinations of historical trauma bring the aforementioned dichotomy back to the fore. When examined historically, trauma transcends generations and informs not only identities but also personalities, habits, and relational dynamics within communities large and small. The concept of historical trauma has been a trope to describe the long-term impacts of historical violence such as the Holocaust and the genocides of Native Americans and the Aboriginal peoples of Canada.[29] However, a consistent caution in advancing this concept is found as well. For example, psychiatrist Laurence J. Kirmayer, psychologist Joseph P. Gone, and anthropologist Joshua Moses question the validity of the analogies drawn between the Holocaust and postcolonial Indigenous experience and problematize the underlying assumption behind the term's popularity, namely, the assumption that the response to trauma is universal.[30]

---

29 Maria Yellow Horse Brave Heart. "The Historical Trauma Response Among Natives and Its Relationship with Substance Abuse: A Lakota Illustration," *Journal of Psychoactive Drugs* 35, no. 1 (2003), 7–13, https://doi.org/10.1080/02791072.2003.10399988; Maria Yellow Horse Brave Heart and Lemyra M. DeBruyn, "The American Indian Holocaust: Healing Historical Unresolved Grief," *American Indian and Alaska Native Mental Health Research* 8, no. 2 (1998), 56–78, https://doi.org/10.5820/aian.0802.1998.60; Allison Crawford, "'The Trauma Experienced by Generations Past Having an Effect in Their Descendants': Narrative and Historical Trauma Among Inuit in Nunavut, Canada," *Transcultural Psychiatry* 51, no. 3 (2013): 1–31, https://doi.org/10.1177/1363461512467161; Eduardo Duran and Bonnie Duran, *Native American Postcolonial Psychology* (Albany, NY: State University of New York Press, 1995); Teresa Evans-Campbell, "Historical Trauma in American Indian/Native Alaska Communities: A Multilevel Framework for Exploring Impacts on Individuals, Families, and Communities," *Journal of Interpersonal Violence* 23, no. 3 (2008): 316–338, https://doi.org/10.1177/0886260507312290; Joseph P. Gone, "Redressing First Nations Historical Trauma: Theorizing Mechanisms for Indigenous Culture as Mental Health Treatment," *Transcultural Psychiatry* 50, no. 5 (2013): 683–706, https://doi.org/10.1177/1363461513487669; Natan P. F. Kellermann, "Psychopathology in Children of Holocaust Survivors: A Review of the Research Literature," *Israeli Journal of Psychiatry Related Science* 38, no. 1 (2001): 36–46; Natan P. F. Kellermann, "Transmission of Holocaust Trauma: An Integrative View," *Psychiatry* 64, no. 3 (2001): 256–267, https://doi.org/10.1521/psyc.64.3.256.18464.

30 Laurence J. Kirmayer, Joseph P. Gone, and Joshua Moses, "Rethinking Historical Trauma," *Transcultural Psychiatry* 51, no. 3 (2014): 299–319, https://doi.org/10.1177/1363461514536358.

Another problem with naming the Holocaust and postcolonial Indigenous experiences as examples of historical trauma lies in the clear demarcation between the perpetrator and the victim in these narratives. In the Holocaust, the Germans were the perpetrators and the Jews were most of their victims. In terms of Indigenous genocide, the Europeans violated the Native Americans. Such a clear demarcation between perpetrator and victim can unify the collective and provide them with certain political power, as in the case of the Jews, by creating a strong historical trauma narrative, whether it is oversimplified or not.

However, such clarity is difficult to achieve in the Korean context. The atrocity of the Korean War was not confined to the military-led destruction but was extended by civilian-led violence that penetrated the very fabric of the society. Historian Ch'an Sŭng Park wrote *Korean War Enters the Villages: Small Battles in Rural Villages During the Korean War Period* (마을로 간 한국전쟁: 한국전쟁기 마을에서 벌어진 작은 전쟁들) based on his field work in several rural villages in the southern provinces of Korea.[31] The micro-history of rural villages reveals that the macro-discourse of the dichotomy of left and right that divided the Korean Peninsula is, in fact, much messier and more complex than the discourse suggests. The conflicts within extended families, between families, and between villages escalated into small battles in the context of the ideological war. The villages composed of villagers with the same last names were often recognized as composed of the Yangban (elite) class. In contrast, the villages with a variety of last names were mostly composed of commoners in the Chosen Dynasty. The caste system was officially abolished in the Gabo Reform during the diplomatic and political turmoil at the end of the Chosen Dynasty in 1895–1896, thus making the abolition of the classes an ambiguous matter. Park notes that the commoners who had gone through the newly introduced modern educational system began to assert their equality to the Yangban in more pronounced ways in the 1920s and 1930s, which created social conflict and anxiety. The communist ideology offered a logical opportunity for them to rise against the classism of the former members of the Yangban

31 Ch'an Sŭng Park, 마을로 간 한국전쟁: 한국전쟁기 마을에서 벌어진 작은 전쟁들 [*Korean War Enters the Villages: Small Battles in Rural Villages during the Korean War Period*] (Paju: Dolbege, 2010).

class. Thus, the class conflict turned into ideological battles between villages or even within a village. In other cases, the anticolonial independence activists from the Japanese colonial period turned into ideologues in wartime, thus complicating the allegiance of family members. Villagers from different towns were connected through marriages and other forms of cooperation. However, during the war, the complicated relational conflicts escalated into betrayal, suspicion, killing, and even massacres among intimate friends and families that undid the communities that had remained closely knitted until then despite the percolating conflicts.

While the official state narrative defined the communists as the perpetrators of the violence against the anticommunists, the inner social dynamics resisted categories with such a clean demarcation and this silenced those who suffered from the violence. The state-sanctioned dualistic definition of perpetrators and victims continued to generate state violence well into the early 1990s, deepening the silence. In the silence of villagers resulting from the powerful repressive mechanism of trauma, the trauma is unnamable because it involves one's own self, family members, friends, and neighbors oscillating between being perpetrators and victims in turn or at once, mixing their trauma with guilt, shame, anger, sadness that is difficult to articulate. Such silence is not far away.

For an example, I can turn to my own family. I asked my parents-in-law, who survived the Jeju April 3 massacre of 1948 and 1949, what they remember about their childhood. They told me the exact phrases so often repeated in my childhood, in interviews conducted with Korean American immigrants, and by my own family members: "It was hard back then. Everyone was having a hard time." This paradoxically simple statement contains unspeakable complexity. It hides the historical trauma that defies the dualism of perpetrators and victims.

A Korean Understanding of Historical Trauma

As psychologists and psychiatrists are honing the concept of historical trauma and testing its clinical validity, the concept has also been used powerfully by historians. Historian Dominick LaCapra used the psychoanalytic terms of transference and empathy to find a way to articulate the fragmented voices of Holocaust trauma survivors.[32] LaCapra's understanding of historical trauma has captivated Korean scholars' imaginations in various attempts to articulate Korean historical trauma. Among them are the interdisciplinary researchers at the Institute for Humanities and Unification at Konkuk University (KUIHU). In conceptualizing historical trauma as a collective experience, they needed to identify the subject who experienced the trauma, or the victims of the historical trauma. As their research agenda lies around the national commonality and identity of Korean people, this research group defined the subjects of the historical trauma experience as "Koreans," a term that includes those in diaspora claiming a Korean ethnic heritage, thus including those beyond the state's boundary. In their search for national commonality and identity, they have published anthologies of research articles on issues such as identity, division and unity, and daily cultural experiences, which they see as formed by the historical trauma of Koreans. They explore these issues in five volumes of anthologies.[33]

The KUIHU research group's working assumption is that they can apply psychoanalytic concepts to history. They base their insights on the historiographic principle laid down by LaCapra in his understanding of

32 Dominick LaCapra, *Representing the Holocaust: History, Theory, Trauma* (Ithaca, NY: Cornell University Press, 1994); Dominick LaCapra, *History and Memory after Auschwitz* (Ithaca, NY: Cornell University Press, 2000); Dominick LaCapra, *History and Reading: Tocqueville, Foucault, French Studies* (Toronto: University of Toronto Press, 2000); Dominick LaCapra, *Writing History, Writing Trauma* (Baltimore, MD: Johns Hopkins University Press, 2001); Dominick LaCapra, *History in Transit: Experience, Identity, Critical Theory* (Ithaca, NY: Cornell University Press, 2004).

33 Konkuk University Institute for Humanities and Unification, 코리언의 역사적 트라우마 [*The Historical Trauma of Koreans*] (Seoul: Seonin, 2012); Konkuk University Institute for Humanities and Unification, 역사가 우리에게 남긴 9가지 트라우마 [*The Nine Traumas History Left Us*] (Hanam: Paradigm Book, 2015); Konkuk University Institute for Humanities and Unification, 식민/이산/분단/전쟁의 역사와 코리언의 트라우마 [*The History of Colonization/Dispersion/Division/War and the Korean Trauma*] (Seoul: Seonin, 2015); Konkuk University Institute for Humanities and Unification, 구술로 본 코리언의 역사적 트라우마 [*The Korean Historical Trauma Examined Through Oral Histories*] (Seoul: Seonin, 2015); Konkuk University Institute for Humanities and Unification, 분단트라우마치유를 위한 고통의 공감과 연대 [*Empathy and Solidarity for Healing Division Trauma*] (Seoul: Hankukmunhwasa, 2016); Konkuk University Institute for Humanities and Unification, 국가폭력 트라우마의 치유 [*The Trauma of State Violence and its Healing*] (Hanam: Paradigm Book, 2018).

historical trauma. They theorize that there is a national libido of the people of Korea and that the flow of this libido is frustrated or severed in historical events such as colonization and war. Each member of the nation suffers from a repressed national libido, even to the point of expressing frustration through aggression against one another during the war. KUIHU researchers Yŏng Kyun Park and Chong Kun Kim claim the healing of this historical trauma will happen when the national libido is unified once again, even with differences in each strand, in the symbolic, imaginary realm.[34] The five historical traumas of Korea are the trauma of colonization, the trauma of dispersing into diaspora, the trauma of division, the trauma of war, and the trauma of state violence. They see the trauma of colonization as the foundational trauma from which all of the other historical traumas stem. Yŏng Kyun Park argues:

> *The posttraumatic stress disorder of historical trauma does not create distortion in individual personality or aggression toward another person but is expressed through a collective character distortion and group aggression. Thus, the aim of psychoanalysis for historical trauma needs to recover the power of life by creating a stream of libido that was blocked between groups, which is different from therapy as a medical treatment of symptoms.*[35]

To reconstruct the national libido, the KUIHU research group uses the English term "Korean" to denote the members of the nation who were dispersed far beyond the boundaries of the current South and North Korea nation-states into various diasporas during the colonial period. Their narrative starts with the narratives they constructed from the quantitative data gathered in the diaspora communities in China, Russia, and Japan and among North Korean defectors.

Based on these premises, KUIHU produced a series of works on historical trauma in 2015. First, drawing on a lecture series, they produced an

34 Konkuk University Institute for Humanities and Unification, 코리언의 역사적 트라우마 [*The Historical Trauma of Koreans*], 61.

35 Konkuk University Institute for Humanities and Unification, 구술로 본 코리언의 역사적 트라우마 [*The Korean Historical Trauma Examined Through Oral Histories*], 89. Translated by the author.

anthology that laid the groundwork for their subsequent historical trauma studies. The lectures articulate the five historical trauma categories they identified in 2012 and trace their remnants in modern Korean history as the reconstruction era, the 518 Gwangju uprising of 1980, the financial crisis of 1996, and the phenomenon of academic elitism. This anthology is called *The Nine Traumas History Left Us* (역사가 우리에게 남긴 9가지 트라우마). The same year, KUIHU published *The History of Colonialism, Dispersion, Division, War, and the Korean Trauma*. In the first part, they argue that the colonial trauma is the foundational trauma for the rest of the historical trauma and theorize the trauma of dispersion and division through comparative studies. The second part of this work is composed of qualitative studies in four trauma sites: Jeju island, where the Cold War conflict morphed into a civilian massacre in 1948; partisan civilian guerrilla unit activities before and after the Korean War; the struggles of a fisherman who was kidnapped by North Korea and returned home only to be treated as a North Korean spy; and narratives of North Koreans who defected to South Korea. The third work that KUIHU published in the same year is a collection of oral histories. The narratives collected include the family history of a socialist activist, the oral history of a North Korean teenage defector who was separated from his family, narratives of a group of Korean Chinese who were exiled to Manchuria, an analysis of in-depth interviews with ten Korean Japanese living in Japan, and an oral history with a Korean Russian living in Sakhalin. This contested Russian island was formerly part of the Qing dynasty but was claimed by the Japanese and the Russians during World War II.

The work done by the KUIHU research team is impressive in its scale and in the richness of its content. However, the concept of national libido that drives this research group has a problematic essentializing undertone. Their conceptualization sounds like a conflation of the psychoanalytic concept of libido and the Eastern philosophical concept of *chi* (氣), which became a totalitarian understanding of libido as an entity that seeks to unite itself by gathering its broken parts. Despite their claim that their notion of libido was inspired by LaCapra, this curious concept is absent in LaCapra's work. The KUIHU research team uses the translated work by LaCapra, where the language of libido comes from the Korean translation of the word "cathected," translated as "libido concentrated."[36] Paradoxically, LaCapra explicitly resists using the term libido in his work. In *History in Transit*, he notes:

> *I try to take from psychoanalysis certain concepts and frames of reference that may be of importance in rethinking both historical understanding and critical theory. This is a limited but, I think, significant project and I am not terribly concerned about whether I am being Freudian, Lacanian, Kleinian, or whatever. Nor do I devote energy to the speculative attempt to determine the intricate flows of affect or libido in the inner psychic plumbing.*[37]

In *Representing the Holocaust*, LaCapra explains that the term *cathected* has to do with the transference of the historian:

> *Here I need to simply reiterate that I am using the concept of transference in a broad and relatively nontechnical sense to refer to the problem of the at times extremely charged or "cathected" implication of the historian in the processes he or she studies. The specific feature of this implication that I insist upon is the tendency to displace—that is, to repeat in variable and often disguised form—aspects of those processes in one's account of them.*[38]

By excavating the term libido from the concept of cathected, the KUIHU team, in fact, unconsciously and uncritically projected their own transference of their cathected emotional energy into the ghostly term libido.

Interestingly, their own research breaks down this assumption and leads them in another direction. In their qualitative research on diaspora Korean communities, KUIHU researchers Chong Kon Kim and Myŏng Ch'ŏl Hŏ, who studied Korean Chinese, observe that "in the effort to put together the national libido to create the imaginary community of one nation, regression

36 Dominick LaCapra, 치유의 역사학으로: 라카프라의 정신분석학적 역사학 [*Toward Therapeutic Historiography: LaCapra's Psychoanalytic Study of History*], ed. and trans. Yeongsu Yuk (Seoul: Pureun Yeoksa, 2008).

37 LaCapra, *History in Transit*, 8.

38 LaCapra, *Representing the Holocaust*, 72.

forms in the shape of division and deprivation."[39] However, in the same volume, the researcher who studied the Korean Japanese community claims that the path to healing lies in international comprehensive unity-building efforts among Korean diasporas through communication and trade.[40] These differing conclusions drawn from the qualitative studies signal a dissonance in the psychoanalytic conceptualization of the need to restore the flow of the national libido.

Search for Subjectivity in Historical Trauma

Such a strong drive to push for this concept beyond the conceptual error and observational findings signifies a critical need in historical trauma studies. The push for the uniqueness of Korean trauma is found in communal narratives and individual trauma narratives. The need for empathy for, and acknowledgment of, specific trauma experiences often shows up in the psychotherapy room. Here in this emotional space, the identity-forming agenda of cultural trauma formation lurks alongside the historical trauma agenda to articulate the collective hardship's inter-generational impact. In this place, in this search for the articulation of the unique experience, the need for healing and restoration seems to seek out the subjectivities of the healer and the one to be healed. The KUIHU research team addressed the question of subjectivity by asking who is included in the nation of Koreans. Is there a different way to explore this subjectivity?

A new possibility for the conceptualization of historical trauma that can reconcile the dissonances named so far began to emerge in KUIHU's next anthology, published in 2016: *Empathy and Solidarity for the Healing the Trauma of Division* (분단 트라우마 치유를 위한 고통의 공감과 연대).[41] Such a possibility appears in the apparition of the ghosts in this

39 Konkuk University Institute for Humanities and Unification, 코리언의 역사적 트라우마 [*The Historical Trauma of Koreans*], 131. Translated by the author.

40 Konkuk University Institute for Humanities and Unification, 코리언의 역사적 트라우마 [*The Historical Trauma of Koreans*], 166.

41 Konkuk University Institute for Humanities and Unification, 분단트라우마치유를 위한 고통의 공감과 연대 [*Empathy and Solidarity for Healing Division Trauma*].

work.[42] The focus on gathering narratives in their psychoanalytic model lead the research group to turn to literary works for the theme of healing. As the researchers looked for the possibility of such healing in the work of novelists Hyŏn Ki Yŏng, Ryu Yŏn San, Im Ch'ŏl U, and Cho Chŏng Rae, what they encountered were deep stories with ghosts. In literature, the problem of fragmented memory surfaces, and the narrative that connects memory and healing invites the presence of specters. Via their ghostliness, these specters bring subjectivity. This spectrality can offer a significant conceptual turning point for the understanding of historical trauma.

Trauma and Spectrality

The fact that specters show up in the creative work of novelists as an important element of working through trauma signals the kind of imaginative field in which spectrality forms. In *History in Transit*, LaCapra notes,

> *A certain ability to engage in play—to joke or to acquire distance (to some extent a safe haven) through explicit dramatization or simulation that frames itself as such—may in certain cases indicate a critical relation to haunting or possessive events and may be related to an attempt to counter acting-out with working-through.*[43]

The imaginary realm for the unification of the national libido that the KUIHU research team envisioned may indeed resemble this area of play or imagination where the haunting can happen. The historical storm of violence and trauma leaves a mess, shattering and dismantling much that formerly had a footing. Such a mess is ugly and complex, requiring a different time and space for its process. In psychoanalyst and pediatrician Donald Winnicott's object relations theory, such a space is called the transitional space, which is also called the liminal space.[44] Any scholarly work that allows

42 Konkuk University Institute for Humanities and Unification, 분단트라우마치유를 위한 고통의 공감과 연대 [*Empathy and Solidarity for Healing Division Trauma*], xviii.

43 LaCapra, *History in Transit*, 102.

44 Ann Belford Ulanov, *Finding Space: Winnicott, God, and Psychic Reality* (Louisville, KY: Westminster John Knox Press, 2001); Donald Woods Winnicott, "Transitional Objects and Transitional Phenomena: A Study of First Not-Me Possession,"

flexibility and engagement with such liminal spaces affords a peek at the specters. They have already been roaming around in this space, in the same way that trauma survivors stated in their conversations with theologian Shelly Rambo that trauma "is always here."[45]

Whether the trauma is historical or individual, such a spectral experience is expected. Rambo quotes philosopher Susan Brison, who called life in the aftermath of trauma a "spectral existence" as "in the aftermath of trauma, death and life no longer stand in opposition. Instead, death haunts life. The challenge for those who experience trauma is to move in a world in which the boundaries and parameters of life and death no longer seem to hold, to provide meaning."[46] With the enmeshed existential boundary, haunting now defies other structural boundaries as well. Sociologist Avery Gordon, in *Ghostly Matters*, notes that "in haunting, organized forces and systematic structures that appear removed from us make their impact felt in everyday life in a way that confounds our analytic separations and confounds the social separations themselves."[47] The KUIHU scholars' call to first construct a safe space where neighbors provide an empathic presence to one another and plan the future without repeating the evil circle of violence for the healing process to begin seems impossible to construct in light of spectrality.[48] Specters will haunt any space, whether it is considered safe or not.

Thus, it is instead a matter of understanding the phenomenon of spectrality. Gordon asks,

> *Could it be that analyzing hauntings might lead to a more complex understanding of the generative structures and moving parts of*

International Journal of Psychoanalysis 34, no. 1 (1953): 89–97; Donald Woods Winnicott, *The Child, the Family, and the Outside World*, 2nd ed. (New York: Perseus, 1992).

45 Shelly Rambo, *Spirit and Trauma: A Theology of Remaining* (Louisville, KY: Westminster John Knox, 2010), 2.

46 Rambo, *Spirit and Trauma*, 3.

47 Avery F. Gordon, *Ghostly Matters: Haunting and the Sociological Imagination* (Minneapolis: Minnesota University Press, 1997), 19.

48 Konkuk University Institute for Humanities and Unification, 국가폭력 트라우마의 치유 [*The Trauma of State Violence and its Healing*], 11.

> *historically embedded social formations in a way that avoids the twin pitfalls of subjectivism and positivism? Perhaps. If so, the result will not be a more tidy world, but one that might be less damaging.*[49]

For such an analysis, we need to ask, Why does the specter haunt? In other words, What does the specter want? The specters come to the space with a subjectivity that haunts Korean historical trauma. The specters seem to demand justice. But this justice, when examined further, points to the damage done to the subjectivity of those wrestling with the historical trauma. The subjectivity of historical trauma victims is confiscated, swapped, and distorted in the complex web of modern historical trauma. The specters, when they appear, claim their needs must be met. Generally, trauma scholars' quest for the healing of historical trauma makes them wonder about the correction of the past. The ghostly desires, however, may point toward something else—the present and the future.

When historical trauma is understood in terms of spectrality, a complex personhood, once buried under the dichotomy of victim/perpetrator, individual/social, and past/present, emerges. Such complex personhood goes through the vicissitudes of their good and bad desires, intentions, intelligence, moral judgments, wit, creativity, and forgetfulness, experiencing life as complicated. Trauma adds complexity, but its mechanism presses it down as if to simplify it as it fragments the person. The fragmented self, memories, and life that were too destructive, distorted, and monstrous to speak of gain a surprising voice in the specters. When spectrality emerges, the complexity of subjectivity rises as well. In this personhood, justice is not simply getting an apology and compensation; it involves restoration of the broken web of relationships. In the Korean historical trauma experience, the destruction involves betrayals within one's family or against intimate neighbors with whom communal ties had been formed, whether in love or hate. Mending such a complexly damaged web of relationships requires understanding the root of the historical trauma.

---

49 Gordon, *Ghostly Matters*, 19.

The Legacy of Colonialization

Behind the common distortion in the traumatized psyche is another layer, which prompted the KUIHU group to search for the foundational historical trauma, which they identified as colonization. In the realm of colonial psychiatry, the colonial subjects were not even considered victims of trauma. They were assigned a "paradigmatic figure of otherness,"[50] which systematically excluded them from medical care. Under this paradigm, for example, treatment of war trauma showed a critical disparity despite the fact that Africans, for example, endured much more suffering than Europeans. The devastating impact of war, which was discussed in terms of shell shock, only applied to Europeans in French and German psychiatric literature. Fassin and Rechtman observe:

> *When disorders were observed in soldiers from the colonies they were interpreted as psychotic manifestations (dismissing any possible causal link between event and symptoms), and patients were sent back to their country, thus evading the issue of compensation and hence of secondary gains around which the debates about European soldiers entered. In other words, African soldiers were apparently not affected by trauma, although it is known that they had more than average exposure to the violence of the conflicts. Conversely, colonial psychiatry offered a wealth of interpretations that aimed to characterize the colonial response to war situations. The various forms of ethnopsychiatry developed in this context explain psychological disorders in terms of malingering.*[51]

Such manipulative colonial psychology deeply penetrated the Korean experience as well. In *Colonial Trauma*, cultural studies scholar Sŏn Yŏng Yu traces the history of the mentality behind the persistent anxiety that permeates contemporary Korean society.[52] The emotional structure of the humiliated nation manifested in the literature and news media during the colonial period. What was referred to as the colonial disposition by

50 Fassin and Rechtman, *The Empire of Trauma*, 228.

51 Didier and Rechtman, *The Empire of Trauma*, 230.

52 Sŏn Yŏng Yu, 식민지 트라우마 [*Colonial Trauma*] (Seoul: Pureun Yeoksa, 2017).

educators in the latter half of the twentieth century was officially opposed by a propagandistic public curriculum that fostered collective narcissism in the form of highlighting the superiority of Korean ethnicity in various fields and areas. Such propaganda included the claim of the homogeneity of the Korean nation and the eugenics-related claim of the intellectual superiority of the Korean people. Such a manufactured sense of superiority is naturally brewed when there is a sense of inferiority and anxiety. Combining sociologist Pierre Bourdieu's concept of habitus and her own construction of the cultural structure of emotions, Yu traces the history of the emotion of anxiety that required such propagandistic measures to patch up the social wounds.[53]

In these colonial experiences, traumatized collective subjects form an amalgam of complex desires to survive or even prosper under the limited and manipulated colonizing power. Such a desire is hybridized with humiliation, frustration, and fear. These emotions are excavated from the records of the everyday life experiences of working, eating, traveling, shopping, treating illness, and helping one another. As subjectivity forms in the relational networks of everyday life, always with the imminent threat of colonial violence, it is formed out of the tangled threads and amalgamated jumble that echoes the spectral question, "Who am I?"

I have introduced elsewhere the scheme of the seventeenth-century Korean novel *Changhwa Hongryŏn Jŏn* as the skeletal structure of spectrality.[54] Here, I offer a brief summary of the book to extend the analogy and to explain the spectral call of historical trauma.

> *The book speaks of the virtuous, loving sisters named* Changwha *and* Hongryŏn *who lost their mother at early age. Their stepmother, after birthing three sons, devises a plot to oust the sisters from the inheritance line to leave more wealth to her own sons. She plants a bloody, dead rat in* Changwha's *sleeping mat to make it look like a miscarriage, an unspeakable crime for*

53 Yu, 식민지 트라우마.

54 Hee-Kyu Heidi Park, "Postcolonializing Practical Theological Methodology as Cartography of Boundary Dynamics," *International Journal of Practical Theology* 22, no. 1 (2018), 63–64, https://doi.org/10.1515/ijpt-2016-0037.

> *a virtuous Confucian girl that disgraces the whole family. To preserve the family honor,* Changwha *is drowned in a lake and* Hongryŏn *follows in* Changwha's *steps after learning the truth and realizing her helplessness under the misguided patriarchal power of her father. The two sisters become specters and haunt not their father's house but the governor's house, which results in each new governor dying on the first night of their installation until one brave governor decides to stay awake during the deadly night. He encounters the specters of the sisters, who report their* Han*-ridden story and plea for an investigation, which eventually reveals the truth. The perpetrators are punished, and the Jade emperor of heaven grants the sisters to be reborn as twins to their father and his virtuous third wife.*

When I introduced this story in 2018, my focus was on the spectral encounter and the probability of carrying out the spectral call. I suggested such spectral engagement as a practical theological method. Avery Gordon uses this method in *Ghostly Matters.*

> *The method here is everything and nothing much really. I do not devise procedures for the application of theories because one major goal of this book is to get us to consider a different way of seeing, one that is less mechanical, more willing to be surprised, to link imagination and critique, one that is more attuned to the task of "conjur[ing] up the appearances of something that [is] absent" . . . A way of seeing is not a rule book for operationalizing discrete explanatory theories. It is a way of negotiating the always unsettled relationship between what we see and what we know.*[55]

Although the gaze of the specter can be deadly enough to kill the surprised governor when the new governor faces the specters face-to-face, once the traumatized specters' suffering is articulated they find a way to move forward. Thus, the pastoral caregiver, whom I posited in 2018 as my intended

55 Gordon, *Ghostly Matters*, 24.

audience, should exercise the Levinasian ethic of seeing the radical other face-to-face in their heights and in their destitution.[56]

In 2018, I saw restoring justice and meting out revenge as the process of answering the specters' call. Today, something else grabs my attention: the sisters reborn into the next generation. Whereas revenge may generate more violence, the ultimate spectral desire seems to be life, realized in the next generation. The call for justice resembles the numerous efforts of the Truth and Reconciliation Commission to find the injustice in the Korean past. However, the latter resembles what I see in the everyday lives of my beloved family members who are navigating the aftermath of the historical trauma of the war. For example, my mother-in-law recounted a scene that took place during the war when she was a little girl, holding her bigger sister's hand, and going to receive a portion of rice from a relief worker. After a long wait in line, right before it was their turn to receive their rice, the girl in line in front of them was hit by a bullet. My mother-in-law, now in her eighties, talks about it without much emotional investment, simply expressing that she felt fear. "How did you process this fear?" I ask. But a familiar answer comes back: "Back then, everybody had a hard time."

My mother-in-law kept this traumatic moment to herself without telling anyone until she and I were driving to a dentist appointment (maybe because she feared the dental work). However, I know that her life revolved around rice; she eventually became a merchant selling rice and grain. When she had accumulated enough savings, she invested in a small apartment building so her family could put down roots there. She rented out what remained from her old rice store to a maker of *kimbap* (seaweed-rolled rice with fillings) and did not raise the rent for a long time, allowing the kimbap maker to sell kimbap at record-low prices. The store always has a long line of people waiting to pick up their daily meals. Now, I also have the answer to the enigma of the pile of huge rice sacks at her doorway, which never seemed to diminish. Like a guardian of the house, the pile stood there, allowing her offspring to take some home whenever they needed to. While she does not describe the tragedy as a trauma, perhaps she has been

56 Emmanuel Lévinas, "Transcendence and Height," in *Basic Philosophical Writings*, ed. Adriaan Theodoor Paperzak, Simon Critchley, and Robert Bernasconi, 11–32 (Bloomington, IN : Indiana University Press, 1996).

answering the spectral call of the rice incident. Her answer to the spectral call of the historical trauma may be pushing her into preparing for the future, not for the past.

My mother-in-law's seeming answer to the spectral call of her historical trauma is a complexly relational and communal process. The Korean War left many marks on her life, and the functional and dysfunctional dynamics that formed amid suffering through the difficult years lurk within the whole family. Families living with historical traumas are never uncomplicated but rather are immensely complex. Nonetheless, my mother-in-law has lived with a passion for the well-being of her children, pushing them forward rather than drawing them back into the past. The image of a swimming octopus comes to mind. With its tentacles hanging behind it, touching and feeling what remains from the past, the head of the octopus swims forward. In that swimming, the victims, the perpetrators, the past, the present, the individual, and the communal are all part of the tentacles, propelling the body to swim forward. This represents a complex being choosing to step into the future.

Implications for Spiritually Integrative Psychotherapy

Despite my effort to name the dissonances in the development of trauma understanding, I have tremendous respect and appreciation for people who work with those with collective historical traumas. In the vicissitude of therapeutic relationships and beyond, all forms of trauma understanding may have a moment in which they shine despite the limitations each understanding holds. Spiritually integrative psychotherapy for collective trauma, if one embarks on it, is a long journey. The journey will be more like a dance than a race, going back and forth with various conceptualizations. I hope this overview of my understanding of historical trauma provides a way to expand such conceptualization.

The spectral call of historical trauma cautions against the unilateral treatment of the silence of trauma victims as pathology, limiting the conceptualization of the trauma experience to its destructive aspects. Such treatment misses the resilient way the silence answers the future-oriented spectral call to move into the next chapter of history. Often in the efforts of communal healing processes, the desire to hear all trauma stories as the prerequisite for working through the historical trauma sometimes frustrates such an effort. It can be helpful to remember that some may have chosen to understand their trauma experience as just one of many, as in the insistence of my mother-in-law that everyone was having a hard time. A more complex, relational understanding of the subjectivity arising from historical trauma may point to the resilience embedded in the seemingly pathological elements of trauma experiences. In such ways, spiritually integrative psychotherapy would allow individuals to face the specters that haunt their historical trauma experience and pay attention to the call.

8

A BUDDHIST PSYCHOSPIRITUALITY OF TRAUMA

A Critical Correlation of Vipassana Meditation and Somatic Experiencing

John B. Freese

THE THEORY AND practice of *vipassana,* or insight, meditation taught by Satya Narayana Goenka (1924–2013), from the Burmese *vipassana* lineage of Ledi Sayadaw (1846–1923), bears a striking resemblance to the theory and practice of Somatic Experiencing (SE), the body-centered trauma therapy developed by neurobiologist and clinician Peter Levine. Based on the teachings on the links of dependent origination (*nidana*) from the Pali Canon, Goenka *vipassana* (GV) teaches that suffering is the experience of being caught in a repeating cycle of becoming or rebirth in which one is overwhelmed by intense body sensations and reactive emotions that lead to unwholesome actions of body, speech, and mind.[1] GV teaches that the way out of this cycle of suffering is to cultivate awareness of, and equanimity toward, body sensations so that one can let go of any reactive emotions that arise from them instead of acting out on them.

Based on the polyvagal theory developed by neurobiologist Stephen Porges in close consultation with Levine, SE theory states that trauma is the experience of being caught in a negative cycle in which one is overwhelmed by intense body sensation and reactive emotion that leads to the reenactment of trauma.[2] SE practice teaches that the way out of this negative cycle is to cultivate awareness of, and equanimity toward, body sensation so that

1 Satya Narayana Goenka, *Discourse Summaries* (Onalaska, WA: Pariyatti Publishing, 2000).

2 Goenka, *Discourse Summaries.*

one can uncouple sensation from reactive emotion and metabolize trauma through the somatic release of stored material.

Despite these similarities between Goenka *vipassana* and Somatic Experiencing theory and practice, the dialogue between Buddhism and trauma therapy in the United States has not yet significantly discussed GV theory and practice. Instead, the dialogue has mainly focused on the teachings of the Burmese Mahasi Sayadaw's (1904–1982) *vipassana* lineage via the teachers of the Insight Meditation Society (IMS) and Spirit Rock.[3] Mahasi *vipassana* is based on the teachings on the four establishments of mindfulness (*satipatthana*), which teach mindfulness of the body (*kaya*), feelings (*vedana*), mind (*citta*), and objects of the mind (*dhamma*).[4] In Mahasi *vipassana,* one practices mindfulness of breathing in the abdomen, cognitively labeling the breath, and cognitively labeling whatever phenomenon that arises in one's awareness using the *satipatthana* framework to categorize phenomena. For *dhamma,* Mahasi *vipassana* focuses on the teachings on the three marks of existence (*tilakkhana*), which state that all conditioned phenomena are impermanent (*anicca*), the source of suffering (*dukkha*) is through attachment, and not self (*anatta*).

The teachings on the three marks are used by Mahasi *vipassana* as a contextual frame to view the first three establishments to attain insight into their true nature. This is said to result in liberation from the habit energies of ignorance, craving, and aversion that cause rebirth. Mahasi *vipassana* promotes the traditional Theravada Buddhist goals of greater welfare and happiness in the present life, favorable rebirth, and liberation from rebirth. IMS and Spirit Rock teachers tend to present an existential

3 John Briere and Catherine Scott, *Principles of Trauma Therapy: A Guide to Symptoms, Evaluation, and Treatment,* 2nd ed. (Thousand Oaks, CA: SAGE Publications, 2014); Mark Epstein, *The Trauma of Everyday Life* (London: Penguin Books, 2014); Victoria M. Follette, Deborah Rozelle, James W. Hopper, John Briere, and David Rome, eds., *Mindfulness-Oriented Interventions for Trauma: Integrating Contemplative Practices* (New York: Guilford Press, 2015); David Allan Treleaven, "Meditation and Trauma: A Hermeneutic Study of Western Vipassana Practice Through the Perspective of Somatic Experiencing" (PhD diss., San Francisco: California Institute of Integral Studies, 2012).

4 Mahasi Sayadaw, *Practical Insight Meditation: Basic and Progressive Stages* (Sri Lanka: Buddhist Publication Society, 1991).

humanist interpretation of Mahasi *vipassana* theory and practice that predominantly focuses on the goal of greater welfare and happiness in the present lifetime and not on the goals of favorable rebirth and liberation from rebirth.[5] The teachings on the three marks are presented by IMS and Spirit Rock as existential insights within the worldview of scientific materialism.

Two main themes within the dialogue between Buddhism and trauma therapy in the United States include: (1) how the teachings on *satipatthana* as taught by IMS and Spirit Rock can be integrated into trauma therapy theory and practice, and (2) how theory and practice from somatic trauma therapy can be integrated into IMS or Spirit Rock *satipatthana* teachings. The dialogue has sought to empower therapists to practice Buddhist-informed trauma therapy and to empower Spirit Rock meditation teachers to teach trauma-informed *vipassana* meditation.

The dialogue has not yet significantly attempted to theorize what trauma is and how to respond to it using non-Mahasi-*vipassana*-IMS-Spirit-Rock Buddhist teachings. The dialogue has overlooked the early Buddhist yogic theory and practice within Goenka *vipassana*. Instead, it has favored the existential humanist interpretation of the later Buddhist scholastic teachings of Mahasi *vipassana* as presented by IMS and Spirit Rock via modern scientific scholastic discourse. In addition, current scholarship has yet to explore how Buddhist ministers could use trauma-informed Buddhist spiritual care based primarily on Buddhist theory and practice to recognize and respond to trauma.

Because of the similarities of the early Buddhist yogic elements of GV and SE, I argue that GV already has much of the essential theory and practice needed to recognize and respond to trauma. What is missing is the social context of trauma-informed Buddhist spiritual care provided by Buddhist ministers who have received clinical training as religious workers, not as licensed mental health clinicians. I make this argument as a Buddhist practical and pastoral theologian whose work focuses on spiritual care and counseling.

---

5 Bhikkhu Bodhi, "The Transformations of Mindfulness," in *Handbook of Mindfulness: Culture, Context, and Social Engagement* (New York: Springer, 2016), 3–15.

Buddhism and Trauma Therapy in the United States

In a chapter entitled "Mindfulness and Trauma Treatment" in their book *Principles of Trauma Therapy: A Guide to Symptoms, Evaluation, and Treatment*, psychiatrists John Briere and Catherine Scott discuss how mindfulness practice can be used in trauma therapy.[6] They state that under the right conditions, the practice of mindfulness of the body, emotions, and thoughts by therapy clients can result in several benefits. Mindfulness can help clients develop "settling skills," which involves recognizing when they are activated by trauma and using mindfulness practice to calm themselves down, or downregulate.[7] Clients can develop greater capacity for exposure to traumatic material. That is, they can tolerate a moderate amount of activated traumatic material without being overwhelmed by it. They can develop *metacognitive awareness*, which means they can be aware of intrusive negative thoughts without being caught up and negatively affected by those thoughts. And they can develop reduced reactivity, which means they can accept and contain conditioned emotional responses that arise when triggered instead of being overwhelmed by them and internally or externally acting out. Those conditioned emotional responses can also diminish in intensity and frequency over time.

Briere and Scott state that trauma therapy clients also can benefit from "existential insights" that come from Buddhist teachings.[8] They posit that the insight of impermanence can help clients let go of being attached to things or situations that are bound to change or are beyond their control. The insight of impermanence can also help clients accept their mortality and the mortality of others so that they can appreciate their relationships and see them in perspective.

Briere and Scott present the insight into suffering as the ability to discern between the unavoidable physical and emotional pain that comes with life and one's reaction to that pain. They use the An Arrow Discourse (*Sallasutta*) SN 36:6 attributed to the Buddha from the Pali Canon on the

---

6 Briere and Scott, *Principles of Trauma Therapy.*

7 Briere and Scott, *Principles of Trauma Therapy*, 223.

8 Briere and Scott, *Principles of Trauma Therapy*, 225–227.

two arrows to make this point.[9] According to Briere and Scott, "the first arrow is the objective pain felt when encountering an adverse event, such as a trauma or loss. The second arrow is the extent to which the pain is exacerbated by the needs and responses that increase suffering—especially those involving nonacceptance."[10]

Finally, Briere and Scott argue that the insight into dependent origination as a theory of complex causes and conditions can help clients become aware that their behaviors and the behaviors of others arise from a complex set of causes and conditions that, if understood, can help explain why interpersonal trauma happens without stigmatizing or pathologizing the clients. Briere and Scott also note that trauma therapists who develop a solid mindfulness practice can benefit by being able to be more attuned to their clients and by being more grounded and compassionate witnesses to their clients.[11] They recommend therapists attend retreats at IMS and Spirit Rock, or attend mindfulness-based stress reduction (MBSR) and mindfulness-based cognitive therapy (MBCT) classes, which are two secular mindfulness spinoffs from IMS and Spirit Rock.

Everyday Suffering and Trauma

Psychiatrist Mark Epstein in his book *The Trauma of Everyday Life* compares the teachings attributed to the Buddha on the Four Noble Truths and on *satipatthana* with psychoanalytic and neuroscientific theory on developmental psychology and early childhood attachment issues.[12] Like Briere and Scott, Epstein interprets the Buddha's teachings on suffering as the reality that life inevitably involves physical and emotional pain, but if a person can learn to accept the pain and let go of their maladaptive reactions to it, the person can suffer less. Trauma is seen as the reaction to the pain. According to Epstein,

> *A critical component of what became known as the Noble Eightfold Path, Realistic View, counseled that trauma, in any of*

9 Bhikkhu Sujato, trans., "An Arrow," in *Linked Discourses: A Plain Translation of the Saṁyutta Nikāya* (n.p., SuttaCentral, 2018), https://suttacentral.net/sn36.6/en/sujato.

10 Briere and Scott, *Principles of Trauma Therapy*, 226.

11 Briere and Scott, *Principles of Trauma Therapy*, 229.

12 Epstein, *The Trauma of Everyday Life*.

> *its forms, is not a failure or a mistake. It is not something to be ashamed of, not a sign of weakness, and not a reflection of inner failing. It is simply a fact of life. This attitude toward trauma is at the heart of the Buddha's teaching, although it is often overlooked in the rush to embrace the inner peace that his teachings also promised . . . The Buddha taught that a realistic view makes all the difference. If one can treat trauma as a fact and not as a failing, one has the chance to learn from the inevitable slings and arrows that comes one's way.*[13]

The early Buddhist yogic teachings do not make the sweeping metaphysical truth claims that all conditioned phenomena are impermanent, suffering, and not self. Such claims are a later scholastic development that became central to Theravada scholasticism. Early yogic Buddhism does not claim that life inherently involves unavoidable physical and emotional pain, but that one can learn to accept that pain and let go of maladaptive reactions to it.

Instead, the early Buddhist yogic teachings describe how suffering is the process of rebirth caused by ignorance, craving, and aversion. Ignorance is not taught as the inability to distinguish between unavoidable pain and one's reactions to it. Instead, it is taught as identifying with, and attaching to, the five aggregates of body, sensation, perception, mental formation, and consciousness. Craving and aversion are seen as relatively unwholesome emotional and intentional reactions to pleasant and unpleasant sensations respectively on a graduated scale of sensations that ranges from gross material to subtle spiritual to even more subtle, more spiritual sensations. At a mundane level, one experiences ignorance, craving, and aversion as the suffering of everyday life. At a supermundane level those habit energies are experienced as the deeply rooted causes of suffering as rebirth itself.

Trauma as post-traumatic stress disorder (PTSD) could be categorized in early Buddhist teachings as a very intense form of mundane suffering. In common trauma therapy parlance, this is often referred to as "big *T* trauma."[14] Less intense levels of trauma could be categorized as less intense

13 Epstein, *The Trauma of Everyday Life*, 2.

14 Elaine Miller-Karas, *Building Resilience to Trauma: The Trauma and Community Resiliency Models* (Oxfordshire: Routledge, 2015), 2.

mundane suffering which, in trauma therapy parlance, is referred to as "small *t*" trauma. The supermundane suffering of rebirth itself could be categorized as "deep *t* trauma," which falls outside the scope of Western trauma therapy.

Epstein speculated that the fact that the Buddha's mother died seven days after he was born may have been a main source of his suffering that drove him to renounce worldly life and become a wandering ascetic.[15] Based on his understanding of developmental psychology, Epstein viewed the Buddha's teachings on *satipatthana* as the Buddha creating a stable, witnessing, relational self that could accept and be with the pain of his early childhood trauma. By practicing mindfulness of his body sensations, emotions, and mind, Epstein posited that the Buddha was able to provide himself with the attuned mothering that was lacking in his infancy. He could accept his pain without trying to change it, which paradoxically, resulted in greater equanimity toward the pain and a gradual diminishment of it.

The Role of Buddhist-Informed Psychotherapists and Trauma-Informed Western Vipassana Movement (WVM) Teachers

In terms of the teachings on no self, Epstein saw the practice of mindfulness of the mind as being in touch with a non-dual witnessing awareness that can become aware of itself.[16] By resting in this witnessing awareness one can be aware of internal and external experience without identifying with and attaching to it. This can result in experiences of no self in which one is just experiencing bare awareness of what is arising in awareness. However, the implied platform of this non-dual awareness that Epstein referenced is a psychobiological one within a theory of evolutionary biology that reduces consciousness to matter. It is not the traditional yogic spiritual platform of Buddhism that contextualizes consciousness within the theory of the links of dependent origination and Right View, which recognizes rebirth and liberation from rebirth. The "realistic view" that Epstein attributes to the Buddha is mindfulness-based existential philosophy, not traditional yogic spiritual Buddhism.

Trauma professional David Treleaven analyzed the teachings on *satipatthana* from IMS and Spirit Rock using the theory and practice of Somatic

---

15 Mark Epstein, *The Trauma of Everyday Life*, 197.
16 Mark Epstein, *The Trauma of Everyday Life*, 129.

Experiencing.[17] He refers to teachers, practitioners, therapists, and therapy clients associated with IMS, Spirit Rock, and its secular spinoffs as the Western Vipassana Movement (WVM).[18] Treleaven argues that the WVM teachings of bare awareness of sensation, emotions, and thoughts as they arise in one's awareness can result in traumatized practitioners becoming overwhelmed and retraumatized. He also argued that silent retreats at IMS and Spirit Rock with their limited access to the teacher lack the trauma-informed social engagement necessary to prevent or downregulate overactivation in traumatized practitioners. In discussing these two critiques of WVM theory and practice Treleaven states,

> *The psychobiological roots of this problem lie in the fear/immobility spiral, where [the sensation of] immobility becomes simultaneously coupled with intense fear, creating a feedback loop in which exiting from immobility begets extreme fear, which begets immobility. This places traumatized meditators in the precarious position of being mindful of sensations that may perpetuate a fear-immobility spiral. The solution to this predicament, as suggested by Levine, is to follow the three sequential building blocks of SE with a trained therapist: Establish safety, support exploration of sensation, and use pendulation and containment to release fear-potentiated immobility. By relying solely on basic guiding principles of the WVM, meditators with a history of trauma may be left vulnerable to retraumatization.*[19]

The process of SE involves establishing attuned social engagement between therapist and client, supporting the client to be in touch with neutral to pleasant sensations, alternating awareness between pleasant and unpleasant sensations, and only taking in small doses of unpleasant sensations at a time. This allows the instinctual drive of the immobility response that was engaged in during the time of perceived unescapable threat to complete itself resulting in the alleviation of trauma symptoms. Treleaven recommends that

17 Treleaven, "Meditation and Trauma."
18 Treleaven, "Meditation and Trauma," 28–30.
19 Treleaven, "Meditation and Trauma," 144.

WVM teacher training include some training in somatic trauma therapy. He also recommends that WVM retreats have a licensed trauma therapist on call to support meditators if they start to become overwhelmed. In her book *American Dharma: Buddhism Beyond Modernity*, religious studies scholar Ann Gleig provides an overview of the WVM and its history. She states that Spirit Rock has made one year of psychotherapeutic training a requirement in its teacher training and that SE is one of the options.[20]

Religious studies scholar Jane Compson echoes Treleaven's concern and argues that intensive meditation retreats can result in meditators becoming overwhelmed and retraumatized.[21] She uses the theory and practice of the trauma resiliency model (TRM) developed by social worker Elaine Miller-Karas to support her claim. TRM is based in large part on SE. Compson argues that the weekly class structure of MBSR with its inclusion of group processing of experience offers a less intense and safer way for traumatized people to learn mindfulness practice.

Levine describes what SE is and how it works, suggesting that SE can help mindfulness meditators understand more clearly what is going on in mindfulness practice. Levine, along with colleagues Peter Payne and Mardi A. Crane-Godreau, notes that by integrating SE principles into their mindfulness meditation practice meditators can more effectively recognize and respond to trauma.[22] Apparently, the authors' understanding of mindfulness meditation is based on the Western Vipassana Movement's presentation of it. They appear unaware of Goenka *vipassana* theory and practice.

To date there has not been substantial research to demonstrate that SE is an effective evidence-based intervention for trauma. In a 2021 scoping literature review exploring the effectiveness of SE and its key factors, the authors found only sixteen out of eighty-three articles that met the standards

20 Ann Gleig, "American Dharma: Buddhism Beyond Modernity," in *American Dharma* (New Haven, CT: Yale University Press, 2019), ch. 4, https://www-degruyter-com.dtl.idm.oclc.org/document/doi/10.12987/9780300245042/html.

21 Jane Compson, "Meditation, Trauma and Suffering in Silence: Raising Questions about How Mediation is Taught and Practiced in Western Contexts in Light of a Contemporary Trauma Resiliency Model," *Contemporary Buddhism* 15, no. 2 (2014): 274–297, https://doi.org/10.1080/14639947.2014.935264.

22 Peter Payne, Peter A. Levine, and Mardi A. Crane-Godreau, "Somatic Experiencing: Using Interoception and Proprioception as Core Elements of Trauma Therapy," *Frontiers in Psychology* 6 (2015), https://doi.org/10.3389/fpsyg.2015.00093.

of the review and were germane to its research questions.[23] According to the authors, "research on SE is in an early stage. So far, it provides promising findings indicating that SE might be effective in reducing traumatic stress, affective disorders, and somatic symptoms and in improving life quality."[24] The authors found only one randomized controlled study on the effectiveness of SE for treating trauma and only one other randomized controlled study that focused on the effectiveness of SE for trauma and comorbid back pain.[25] It is unclear why the proponents of SE have not more aggressively sought to research the effectiveness of SE on trauma as compared to say cognitive behavioral therapy (CBT) or eye motion desensitization reprocessing (EMDR).

The Theoretical Framework of the Three Modes of Knowledge Production

Engaging in mutual critical correlation between Goenka *vipassana* and Somatic Experiencing theory and practice is supported by a theoretical framework, which I call the *three modes of knowledge production*. GV teachings on mindfulness of breathing and of body sensations in the context of the links of dependent origination can be contextualized within the early Buddhist teachings on meditation from the Connected Discourses (*Samyutta Nikaya*) in the Pali Canon.[26] The discourses of the *Samyutta*

23 Marie Kuhfuß, Tobias Maldei, Andreas Hetmanek, and Nicola Baumann, "Somatic Experiencing—Effectiveness and Key Factors of a Body-Oriented Trauma Therapy: A Scoping Literature Review," *European Journal of Psychotraumatology* 12, no. 1 (2021), https://doi.org/10.1080/20008198.2021.1929023.

24 Kuhfuß, Maldei, Hetmanek, and Baumann, "Somatic Experiencing."

25 Tonny Elmose Anderson, Yael Lahav, Hanne Ellegaard, and Claus Manniche, "A Randomized Control Trial of Brief Somatic Experiencing for Chronic Low Back Pain and Comorbid Post-Traumatic Stress Disorder Symptoms," *European Journal of Psychotraumatology* 8, no. 1 (2017), https://doi.org/10.1080/20008198.2017.1331108; Danny Brom, Yaffa Stokar, Cathy Lawi, Vered Nuriel-Porat, Yuval Ziv, Karen Lerner, and Gina Ross, "Somatic Experiencing for Posttraumatic Stress Disorder: A Randomized Controlled Outcome Study," *Journal of Traumatic Stress* 30, no. 3 (2017): 304–312, https://doi.org/10.1002/jts.22189.

26 The Pali Canon is comprised of three collections of texts known as the "basket of discourses" (*Suttapitaka*), the "basket of monastic rules" (*Vinayapitaka*), and the basket of systematic teachings or "higher *Dhamma*" (*Abidhammapitaka*). Thus, the Pali

Nikaya are the product of an *early Buddhist yogic* mode of knowledge production that originally relied on an oral tradition to maintain and transmit its teachings. The *satipatthana* teachings of Mahasi *vipassana* are a product of later Theravada scholastic teachings based on the Discourse on the Four Establishments of Mindfulness (*Satipatthana Sutta*) MN 10 from the Middle Length Discourses (*Majhima Nikaya*) and on the Path of Purification (*Visuddhimagga*), a commentary on the Pali Canon from the fifth-century scholar monk Buddhaghosa. This *later Buddhist scholastic* mode of knowledge production has relied on reading and writing to maintain and transmit its teachings.

The Western Vipassana Movement's existential humanist interpretation of Mahasi teachings and the theory and practice of SE are the products of the *modern scientific scholastic* mode of knowledge production, which also relies on reading and writing to maintain and transmit its teachings. The main hermeneutic trend in the WVM has been to import Theravada teachings from the later Buddhist scholastic mode into existential humanist teachings on mindfulness based on doctrine from the modern scientific scholastic mode. The teachings from the early Buddhist yogic mode appear to have been overlooked or filtered out by the WVM.

Thanissaro Bhikkhu, a scholar practitioner monk from the Thai Forest tradition, has argued that the Theravada scholastic teachings on the three marks of existence as metaphysical truth claims about the nature of reality—that is, that all conditioned phenomena are impermanent, suffering, and not self—represent a later development in Buddhism.[27] He argues that the early Buddhist teachings on impermanence, suffering, and not self were originally taught as skillful perceptions one took up at a certain stage of meditation practice to disrupt the process of rebirth. He also argues that they were not originally meant to be universal truth claims about the nature of reality.

Canon is referred to as the "three baskets" (*Tipitaka*). The *Suttapitaka* is primarily made up of four main collections of discourses, namely the Connected Discourses (*Samyutta Nikaya*), the Numbered Discourses (*Anguttara Nikaya*), the Middle Length Discourses (*Majhima Nikaya*), and the Long Discourses (*Digha Nikaya*). The Pali Canon is the Canon used by Theravada Buddhism, the predominate form of Buddhism in Southeast Asia.

27 Thanissaro Bhikkhu, *First Things First: Essays on the Buddhist Path* (Mountain View, CA: Creative Commons, 2018).

Ajhan Sujato, another scholar practitioner monk from the Thai Forest tradition, has argued that the *Samyutta Nikaya* is by and large the oldest collection of discourses in the *Suttapitaka*.[28] His claim is based on his comparative study of the extant early Buddhist canons in Pali, Sanskrit, Tibetan, and in classical Chinese translated from Sanskrit. He therefore argues that the shorter discourses in the *Samyutta Nikaya* on mindfulness of breathing (*anapanasati*) and on *satipatthana* are older than the teachings on *satipatthana* from the longer *Satipatthana Sutta* MN 10 in the *Majhima Nikaya*. He states that this reverses a commonly held view on research into *satipatthana* teachings in the Pali Canon that has seen the longer *Satipatthana Sutta* as the earlier and more important root text on *satipatthana* and the shorter texts on *satipatthana* in the *Samyutta Nikaya* as later and less important commentaries of the root text.[29]

Based on the Theravada scholastic understanding of Buddhist meditation from the *Visuddhimagga*, Mahasi *vipassana* presents itself as a path of "dry insight" in which one only develops access concentration before proceeding to insight meditation (*vipassana*).[30] This differs from the Theravada scholastic understanding of the meditation path that involves first developing the states of meditative absorption (*jhanas*) through tranquility meditation (*samatha*) before practicing *vipassana* meditation. The Theravada scholastic view sees the *jhanas* as states of concentration in which one is aware of a subtle mental object of meditation known as the counterpoint sign (*paṭibhāga-nimitta*) and is not aware of one's body and mind.[31] Because, according to Theravada scholasticism, one is not aware of one's body and mind when in *jhana*, one is unable practice *vipassana* while one is in *jhana*. Thus, the practitioner has two choices of path: developing access concentration before practicing *vipassana* or developing the *jhanas* first and then practicing *vipassana*.

---

28 Bhikkhu Sujato, *A History of Mindfulness, How Insight Worsted Tranquility in the Satipatthana Sutta*, 2nd ed. (n.p., Santipada: 2012), 47–49.

29 Sujato, *A History of Mindfulness*, 3

30 Bhikkhu Sujato, *How Early Buddhism Differs from Theravada* (n.p.: Publisher at the End of the World, 2022), 26.

31 Ledi Sayadaw, *Manual of Mindfulness of Breathing: Anapana Dipani* (Sri Lanka: Buddhist Publication Society, 2000), 32–42.

Sujato argues that the early Buddhist teachings on meditation do not make this distinction between a path with *jhanas* and a path without *jhanas*.[32] There is only the path with *jhanas*. The *jhanas* are understood to be the four *jhanas*, and the teachings on the sixteen exercises of mindfulness of breathing (*anapanasati*) are understood to contain a progression through the four *jhanas*. The *satipatthana* teachings are used as a contemplative structure that includes this progression. Thanissaro Bhikkhu argues that the early Buddhist teachings on *jhana* describe states of meditative absorption in which one *is* aware of one's whole body and mind, and that *jhana* is primarily cultivated through awareness of the breath, breath energy, body sensations, and mind.[33] Thanissaro cited the descriptions of the four *jhanas* in the With Five Factors Discourse (*Pañcaṅgikasutta*) AN 5:28 from the *Anguttara Nikaya* to support his claim. Here is Thanissaro's translation of the Buddha's description of the first *jhana* from that discourse:

> *There is the case where a monk—quite withdrawn from sensuality, withdrawn from unskillful qualities—enters and remains in the first jhana: rapture and pleasure born from withdrawal, accompanied by directed thought and evaluation. He permeates and pervades, suffuses and fills this very body with the rapture and pleasure born from withdrawal. There is nothing of his entire body unpervaded by rapture and pleasure born from withdrawal.*
>
> *Just as if a skilled bathman or bathman's apprentice would pour bath powder into a brass basin and knead it together, sprinkling it again and again with water, so that his ball of bath powder—saturated, moisture-laden, permeated within and without—would nevertheless not drip; even so, the monk permeates, suffuses and fills this very body with the rapture and pleasure born of withdrawal. There is nothing of his entire body unpervaded by rapture and pleasure born from withdrawal.*[34]

---

32 Sujato, *How Early Buddhism Differs from Theravada*, 26.

33 Thanissaro Bhikkhu, *With Each & Every Breath: A Guide to Meditation* (Valley Center, CA: Metta Forest Monastery, 2013).

34 Thanissaro Bhikkhu, "Jhana," Access to Insight, 2005, para. 1–2 https://www.accesstoinsight.org/ptf/dhamma/sacca/sacca4/samma-samadhi/jhana.html.

Withdrawal refers in part to the renunciant precepts that monastics keep in which they renounce physical and verbal behavior that seeks worldly sensual pleasure; the practice of withdrawing to secluded places in the forest to practice meditation; and the practice of withdrawing internally from physical and emotional habit energies that are based on sensual craving and aversion. Based on that withdrawal from more gross external and internal sensory pleasures one cultivates more subtle sensations of internal spiritual pleasure throughout one's body.

Sensation and Mindfulness Breathing

In the Spiritual Discourse (*Nirāmisasutta*) of the *Samyutta Nikaya*, SN 36:31, from the Chapter on Sensation (*vedanasamyutta*) SN 36, the Buddha describes his path of meditation as being based on three different levels of sensation (*vedana*), namely material (*sāmisā*), spiritual (*nirāmisā*), and more spiritual (*nirāmisatarā*). For each level of sensation, he describes a progression of sensation, namely rapture (*pīti)*, pleasure (*sukhaṁ*), equanimity (*upekkhā*), and liberation (*vimokkho*).

> *Mendicants, there is material rapture, spiritual rapture, and even more spiritual rapture.*
> *There is material pleasure, spiritual pleasure, and even more spiritual pleasure.*
> *There is material equanimity, spiritual equanimity, and even more spiritual equanimity.*
> *There is material liberation, spiritual liberation, and even more spiritual liberation.*[35]

The path of practice involves renouncing material sensations of rapture, pleasure, equanimity, and liberation; cultivating spiritual sensations of rapture, pleasure, equanimity, and liberation through the four *jhanas*; and then cultivating more spiritual sensations of rapture, pleasure, equanimity, and liberation through realizing *nibbana*. Based on the foundation of keeping the

35 Bhikkhu Sujato, trans., "Spiritual Discourse (Nirāmisasutta)," in *Linked Discourses: A Plain Translation of the Saṁyutta Nikāya* (n.p., SuttaCentral, 2018), https://suttacentral.net/sn36.31/en/sujato.

renunciant precepts taught in the *Vinayapitaka*, the teachings on the sixteen exercises of mindfulness of breathing concentration (*anapanasati samadhi*) from the *Samyutta Nikaya* teach the practice of working with material, spiritual, and more spiritual sensations. The four establishments of mindfulness, *satiphatthana*, which literally translates as "mindfulness (*sati*) establishment (*pathana*)," provides the contemplative structure for the progression of four sets of four mindfulness of breathing exercises.

Table 8.1 presents Sujato's translation of the sixteen exercises based on the discourses in the chapter on the mindfulness of breathing (*anapanasamyutta*) in the *Samyutta Nikaya* SN 54.

Table 8.1. The Sixteen Exercises of Mindfulness of Breathing (*Ānāpānāsati*) in Relation to the Four Establishments of Mindfulness (*Satipaṭṭhāna*) (adapted from Sujato).[36]

Satipaṭṭhāna	***Ānāpānāsati***
Contemplation of the body	Breathing long
	Breathing short
	Experiencing the whole body
	Tranquillizing the bodily activities
Contemplation of feelings	Experiencing rapture
	Experiencing bliss
	Experiencing mental activities
	Tranquilizing mental activities
Contemplation of the mind	Experiencing the mind
	Gladdening the mind
	Centering the mind in samādhi
	Releasing the mind
Contemplation of dhammas	Contemplating impermanence
	Contemplating fading of lust
	Contemplating cessation
	Contemplating relinquishment

36 Sujato, *A History of Mindfulness*, 141–142.

The first four exercises are about establishing access concentration through mindfulness of breathing and body sensations (*vedana*). Exercises five though eight are about cultivating the spiritual sensations of the four *jhanas*. With the fourth *jhana* as the basis, exercises nine through twelve are about contemplating the heart-mind in order to calm its movements and liberate if from identifying with and attaching to the five aggregates as self. Exercises thirteen to sixteen are about contemplating the impermanence of the process of becoming via the links of dependent origination in order to give rise to the more spiritual sensations of rapture, pleasure, equanimity, and liberation that come with realizing *nibbana*.

Rebirth and Liberation from Rebirth

The discourses (*suttas*) on the links of dependent origination in the chapter on the links (*nidanasamyutta*) SN 12 in the Book of the Links (*Nidana Vagga*) in the *Samyutta Nikaya* describe the mechanics of the process of rebirth and liberation from rebirth. The Buddha presents a twelve-linked chain to provide an overview of his teachings on the links of dependent origination. The twelve-linked chain is ignorance (*avijja*), intention (*sankhara*), consciousness (*vinnana*), name-and-form, that is, psyche-soma (*namarupa*), sense bases (*salayatana*), contact (*phassa*), sensation (*vedana*), craving (*tanha*), grasping (*upadana*), becoming (*bhava*), birth (*jati*), and old age sickness and death (*jarmaranam*). He focuses on certain sections of the chain to describe two primal phenomenological rhythms that cause rebirth. One is the rhythm of intention that leads to consciousness manifesting as psyche-soma. The other is the rhythm of sensory and mental contact that leads to sensations giving rise to intentions/emotions, which lead to actions and their embodied results.

In the Second Discourse on Intention (*Dutiyacetanāsutta*) SN 12:39, the Buddha focuses on the territory of the first phenomenological rhythm via the first four links.

> *Mendicants, what you intend or plan, and what you have underlying tendencies for become a support for the continuation of consciousness. When this support exists, consciousness becomes*

> *established. When consciousness is established, name and form are conceived.*[37]

This passage describes how a person's karmic trajectory lands on their present lifetime to be reborn. It can also be seen as describing the ongoing process of rebirth within the present lifetime in terms of a person's consciousness continuously identifying with and attaching to their body and mind as self. The process of rebirth here includes conscious intentions as well as unconscious underlying tendencies. Liberation from rebirth here involves disrupting the process of intention and uprooting the underlying tendencies of ignorance, craving, and aversion.

In the Suffering Discourse (*Dukkhasutta*) SN 12:43, the Buddha focuses on the territory of the second phenomenological rhythm via links five through eight.

> *And what, mendicants, is the origin of suffering? Eye [ear, nose, tongue, body, and mind] consciousness arises dependent on the eye [ear, nose, tongue, body, and mind] and sights [sound, smells, tastes, touch, and objects of mind]. The meeting of the three is contact. Contact is a condition for feeling. Feeling is a condition for craving. This is the origin of suffering.*[38]

This describes how a person's embodied karmic trajectory within their present lifetime involves sensory or mental contact (*phassa*), sensation (*vedana*; i.e., feeling), and craving (*tanha*). Craving leads to grasping (*upadana*) which leads to becoming (*bhava*). Becoming can be seen as the process of rebirth that one goes through over and over again in one's present lifetime. In more neutral general terms this phenomenological rhythm can be expressed as contact (*phassa*), sensation (*vedana*), intention/emotion (*sankhara*), action (*kamma*), and the embodied result of that action, (i.e., becoming; *bhava*).

37 Bhikkhu Sujato, trans., "Dutiyacetanāsutta," in *Linked Discourses: A Plain Translation of the Saṁyutta Nikāya* (n.p., SuttaCentral, 2018), https://suttacentral.net/sn12.39/en/sujato.

38 Bhikkhu Sujato, trans., "Dukkhasutta," in *Linked Discourses: A Plain Translation of the Saṁyutta Nikāya* (n.p., SuttaCentral, 2018), https://suttacentral.net/sn12.43/en/sujato.

Liberation from rebirth here involves abandoning conscious craving and aversion—aversion is the craving to get rid of something—as well as the unconscious underlying tendencies of craving and aversion.

The first eight of the sixteen exercises of mindfulness of breathing can be seen as a systematic process of abandoning craving and aversion that arises from contact and sensation. Exercises nine through twelve are focused on mindfulness of the heart-mind (*citta*) and liberating it from identifying with and attaching to any conditioned phenomena. The final four exercises are about realizing *nibbana* through contemplating the impermanence of both of the above-mentioned primal phenomenological rhythms experienced via the links of dependent origination. This results in the cessation of ignorance, craving, and aversion resulting in the cessation of rebirth.

Even though Ledi Sayadaw, the founder of the GV lineage, used Buddhaghosa's Theravada scholastic theoretical framework to teach dry insight *vipassana* meditation, the fact that he taught mindfulness of breathing and mindfulness of the body sensations as the four elements makes his teachings similar to the early Buddhist yogic understanding of the first four of the sixteen exercises of mindfulness of breathing.[39] Even though Goenka and his teacher U Ba Khin also used the Buddhaghosa framework to teach dry insight *vipassana* meditation, the fact that they taught mindfulness of breathing and the bodyscan practice within the context of the links of dependent origination also makes their teachings similar to the first four of the sixteen exercises.[40] The main differences between Goenka *vipassana* and the sixteen exercises are that GV does not teach simultaneous awareness of the breath and body sensations; GV does not teach the *jhanas* since its understanding of *jhana* is the later Theravada scholastic understanding and not the early Buddhist yogic understanding; and GV does not teach mindfulness of the heart-mind. However, since GV does teach mindfulness of body sensations in the context of the links of dependent origination, one could say that the Ledi Sayadaw *vipassana* lineage came close to reinventing early Buddhist yogic meditation without knowing it.

39 Sayadaw, *Manual of Mindfulness of Breathing.*

40 Sayagyi U Ba Khin and Satya Narayana Goenka, *Sayagyi U Ba Khin Journal: A Collection Commemorating the Teaching of Sayagyi U Ba Khi* (India: Vipassana Research Publications, 2017).

A Mutual Critical Correlation of Goenka Vipassana and Somatic Experiencing

The Four Noble Truths can be used to compare how GV and SE understand suffering and trauma, the cause of suffering and trauma, the cessation of suffering and trauma, and the path leading to the cessation of suffering and trauma.

Understanding Suffering and Trauma and Their Causes

The core theory of GV is the teachings on the links of dependent origination while the core theory of SE is the polyvagal theory. GV sees suffering as the constantly repeating cycle of rebirth experienced via the links of dependent origination. In particular, it focuses on the links of contact (*phassa*), sensation (*vedana*), craving (*tanha*), grasping (*upadana*), and becoming (*bhava*).[41] GV understands suffering as being caught in a negative cycle in which one is overwhelmed by intense body sensations, which give rise to reactive intentions and emotions, which lead to unskillful acting out. GV sees pleasant sensations as tending to give rise to craving, unpleasant sensations as tending to give rise to aversion, and neutral sensations as tending to give rise to ignorance.

SE sees trauma as being caught in a negative cycle in which one is overwhelmed by intense body sensations and reactive emotions, which leads to the reenactment of trauma instead of the metabolization of trauma. The intense sensations and reactive emotions are seen as the instinctual drive of the immobility response trying to complete itself after it has been engaged in the face of a perceived life threat. The polyvagal theory posits that the human nervous system has three sets of vagal nerves in the body that govern three different aspects of the nervous system. According to Levine:

> *The* dorsal-vagal system *[. . . governs] immobilization, metabolic conservation, and overall shutdown. Its target is the internal visceral organs. The* sympathetic nervous system *[governs]*

41 In Buddhist terminology, craving is an intention/emotion (*sankhara*) and grasping is an action (*kamma*). I find it useful to update the Buddha's original list of these links as contact (*phassa*), sensation (*vedana*), intention/emotion (*sankhara*), action (*kamma*), and becoming, i.e., the embodied result of action (*bhava*).

> *mobilization and enhanced action (as in fight or flight); its target in the body is the limbs. [. . . .] The ventral branch of the parasympathetic nervous system [. . .known] as the* social engagement system *[. . . is] linked neuroanatomically to the cranial nerves that mediate acoustic tuning, vocalization, and facial expression.*[42]

When faced with a threat, an animal's body activates the fight or flight drive. If the animal is unable to fight or flee from the foe, then the animal's body activates the immobility drive. This causes the animal's body to shut down as if it is dead. The predator may think the animal is already dead and therefore not kill it giving the prey a chance to later escape. Or, if the predator does kill the prey, the prey's consciousness is disassociated from its body and therefore will not feel as much pain.[43] If the animal is able to come out of immobility and escape, its body will uncontrollably shake when it gets to safety in order to release the supercharged energy of fight and flight that got frozen in its body when it went from fight or flight into immobility.

According to Levine, trauma in humans is caused when their immobility response tries to complete itself and the person is overwhelmed by the intense body sensations and emotions. Instead of allowing their body to organically shake off the trauma, they get caught up in the reactive emotion and thwart the drive from completing itself. The tension caused by blocking the drive is what results in hyperarousal, hypo-arousal, or dissociation, all symptoms of post-traumatic stress disorder.

Although GV sees suffering as the twelve links of dependent origination, it isolates the link of craving (and aversion, which is the craving to get rid of something) as the functional cause of suffering. The links of contact and sensation are the results of one's past actions and are already happening. One has no control over them. Once craving or aversion has been acted on through the link of grasping, becoming automatically results. The arrow

---

42 Peter A. Levine, "Polyvagal Theory and Trauma," in *The Polyvagal Theory: The Emergence of Polyvagal-Informed Therapies* (New York: W. W. Norton, 2018), 14–15 (emphasis in original).

43 Peter A. Levine, *Waking the Tiger: Healing Trauma* (Berkeley, CA: North Atlantic Books, 1997), 15–22.

has left the bow and cannot be called back. However, if one can cultivate awareness of and equanimity toward body sensation one has the chance to abandon craving and aversion instead of acting on them. According to Goenka, "here, at the link of sensation, one can break the chain."[44] Thus, the inability to separate sensation from craving and aversion is seen as the cause of suffering.

In a similar way, Levine posits that the cause of trauma is the inability to uncouple the sensations of immobility from intense reactive emotions that arise from those sensations, especially fear. According to Levine,

> *I believe that it is only when the immobility becomes inextricably and simultaneously coupled with intense fear and other strong negative emotions that we get the entrenched feedback loop in the form of persistent posttraumatic stress disorder. My experience [. . .] has taught me that the very key to resolving trauma is being able to* uncouple and separate the fear from the immobility.[45]

Thus SE, like GV, describes trauma as being caught in a negative repeating cycle in which one is overwhelmed by intense sensation and reactive emotions. Like SE, GV isolates the experience of being unable to uncouple sensation from reactive emotion as the root functional cause of the negative cycle.

Ending Suffering and Trauma and Pathways toward Cessation

GV sees the cessation of suffering as being an organic release of present and stored past reactive intentions and emotions (*sankharas*) that arise in one's awareness and are released once awareness of and equanimity toward body sensations has been achieved. According to Goenka:

> *Any moment in which one does not generate a new* sankhara, *one of the old ones will arise on the surface of the mind, and along with it a sensation will start within the body. If one remains*

---

44 Satya Narayana Goenka, *Discourse Summaries* (Onalaska, WA: Pariyatti Publishing, 2000), 43.

45 Peter A. Levine, *In an Unspoken Voice: How the Body Releases Trauma and Restores Goodness*, 1st ed. (Berkeley: North Atlantic Books, 2010), 56 (emphasis in original).

> *equanimous, it passes away and another old reaction arises in its place. One continues to remain equanimous to physical sensations and the old* sankhara[s] *continue to arise and pass away, one after another. If out of ignorance one reacts to sensations, then one multiplies the* sankhara[s], *multiplies one's misery. But if one develops wisdom and does not react to sensations, then one after another the* sankhara[s] *are eradicated, misery is eradicated.*[46]

Thus, GV distinguishes between *sankharas* that have to do with the present moment based on sensations that arise from contact with the sense bases and their objects, and *sankharas* from the past that arise in one's awareness along with body sensation. In other words, some body sensations have to do with what is happening in the present and some body sensations have to do with what has happened in the past. Sensations and emotions from the past can be seen as implicit memories. GV refers to them as "latent tendencies" (*anusaya kilesa*).[47] The ultimate goal of GV is to uproot the deeply rooted latent tendencies that cause rebirth.

The goal of SE practice is to cultivate awareness of and equanimity toward body sensations so that the sensations of immobility can be uncoupled from the reactive emotions of fear and anger, allowing the immobility drive to complete itself. In SE sessions the therapist works with the client to get in touch with manageable amounts of sensation and emotion so that the immobility drive can be completed in small doses. This results in tolerable amounts of the person's body organically releasing the trauma through such experiences as shaking, sweating, moderate crying, and completion of thwarted fight or flight movements. Levine refers to this as bottom-up processing because it is the natural experience of the person's nervous system rebalancing through awareness of sensations that metabolizes the trauma.[48] This is opposed to the more traditional "top-down processing" of trauma through cognitively remembering and retelling the story and feeling the emotions. Thus, like GV, SE states that stored past material is organically released via awareness of and equanimity toward body sensation.

---

46 Goenka, *Discourse Summaries*, 43.

47 Goenka, *Discourse Summaries*, 115

48 Payne, Levine, and Crane-Godreau, "Somatic Experiencing."

Both GV and SE take a staged approach to practice. The foundation of GV practice is keeping the five precepts of not killing, not stealing, no sexual misconduct, no false or harmful speech, and no intoxicants. This is similar to the stage of establishing safety that is common in trauma therapy. The therapist works with the client to try and ensure that the client is not still living in a situation that is traumatizing nor are they harming themselves through acting out on addiction or harmful compulsive behavior. If one were to engage in trauma-informed Buddhist counseling, the five precepts could be used to assess for trauma by asking if the person has broken any of the precepts or has had them broken against the person. One would assume that an SE therapist would include establishing safety as part of their trauma therapy practice.

The next stage of practice in GV is mindfulness of breathing at the nose. This gets the practitioner in touch with neutral to pleasant sensations that have the tendency to calm and stabilize the body and mind. In a standard ten-day course, one practices this for the first three days and then one switches to the bodyscan practice. One is instructed to return to mindfulness of breathing as needed to restore calm and stability. The next stage in SE is known as "resourcing."[49] The therapist works with the client to help them get in touch with neutral and pleasant sensations. This is done through attuned social engagement between the therapist and client and by directing the client's awareness to neutral and pleasant sensations.

In GV, once calm and stability are established through mindfulness of breathing one then engages in a systematic bodyscan where one moves one's awareness throughout one's body. One is taught to observe whether sensations are pleasant, unpleasant, or neutral. If one has a reactive emotion arise from sensation one is instructed to bring awareness back to sensation and let go of the reactive emotion. Because one is taught to keep moving one's awareness through one's body one does not linger long on any one sensation. In SE once resourcing has been established one starts working with unpleasant sensations. One it taught "pendulation" which means alternating awareness between pleasant and unpleasant sensations. One is also taught "titration" which means only taking in small doses of unpleasant sensations

---

49 Payne, Levine, and Crane-Godreau, "Somatic Experiencing."

at a time.[50] This is similar to mindfulness of breathing in GV where one is taught to return to resourcing whenever one needs to restore calmness and stability.

Goenka *Vipassana*, Somatic Experiencing, and the Spectrum of Suffering

A core tenant in psychiatrist Judith Herman's seminal book *Trauma and Recovery: The Aftermath of Violence—from Domestic Abuse to Political Terror* is that it takes a sociopolitical movement for society to be able to recognize and respond to trauma.[51] She traced the origins of trauma therapy to the origins of Western psychiatry and psychology itself through the figures of Jean Martin Charcot, Pierre Janet, William James, and Sigmund Freud. Janet, James, and Freud studied under Charcot in Paris toward the end of the nineteenth century. The anticlerical movement of the French Third Republic gave them the sociopolitical support to explore the cause of hysteria in women from a modern medical perspective instead of from the previous feudal Catholic perspective.

However, when Freud discovered that childhood sexual abuse was the primary cause of hysteria in women, the sociopolitical support for his work evaporated because the men in charge of the medical community in France and Austria did not want to admit that sexual abuse of women as girls was a widespread societal phenomenon. Herman argues that it took the antiwar movement and the women's liberation movement in the twentieth century to provide the sociopolitical support to re-recognize trauma in society and to revive trauma therapy within Western psychiatry/psychology. Her and her colleagues such as Bessel Van Der Kolk, John Briere, and Catherine Scott fought a long fight to get PTSD recognized in the American Psychiatric Association's *Diagnostics and Statistics Manual* (DSM). Trauma therapists are currently fighting to get complex trauma recognized by the DSM instead of just acute trauma. They are also fighting to get not just life-threatening

50 Payne, Levine, and Crane-Godreau, "Somatic Experiencing."

51 Judith Lewis Herman, *Trauma and Recovery: The Aftermath of Violence—From Domestic Abuse to Political Terror* (New York: Basic Books, 2015), ch. 1.

incidents recognized as the cause of trauma, but also non-life-threatening incidents.

In actual practice, trauma therapists commonly see trauma as occurring along a spectrum of intensity. According to Briere and Scott, "Our own conclusion is that an event is traumatic if it is extremely upsetting, at least temporarily overwhelms the individual's internal resources, and produces lasting psychological symptoms."[52] Somatic trauma therapist Pat Ogden has defined trauma as follows, "Unresolved trauma can be conceptualized as deriving from overwhelming experiences that cannot be integrated."[53] Elaine Miller-Karas has distinguished between 'large *T* trauma" caused by war or sexual violence and "small *t* trauma" caused by incidents such as a dog bite or a surgery.[54]

Levine and his coauthors have described an even more refined spectrum of trauma based on the imbalance of the nervous system instead of the external event(s) that caused the trauma. They also state that an event may be more traumatizing to one person versus another based on the resiliency of the person's nervous system or the support that is available for the person after the incident(s). They summarized their understanding of this spectrum of trauma by stating,

> *This view implies a continuum of stress conditions; a chronic but mild elevation of sympathetic response at one end, and a chronic extreme activation of both sympathetic and parasympathetic (or more exactly, ergotropic and trophotopic) systems at the other. At precisely what point the stress should be regarded as "traumatic" is less important than the understanding of the nature of the dysregulation of the nervous system.*[55]

From an early Buddhist yogic perspective, big *T* trauma can be seen as an extreme form of mundane suffering (*dukkha*). In the language of Goenka *vipassana*, big *T* trauma could be categorized as very intense

52 Briere and Scott, *Principles of Trauma Therapy*, 10.

53 Pat Ogden and Janina Fisher, *Sensorimotor Psychotherapy: Interventions for Trauma and Attachment*, CSM ed. (New York: W. W. Norton, 2015), 28.

54 Miller-Karas, *Building Resilience to Trauma*, 2.

55 Payne, Levine, and Crane-Godreau, "Somatic Experiencing," 5.

sankharas (intentions/emotions) that co-arise with very intense body sensations (*vedana*) that are experienced within the primal phenomenological rhythms of the links of dependent origination (*nidana*). In terms of trauma caused by interpersonal interaction, early Buddhist yogic teachings could categorize those as breeches of the five precepts of not killing, not stealing, not engaging in sexual misconduct, not using false or harmful speech, and not abusing intoxicants. Small *t* trauma could be categorized as less intense forms of mundane suffering (*dukkha*) that manifest as less intense body sensations (*vedana*) and less intense intentions/emotions (*sankharas*) within the narrative of the links of dependent origination. From a traditional Buddhist perspective, deep *t* trauma could be categorized as the process of rebirth itself which puts a person in the situation of being vulnerable to small *t* and big *T* trauma in the first place.

9

A REFRAMED PSYCHOSPIRITUALITY OF STRESS AND TRAUMA

Honoring the Complexity of Lived Experience

M. Jan Holton and Jill L. Snodgrass

REFRAMING THEORETICAL AND theological understandings of stress and trauma draws upon individual, intergenerational, intercultural, and communal lived experiences. Amid the messiness of human embodied, spiritual, and psychological experience, this project endeavors to navigate spaces of uncertainty and ambiguity. *Reframing Trauma* is not an attempt to abolish or revise diagnostic definitions of trauma, nor does it contest systematic theologies of trauma. Both are quite necessary and bring important insight and a sense of order to what can often feel chaotic. However, *Reframing Trauma* is situated, unapologetically, in the push and pull, from and between, both psychology and theology. It honors the complexity of lived experience as a vital place of learning and growth. It is from this reality that we posit a constructive theological perspective of trauma, highlighting revised understandings of God and humanity. Though firmly grounded in the Christian tradition, this reframed theology weaves together a variety of insights from the work to reframe trauma in a way that also respects the distinctiveness of Islamic and Buddhist perspectives without being reductionistic.[1]

A Reframed Christian Theology of Trauma

Reframing trauma invites us to revise our theological understandings of the causes of, implications for, and responses to trauma. When trauma is

1 This is not an attempt to exclude wisdom from other religious traditions. It simply reflects that the contributing authors identify as Christian, Muslim, and Buddhist and write from these perspectives.

reframed as part of a stress-trauma continuum,[2] our sense of the chronology of trauma shifts. Hyper-individualized conceptions of trauma that focus solely on humans as atomistic beings are reframed to also include the collective, cumulative impact of distress over time. By challenging doctrinal and embedded theologies of God's perceived role in trauma, through direct or indirect action, we can shift to construct more life-giving, deliberative theologies of trauma and suffering.

Beyond Event-Based Trauma

Traditional biomedical conceptions of trauma, such as those put forth in the DSM-5-TR, define trauma as the result of a "terrible event."[3] Such events occur in chronological time, implying a discrete period pre-trauma, a "moment of injury,"[4] and a discrete period post-trauma (see Cho, chapter 5). Reframing trauma as part of a stress-trauma continuum acknowledges that not all trauma is event-based and, as humans, we may experience trauma as part of an ongoing, collective, and spiritual experience that is always already occurring. This potential disruption of the temporality of trauma pushes back against what Keith A. Menhinick and Cody J. Sanders refer to in chapter 3 as the "tyranny of the present over the future." Individuals and communities experiencing ongoing, collective stress and trauma often look toward potential futures as foreclosed. The oppressive present is all that can be conceived in any given moment. Yet Jesus pushed back against the tyrannies of the present over the future by disrupting the temporal arc that threatens to maintain unjust structures forever and always. Understanding trauma as part of a stress-trauma continuum challenges conceptions of trauma as the result of a moment of injury and shifts the focus from chronological time, or *chronos*, to God's time, or *kairos*. This invites humans to join Jesus in pushing

---

2 Catherine N. Dulmus and Carolyn Hilarski, "When Stress Constitutes Trauma and Trauma Constitutes Crisis: The Stress-Trauma-Crisis Continuum," *Brief Treatment and Crisis Intervention* 3, no. 1 (2003): 27–35, https://doi.org/10.1093/brief-treatment/mhg008.

3 American Psychiatric Association, *Diagnostic and Statistical Manual of Mental Disorders*, 5th ed., Text Revision (Washington, DC: American Psychiatric Association, 2022), https://doi.org/10.1176/appi.books.9780890425787.

4 Rebecca Lester, "Back from the Edge of Existence: A Critical Anthropology of Trauma," *Transcultural Psychiatry* 50, no. 5 (2013): 758, https://doi.org/10.1177/1363461513504520.

back against the resignation of presentism and instead embrace God's continuous engagement in the fight against life-limiting, oppressive forces.

Beyond Individual Trauma

Reframing trauma as part of a stress-trauma continuum shifts our understanding of both when trauma occurs, broadening limited chronological conceptions, and who experiences trauma. A reframed understanding acknowledges the collective and communal stress and trauma experienced in communities around the globe. We can look to long-term systemic oppression, war, and conflict, including the experiences of African American women in the United States (see Chapman Lape, chapter 2), intergenerational injuries of colonization (see Park, chapter 7), immigrants and refugees (see Cho, chapter 5), and victims of mass rape and genocide (see Isgandarova, chapter 6). Individuals and communities navigate distress and trauma that is not solely their own, but a collective experience that is prolonged and sustained by oppressive forces.

Biomedical, event-based conceptions of trauma focus on individuals as victims of traumatic events and their cognitive appraisal of an event as life threatening, or not. Yet such hyper-individualized conceptions of trauma fail to see how our personal identities are constructed and defined by and in community, present and past. Our cognitive appraisals of acute and enduring events are not created in a vacuum, but always co-constructed in and with community. Larger cultural narratives shape the ascribed meaning of stress and trauma. Because experiences of oppression and attempted annihilation by the dominant, white, colonialist, capitalist, heteronormative culture impact communities in insidious, pervasive ways, individuals and communities alike are the victim-survivors of trauma.

Beyond Human Trauma

Reframed understandings of trauma also invite us to see the ways that humans are not the only species suffering from stress and trauma. In Chapter 4, Ryan LaMothe describes the ontological rift between humans and other species that facilitates our failure to see how trauma in the Anthropocene Age is experienced by other-than-human species and the way that human action directly and indirectly perpetuates such traumas. The ontological rift between humans and other species, and other humans for that matter, is perpetuated by false theological understandings of God, creation, and perceived human power.

The idea that God created humans with superiority over other species, a theological anthropology traditionally supported by the first creation story in Genesis 1:1–2:4a, leads to an ontological rift between those who have power (humans) and those who are deemed "subordinate, inferior, and different" (other-than-human species).[5] This exegesis contributes to anthropocentric understandings of creation wherein humans are considered the only beings with inherent value. Humans are the only aspect of creation reflecting the divine nature (i.e., made in the image and likeness of God), and humans are granted tremendous power and control over nature. This narrative is in tension with the second creation story found in Genesis 2:4b–25 wherein humans and animals share inherent interdependence and mutuality; humans and "every animal of the field and every bird of the air" (Genesis 2:19) are made of the same "dust of the ground" (2:7). According to biblical scholar Thomas Mann, "What we distinguish as animal, vegetable, and mineral, in this anthropology are all intimately and inextricably related. Human beings are 'mud kin' with all other earth creatures (*fauna*), and with the trees of the orchard (*flora*)."[6] Nevertheless, the ontological rift between humans and other-than-human species distorts the goodness of creation by withholding the full blessing of belonging for other-than-human species. Other species are objectified, and disidentification makes the withholding of dignity and care possible, except where required for humans' own sake.

Beyond Individualism and Ruptures in Belonging

Sadly, it is not only other-than-human species who are often considered outside the obligation of respect and care except when benefitting humans in power. Humans engage in callous disregard for and disidentification with fellow humans.[7] Black persons throughout enslavement

5 Ryan LaMothe, "Ontological Psychospirituality: The Stress and Trauma of Other Species," in *Reframing Trauma: A Psychospiritual Theory and Theology*, eds. M. Jan Holton and Jill L. Snodgrass (Minneapolis: Fortress, 2025), 87.

6 Thomas W. Mann, *The Book of the Torah*, 2nd ed. (Eugene, OR: Cascade Books, 2013), 23.

7 LaMothe, "Ontological Psychospirituality," 97.

and beyond, LGBTQ+ persons, victim-survivors of genocide, immigrants, and more have likewise been "othered," treated as unworthy of full inclusion as is due all those reflecting the image of the creator God. A rift was instituted and maintained among and between humans. Stress and trauma are not a punishment from God or merely a byproduct of humans' innately sinful nature. Rather, stress and trauma can be engendered by our failure to live righteously and acknowledge that we belong to one another. Humans fail to accept our interdependence with all creation, including other humans.

Consider the story of Cain and Abel found in Genesis 4:1–16. Jealous that his brother Abel's offering was more pleasing to God, Cain lured Abel to a field and killed him. After the murder, God's first response to Cain was the question, "Where is your brother Abel?" Cain was certainly aware of God's omniscience, yet he responded rhetorically, saying, "I do not know; am I my brother's keeper?" Cain fails to acknowledge his interdependence with Abel, that is, to see that as a human, as a sibling, as part of God's creation, *we all belong to one another.*

Biblical scholar Brent Strawn notes that the story of Cain and Abel features the first use of the word sin, *hattat,* in the Bible, which then provokes a series of firsts.[8] According to Strawn, "sin is associated with the first violent act of human history, the fratricide occurs between the first two brothers, the first children of the first human couple. After the very first murder we read immediately of the very first prayer as Abel's blood gurgles into the ground."[9] The blood is crying out in prayer to the One who "has an ear for precisely these kinds of prayers."[10] Perhaps this act of spilling human blood into the earth is another shameful first act, that of human violence against creation, one that has continued with every war since and expanded even to the ecological violence with which we must contend today. Nevertheless, this violent rupture of relationship between these siblings, and between humans and the Earth, demonstrates, in the most visceral of ways, what

8 Brent A. Strawn, *Honest to God Preaching: Talking Sin, Suffering, and Violence* (Minneapolis: Fortress, 2021). While the story of Adam's and Eve's disobedience in the garden is long associated with original sin, Strawn's point here refers to the first use of the Hebrew word for sin, *hattat.*

9 Strawn, *Honest to God Preaching,* 99.

10 Strawn, *Honest to God Preaching,* 100.

Strawn calls the unholy trinity of sin, suffering, and violence.[11] As humans, we inflict stress and trauma upon our siblings, truly upon creation writ large, by "otherizing" aspects of God's creation rather than acknowledging and celebrating our belonging.

Such considerations point toward several implications about what it means to belong in the ways that God intended. First, it is evident that belonging is reciprocal. We must desire to belong, but others must claim us as well.[12] This is true even in relationship with God. God surely searches for us and knows us (Psalm 139). God assures us, "you are mine" (Isaiah 43:1b), and God promises that nothing can separate us from the love of God (Romans 8:38). Practical theologian John Swinton elucidated the theological distinction between inclusion and belonging.[13] According to Swinton, as humans we will always be naturally drawn to some people and disinclined toward others, particularly those we deem different. Belonging does not simply mean including those who are different. Rather, "belonging is a gift of the Spirit of Jesus that is experienced within the community that Jesus gathers to himself through himself, and which seeks to model God's continuing redemption of creation in and through Christ."[14] Swinton argues that belonging is not fostered by turning to others and welcoming them. Belonging is fostered by turning to God and then welcoming in everyone who is God's beloved, thus everyone. When we fail to turn first to God, we then fail to acknowledge and act out of mutual belonging, and we lay the foundation upon which the structures of sin are built.

There is another messy matter about being human. Turning to God is always filtered through our human lens and the communities that shape us. Many communities, even communities of faith who believe themselves to be righteous and trusting believers in and interpreters of God's call to us as humans, exclude and other those on the margins, perhaps even creating stress and traumatic experiences for them in the process. This is certainly

---

11 Strawn, *Honest to God Preaching*, 100.

12 M. Jan Holton, *Longing for Home: Forced Displacement and Postures of Hospitality* (New Haven, CT: Yale University Press, 2016), 81, 88.

13 John Swinton, "From Inclusion to Belonging: A Practical Theology of Community, Disability and Humanness," *Journal of Religion, Disability & Health* 16, no. 2 (2012): 172–190, https://doi.org/10.1080/15228967.2012.676243.

14 Swinton, "From Inclusion to Belonging," 184.

true for the LGBTQ+ and immigrant communities (see Menhinick and Sanders, chapter 3 and Cho, chapter 5). But even when our belonging to God is "sanctioned" by our communities of faith, belonging can be complex. Trauma is one of the factors and experiences that can hinder feelings and beliefs that we actually do belong to God, and at times may thwart even the very desire to belong to God. But, while God's promise of belongingness is sure for all the ages, the same is not true for belonging among humans.

How Humans Rupture Belonging

Reframed understandings of trauma enable us to conceive of suffering, stress, and trauma not as punishments from God but, in part, as the outcome of humanity's exercise of God-given agency and free will. Humans are free to turn away from God to create and perpetuate structures of sin. Despite God's desire for us, we inflict violence on other humans, other species, and all of creation. Humans are, as LaMothe notes in chapter 4, "gratuitously destructive."[15] Covert violence like the "insidious trauma"[16] that results from colonialism, racism, homophobia, trans-antagonism, and other oppressions goes against the will of God and violates righteous living. This destruction, the covert and overt violence, leaves those who suffer at risk of isolation. As Cathy Caruth, scholar on the languages of trauma, argues, at the core of trauma is a "lack of support, of help, of comfort; being utterly left alone with the experience of having no one to listen."[17] This can shatter our assumptive world and goes against God's intended creation. "Trauma, especially trauma at the hands of other human beings, is completely at odds with the assumptive embodied, pre-representational world of trust and vulnerability."[18] God honors human agency, even the violent destructive failings of human beings, not because God creates evil or wishes harm or punishment for humans, but because we are free to make poor, even violent, choices.[19]

---

15 LaMothe, "Ontological Psychospirituality," 89.

16 Maria P. P. Root, "Reconstructing the Impact of Trauma on Personality," in *Personality and Psychopathology: Feminist Reappraisals*, ed. Laura S. Brown and Mary Ballou (New York: Guilford Press, 1992), 240.

17 Cathy Caruth, *Unclaimed Experience: Trauma, Narrative, and History* (Baltimore, MD: Johns Hopkins University Press, 1996), 202.

18 LaMothe, "Ontological Psychospirituality," 93.

19 Paul Tillich, *Systematic Theology*, vol. 2, *Existence and The Christ* (Chicago: The University of Chicago Press, 1957).

When we participate in structures of sin, our sense of belonging is ruptured, which impacts not only how we claim others, but also how others claim us. Swinton, as referenced above, uses the term *thin*, in contrast to the richness of thick, to describe how humans create "thin definitions of disability and thin understandings of disabled people [that] lead to thin forms of inclusion."[20] This thin inclusion keeps people at a distance by only including others in temporary or performative ways and failing to move toward rich relationship and thick belonging. When belonging is ruptured, relations become thin. We do not claim others. As Swinton argues, "*to belong you need to be missed.* People need to be concerned when you are not there; your communities need to feel empty when you are not there [. . .] It is precisely in these ways that we are called to long for one another even amid of all our differences."[21]

A revised theology of trauma disputes that the suffering resulting from stress and trauma, or any other kind, stems from a collective human moral failing, be it innate or acquired. However, stress and trauma can result in thin relationships, lack of belonging, and spiritual dis-ease, a lack of harmony in relation to self, others, creation, and God. In such experiences, humans are brought face-to-face with our finitude and the threat of nonbeing. We experience finitude through the "unending projections of violent futures in which there is no possibility for the flourishing of life."[22] We face our finite nature in ways that contribute to uncertainty, angst, and existential anxiety.

Trauma, Free Will, and Meeting God

But that is not the end of the story. Humans are more than fallen, sinful creatures. While we are finite and free to fail, we are also free to actualize our

20 Swinton, "From Inclusion to Belonging," 180. Swinton borrows the language of thick and thin from anthropologist Clifford Geertz who delineated between thick and thin descriptions of phenomena in ethnographic research. Clifford Geertz, *Interpretation of Cultures: Selected Essays* (New York: Basic Books, 1973).

21 Swinton, "From Inclusion to Belonging," 183.

22 Keith A. Menhinick and Cody J. Sanders, "The Psychospiritual Trauma of LGBTQ+ People and Communities: Depathologizing Queer Lives and Experiences," in *Reframing Trauma: A Psychospiritual Theory and Theology*, eds. M. Jan Holton and Jill L. Snodgrass (Minneapolis: Fortress, 2025), 75.

divinely bestowed potential.[23] It is within the messiness of this freedom that goodness and evil coexist. Of course, living into our divine potential is not a simple matter of making good choices. It is an unjust world that we have created and not all have the same freedoms to choose. We must recognize how the failure to live righteously has aided the creation and sustaining of structural sin of all forms including capitalism, colonialism, white supremacy, homophobia, and the oppression of sexual and gender minorities.

Humans are able to actualize their potential, even in the threat of their finitude and all the forces of violence and oppression that stand in their way, by finding "the courage to be in the face of nonbeing."[24] God is the source of this courage that makes it possible for humans to face stress and trauma with simultaneous hope and resilience. We search for God and God searches for us. God met Hagar and Ishmael as they navigated the wilderness in danger and gave them sustenance, hope, and the promise of a future. God was and is the source of spiritual tenacity that has given African American women the strength to face the stressors and traumas imprinted from generations and those imposed upon them every day (see Chapman Lape, chapter 2). God meets migrants and immigrants in the literal wilderness of fleeing famine, war, and conflict (see Cho, chapter 5) and LGBTQ+ persons in all the wilderness spaces of rejection (see Menhinick and Sanders, chapter 3). For some, God stands in to provide the security and safety that is breached via experiences of stress and trauma. But God does not act alone. God does this in and through God's creation.

We arrive then at the paradox of stress and trauma. Although much stress and trauma is caused by humans' failure to live righteously, stress and trauma can simultaneously repair the relational ruptures by bringing people into authentic communities of resistance and resilience. Community functions as a protective measure to mitigate the effects of stress and trauma and to foster resilience even as stress and trauma occur. Community offers a counternarrative to biomedical models of trauma that frame trauma as a hyper-individualized experience with a hyper-individualized cure. Community helps to externalize the source of the problem as a collective

23 Tillich, *Systematic Theology*, 32–33.

24 Paul Tillich, *The Courage to Be*, 2nd ed. (New Haven, CT: Yale University Press, 2000).

predicament and not an individual pathology, although individuals may still endure unique neurobiological and somatic responses.

A Theology of Trauma and Resilience

Understanding resilience and trauma from a theological perspective is complex. Since the early 2000s, psychologists have affirmed that resilience in the face of significant loss and trauma is relatively common. For example, in a study following the September 11, 2001 terrorist attacks in New York, 35 percent of participants in or near the World Trade Center displayed remarkable resilience.[25] According to clinical psychologist George Bonanno, "resilience in the form of a trajectory of 'relatively stable, healthy levels of psychological and physical functioning' was far more prevalent in the aftermath of potentially traumatic events (PTEs) than had previously been assumed."[26] Yet, as we discussed previously, the stress-trauma continuum helps us expand our understanding of trauma beyond being solely event-based. It also reminds us that resilience is not an outcome.

In chapter 1, we noted several scriptural examples of how resilience, stress, and trauma can co-occur. Furthermore, resilience, supported by and facilitated in community, can be experienced alongside suffering by victim-survivors of genocidal rape, by members of LGBTQ+ communities, by African American women enduring the legacies of slavery in the United States, and more. In each of these examples, we see how social support is crucial to resilience. Social support is not merely accompaniment but provides a deep sense of belonging. Belonging is not made possible simply because humans attempt to include one another. Rather, belonging is made possible and engendered by God. It is because of God, and God's desires for creation, that humans experience belonging with God and with one another and all creation. Ultimately, God is the root source of resilience. God meets God's beloved in the wilderness of stress and trauma

---

25 George A. Bonanno, Courtney Rennicke, and Sharon Dekel, "Self-enhancement Among High-Exposure Survivors of the September 11th Terrorist Attack: Resilience or Social Maladjustment?" *Journal of Personal Social Psychology*, 88, no. 6 (2005): 984–998, https://doi.org/10.1037/0022-3514.88.6.984.

26 George A. Bonanno, "The Resilience Paradox," *European Journal of Psychotraumatology* 12, no. 1 (2021): 1942642, https://doi.org/10.1080/20008198.2021.1942642.

and emboldens us with spiritual tenacity and the courage to face finitude and persevere.[27] Moreover, God created humans in communal interdependence, with belonging. When humans recognize and live out our innate belonging, resilience is facilitated not only within individuals but within the wider community.

Christian theology, and perhaps even especially a Christian theology of resilience, should bear a healthy dose of humility in its claims as an ultimate source of knowledge. We acknowledge and celebrate that other religious and spiritual traditions have equally valid perceptions of the source of resilience and how it shapes the human spirit in the face of trauma. Traditional religions, or beliefs of Indigenous peoples around the globe, whether serving as a lone spiritual authority or one that works in conjunction with Christian or other beliefs, also posit important insights regarding the origins of resilience.

Christianity is both a deeply held faith tradition and a religion that brings with it a legacy of violence and oppression. Pastoral theologians Emmanuel Lartey and Helena Moon remind us that:

> *Religion has been a tool, a methodological weapon for colonizing the two-thirds world by creating and constructing categories of what were considered secular, sacred, and profane—obliterating practices that were considered unrecognizable and illegible to the civilized Western knowing subject; as well as dehumanizing the practices of local communities in the Americas, Africa, and Asia.*[28]

Yet, precolonial traditional religions and healing practices, even though not acknowledging the "white God," wove deep interconnections between the sacred and profane such that it was not possible to separate the two.[29] Lartey notes that the organizing principle of the human being, in African tradition, is that of the divine-given essence, bestowed in every person before their

---

27 N. Lynne Westfield, *Dear Sisters: A Womanist Practice of Hospitality* (Cleveland, OH: Pilgrim Press, 2007).

28 Emmanuel Y. Lartey and Helena Moon, eds., *Postcolonial Images of Spiritual Care: Challenges of Care in a Neoliberal Age* (Eugene, OR: Pickwick, 2020), 5.

29 Emmanuel Y. Lartey, "Be-ing in Relation," in *Postcolonial Images of Spiritual Care; Challenges of Care in a Neoliberal Age*, ed. Emmanuel Y. Lartey and Hellena Moon (Eugene, OR: Pickwick, 2020), 18.

entry into this world that gives them their drive and purpose in life.[30] Similar to Christian understandings of God as an ultimate source of belonging and relationship, African traditions understand that the essence that originates in the divine and is instilled in humans is what drives them to seek relationship with others.

In the Americas, Native American traditions also celebrate the interconnectedness between the sacred and the profane, the divine and human, the land and all of creation.[31] Scholars of social work Michelle Johnson-Jennings, Shanondora Billiot, and Karina Walters state, "Original Instructions [ancient teachings] are tied to land and cosmos and require a relationship between person and place with specific obligations and responsibilities. . ."[32] This deep connection to place makes the brutal forced displacement by settlers and outlawing of traditional practices particularly tragic. Repair of this rupture is bringing forth a form of resilience. Johnson-Jennings and colleagues explain: "As these threads of knowledge are engaged and ancient teachings (aka Original Instructions) are revitalized and regenerated in Indigenous community practices, *thrivance* is activated, and Indigenous community wellbeing is actuated."[33] A reframed Christian theology of trauma recognizes that this spiritual frame is one among many others that can build resilience among its believers.

From the perspective of Christian theology, we honor that resilience is grounded in God and the ways God created humans in relationship. Resilience, then, is not simply an outcome of event-based trauma, nor a personality trait. Decades of empirical psychological research has attempted to identify the factors that facilitate resilience following exposure to potentially traumatic events. However, more predictive than personality traits and demographic variables are social and economic resources and worldviews and meaning making, factors that are derived from and fostered by

30 Lartey, "Be-ing in Relation," 18.

31 There is no singular Native American tradition or African religion. Rather, these are traditions that are unique in some ways to specific tribes or communities but that also share essential commonalities.

32 Michelle Johnson-Jennings, Shanondora Billiot, and Karina Walters, "Returning to Our Roots: Tribal Health and Wellness through Land-Based Healing," *Geneology 4*, no. 3 (2020): 91, https://doi.org/10.3390/genealogy4030091.

33 Johnson-Jennings, Billiot, and Walters, "Returning to Our Roots."

belonging.[34] Resilience is not solely the outcome of our individual, God-given natures or our personalities and intersecting identities. Resilience is an act made possible and facilitated by God in community. In response to the insidious trauma resulting from legacies of capitalism and colonialism, resilience is quite often an act of resistance. But given the ruptures experienced in belonging, working to foster resilience amid stress and trauma by and in community becomes imperative. Here we turn to look at four factors that can facilitate resilience amid stress and trauma: somatic practices, biblical trauma narratives, meaning making, and post-traumatic growth (PTG).

Somatic Practices of Resilience

Resilience amid stress and trauma can be facilitated by somatic practices, including mindfulness of breathing and of body sensations, that facilitate self-regulation in multiple domains. Humans experiencing stress and trauma can become caught in a negative cycle of overwhelming body sensations and reactive emotions that lead to "unwholesome actions of body, speech, and mind" and "reenactment of trauma."[35] In Chapter 8, John B. Freese demonstrates the similarities between the early Buddhist yogic theory and practice within Goenka *vipassana* and Somatic Experiencing theory and practice. When critically correlated, these two theories evidence how trauma can be metabolized toward greater resilience. In a Buddhist framework, this entails cultivating awareness of and equanimity toward body sensations as a means of abandoning craving and aversion rather than acting on them. In the language of Somatic Experiencing, this entails uncoupling and separating the reactive fear engendered by stress and trauma from sensations of immobility, thus allowing the immobility drive to complete itself.[36] Engaging in mindfulness practices can enable individuals to work with manageable

---

34 George A. Bonanno, Maren Westphal, and Anthony D. Mancini, "Resilience to Loss and Potential Trauma," *Annual Review of Clinical Psychology*, 7 (2011): 511–535, https://doi-org/10.1146/annurev-clinpsy-032210-104526.

35 John B. Freese, "A Buddhist Psychospirituality of Trauma: A Critical Correlation of Vipassana Meditation and Somatic Experiencing," in *Reframing Trauma: A Psychospiritual Theory and Theology*, eds. M. Jan Holton and Jill L. Snodgrass (Minneapolis: Fortress, 2025), 179.

36 Peter A. Levine, *In an Unspoken Voice: How the Body Releases Trauma and Restores Goodness* (Berkeley, CA: North Atlantic Books, 2010).

amounts of sensation and emotion toward rebalancing the nervous system. These practices include breathwork and bodyscan exercises that facilitate acknowledging reactive emotions and bringing awareness back to sensation. Because these are practices, once they are learned they can be re-engaged whenever one encounters stress and trauma. The ability to skillfully self-regulate and rebalance the nervous system facilitates resilience and allows one to return to "relatively stable, healthy levels of psychological and physical functioning."[37]

Theology and Trauma Narratives

In her seminal book *Trauma and Recovery: The Aftermath of Violence—From Domestic Abuse to Political Terror*, Judith Herman stresses three conditions and their order for healing from trauma: establishing safety, telling the story of the trauma, and creating a future.[38] More recently she considers a "fourth and final" condition, justice.[39] This formula for recovery is fraught with difficulty, especially for persons from non-Western cultures, those who live under continued threat in conflict zones, or those simply trying to survive in a violent culture that ostracizes them. Telling individual stories can, for many, lead to further danger. For communities living under the continued imprint of oppression, a hopeful future may be difficult to imagine. Justice around the globe is more often on the far horizon than a near reality. Does this mean that there is no hope for healing the stress and trauma endured by these persons and communities? To this we answer, no.

Though the appropriateness of telling stories about trauma is deeply culturally bound, Christian trauma narratives are a notable exception. Christian communities in churches, cities, villages, and refugee and displacement camps around the world often turn to the Bible to find solace. This is one of the finest examples of how, as argued by theologian Rebecca S. Chopp, the Word serves as the "perfectly open sign" that at once defines and pushes

---

37 Bonanno, "The Resilience Paradox," 2.

38 Judith Herman, *Trauma and Recovery: The Aftermath of Violence—From Domestic Abuse to Political Terror* (New York: Basic Books, 1997).

39 Judith Herman, *Truth and Repair: How Trauma Survivors Envision Justice* (New York: Basic Books, 2023), 3.

against that definition.[40] While in Western churches stories of violence and terror often do more harm than good to trauma survivors, in other parts of the world more culturally bound to resist personal "trauma narratives," the biblical stories of war, exile, and the violence they entail becomes the sustenance that feeds faith and hope. For some, these are the trauma narratives they most identify with and can use in lieu of their personal stories.

Understanding the power of these biblical narratives in other cultures is just as important as understanding how they can be harmful if used carelessly in Western churches. Brent Strawn reinterprets the purpose of the many violent stories in the Old Testament and suggests that they act as detailed confessions that serve a collective purpose of naming, in every gory detail, the violence they have committed and the violence they have endured.[41] Indeed, according to Herman, "The completed narrative must include a full and vivid description of the traumatic imagery."[42] She is adamant that without the spoken word that includes these details and accompanying affect, the effort is "barren and incomplete."[43] Herman fails to take into account, however, that there is simply more than one way to tell a trauma narrative. She does not find valid or even consider all the ways that oppressed people, unable to speak the unspeakable for risk of death for themselves or their beloveds, have used dance, poetry, songs, hymns, story, and other cultural traditions to speak of their pain and to forge hope for a future.

Heidi Park offers a powerful example of this way of subversive speaking in chapter 7 with her description and analysis of how the spectral presence in literature and art serves to carry the wounds of colonialism and violence that generations have absorbed. In her book *Joy Unspeakable: Contemplative Practices of the Black Church*, Barbara Holmes describes the contemplative practices in the Black church that through generations have told the stories of violence, suffering, and survival. She notes, for example, the power of the *ring shout* during enslavement that could carry multiple layers of meaning from deliverance to disappointment to celebration of survival, in which the

40 Rebecca S. Chopp, *The Power to Speak: Feminism, Language, and God* (Chestnut Ridge, NY: Crossroad, 1991), 125.

41 Strawn, *Honest to God Preaching*, 6.

42 Herman, *Trauma and Recovery*, 177.

43 Herman, *Trauma and Recovery*, 177.

story is told, not in words, but through the moving body.[44] Holmes demonstrates how hope, courage, and resilience can co-occur with the trauma of enslavement. She says of the ring shout, "Stories of torture and oppression, meant to discourage and create fear, became the grist for storytellers who shared mythic narratives of courage, even the very tools of torture were divested of their power through inversion and sacred ritual."[45]

Meaning Making

Re-storying one's own trauma narrative by turning to any of the many biblical narratives of stress and trauma is a form of meaning making that can facilitate resilience. This is not to say that experiences of stress and trauma should always be reframed as opportunities for growth, although that may be the meaning one makes of such experiences. Rather, as Crystal L. Park argues, distress often results when the situational meaning ascribed to an experience of stress or trauma does not align with one's global meaning.[46] "Highly traumatic events are commonly appraised as unpredictable, unfair, and uncontrollable and as having pervasive adverse implications for survivors and their futures [. . .] The meaning making model asserts that distress is not generated by the appraised meaning itself but rather by discrepancies between that appraised meaning and the individual's global meaning system."[47] The greater the discrepancy between the appraised meaning and one's individual global meaning system, the greater the perceived violation. Individuals and communities have the power to make meaning of stress and trauma in ways that are more life-giving. This can be done by ascribing situational meaning to experiences of stress and trauma that align with their global meaning system. At times it may also be necessary to revise their "global meaning to accommodate the trauma."[48] When stress and trauma

44 Barbara A. Holmes, *Joy Unspeakable: Contemplative Practices of the Black Church*, 2nd ed. (Minneapolis: Fortress Press, 2017), 62. See also, David D. Daniels, *The Cultural Renewal of Slave Religion: Charles Prince Jones and the Emergence of the Holiness Movement in Mississippi* (PhD diss., Union Theological Seminary, New York, 1992), 85.

45 Holmes, *Unspeakable Joy*, 62.

46 Crystal L. Park, "Meaning Making Following Trauma," *Frontiers in Psychology* 13 (2022): 844891, https://doi.org/10.3389/fpsyg.2022.844891.

47 Park, "Meaning Making Following Trauma," 2.

48 Park, "Meaning Making Following Trauma," 3.

result in discrepancy between the situational meaning and the global meaning, reducing the discrepancy via meaning making leads to better adjustment and resilience. For example, in experiencing stress and trauma, it is not uncommon for individuals to realize they possess strengths, skills, and resources they previously did not know they had. A child may endure years of physical and psychological abuse and cultivate resilience amid such stress and trauma by appraising the abuse as an event that evidenced their innate strength and grit.

Post-Traumatic Growth

Post-traumatic growth (PTG) suggests that growth can co-occur with suffering. PTG is similar to resilience, but the two are not the same. Pastoral theologian Mary Beth Werdel helps us understand several things about PTG. First, while resilience can be present from the earliest moments and onward throughout stress and trauma, growth requires time and reflection. Second, Werdel likens this growth to wisdom. Of this she says, "The road to wisdom is not one in which a person in darkness can solely focus on light. Nor is wisdom found by trying to make darkness light. Rather . . . traumatic growth is seen only by allowing dark and light to coexist, recognizing how they correlate, and finding a way to synthesize new meanings . . . For some people, this newly synthesized meaning leads to growth."[49] While the framing of light as good and dark as bad is unfortunate, the point is well taken. The idea of PTG can be a liberating one. However, one need not believe that growth can happen only after some far horizon of healing has been met. Finally, while resilience is not an outcome PTG can help build or enhance resilience that can be beneficial in facing future challenges.[50]

---

49 Mary Beth Werdel, *The Paradox of Trauma and Growth in Pastoral and Spiritual Care: Night Blooming* (Lanham, MD: Lexington Books, 2024), 26.

50 Werdel, *The Paradox of Trauma*, 34.

CONCLUSION

Moving from Theory to Practice

M. Jan Holton and Jill L. Snodgrass

MITIGATING STRESS AND trauma, and fostering resilience amid trauma, requires that we, as humans, make inoperative the apparatuses that create and maintain the ontological rift between humans and creation. This means accepting that in all our uniqueness, we are also like all other animals and like all other humans. This means accepting our collective existential vulnerability, insignificance, and impermanence, yet embracing the courage to be in the face of such finitude. The first step in doing this is to resist the legacies of capitalism and colonialism by turning first to God and then to neighbor. This is work we cannot do alone, but that must be done in communion with God and all creation. The second step is to accept that we will continuously fall short. Jesus is the only one, in his divine perfection, who is capable of defeating the power of stress and trauma. We cannot. Yet by embracing our interdependence with all creation, living out our mutual belonging, facilitating resilience, and turning to liberative theological trauma narratives, we can face our finitude with courage.

Four case studies help us to consider the implications of this reframed psychospiritual theory for the practice of spiritual caregiving. The case studies privilege an intercultural approach, stressing the importance of contextual caregiving that values multiple perspectives and authentic participation. They focus on distinctive contexts and modalities of care, including congregational care, spiritually integrated psychotherapy, nonprofit/NGO care, and hospital chaplaincy.

Case Study 1: Congregational Care

Sam, a Black man in his mid-forties, describes himself as "a mess" during the first months after his seven-year-old daughter, Sara, died. She ran into the road and was struck by a car. It was a tragic accident. A sitter was watching Sara and her eleven-year-old sister Lily, and it just happened so fast. Sam is only now, a year later, starting to regain his footing in any real way. He and Kim, his wife and Sara's mom, depended so much on each other and God to help carry them through the tragedy and help Lily through it as well. It was such a senseless death. He is still shaken by how unjust it all feels. Why would God take his sweet Sara? It still doesn't make sense.

For the first time since Sara's death, Sam took on a new project at work. His prayer life has been challenged, but he feels like he's starting to connect with God again. Sam finds himself occasionally wanting to go out without worries about the awkwardness of running into acquaintances who do not know what to say.

Sam feels that Kim is having a harder time adjusting. He tries not to be frustrated but sometimes it's difficult. What used to be small disputes they'd work through now frequently end in an argument that never gets resolved. Sara's room is still pretty much as it was the day she died. Sam and Kim both worry about Lily, now twelve years old. She is distant at times, but it's difficult to know if that's because of the grief or just because she's being a normal adolescent. Sam doesn't think he can share all that he feels with Kim without being disrespectful of her own grief. Most of all, Sam doesn't want Kim to think that he doesn't love Sara just as much as she does. A silly thought, maybe, but he can't shake it.

Kim, a white woman in her early forties, says that she is doing the best she can after Sara's death. But she can't stop seeing her baby's broken, lifeless body. And though her family and community keep calling it an "accident," it was more like murder, whether intended or not. Such a senseless death. She and Sam have clung to each other and to God to get through this. She knows they should forgive the driver of the car, but she doesn't see how. She doesn't know how to forgive God, either. Why would God do such a thing? What had she done to deserve this? Sara certainly didn't do anything—she was just a child! Kim is hard-pressed to find an answer. It's hard to love a God who does such things. But she also can't afford not to.

Kim says that she keeps up with things around the house but feels sure that she was a better mother, wife, and homemaker before the chaos of paralyzing grief turned her life upside down. She worries about Lily. Thankfully she is doing well in school and seems to be getting along with her friends.

It seems to Kim like Sam is moving along faster in sorting through his grief. Some days she envies this. But in a strange way grief makes her feel closer to Sara. Isn't that a funny thing? She is grateful for her early morning time when she thinks of Sara and tries to talk to God. The psalms are sometimes helpful, sometimes not. They seem as confused as she is with their mixture of sorrow, anger, and joy. She hasn't taken apart Sara's room yet, but it's time. They need the storage space. There are boxes just waiting to go in there. It's a little overwhelming to think of sorting through Sara's things. Kim knows it will bring back so many memories, and she's already struggling with thoughts she doesn't want to have.

Suggested Questions for Reflection

Imagine you are Kim and Sam's religious leader. The couple asks if they can meet with you to talk about the impact of Sara's death on their marriage. You are focused on assessing and caring for Kim's and Sam's spiritual well-being. You may be considering referring them to a mental health professional because marriage therapy is outside your scope of practice.

1. How would you conceptualize their experiences along a stress-trauma continuum?
2. Would a stress-trauma continuum be a helpful framework for affirming the uniqueness of their grief and healing? Why, or why not?
3. Religious leaders often employ the language used by care-seekers. Kim repeatedly refers to Sara's death as traumatic while Sam does not. How can you care for their divergent perceptions?
4. Spiritually, what might a stress-trauma continuum offer you that would help you to frame their experience theologically?
5. What themes from your tradition's sacred texts would you employ to speak to *both* Kim's and Sam's experiences?

Additional Thoughts for Consideration

In engaging case study 1, you might also reflect upon the following: how being a mixed-race family might impact Kim's and Sam's experiences; how religious and spiritual traditions approach forgiveness in both helpful and harmful ways; and how the myths of grief (i.e., grief as a linear, progressive journey; achieving closure; acceptable and unacceptable ways to grieve; etc.) interfere with expectations for coping with loss.

Case Study 2: Spiritually Integrated Psychotherapy

Andrew Reyes, a thirty-year-old, Catholic, Filipino American male, is a unit supply specialist in the US Army.[1] Reyes is tall, athletic, and takes pride in his appearance. He is responsible for managing ten soldiers and is well-respected by peers and his corporal. Three weeks after being deployed overseas, Reyes joined his buddies for drinks at a local bar. After a stressful day, he drank far more than intended and became quite inebriated. Mark Watson, a fellow army specialist, told their buddies he would look out for Reyes then left to escort him back to his sleeping quarters. Reyes considered Watson a friend and faithful counterpart. Upon entering Reyes's command launch unit, Watson raped and sodomized Reyes. As the assault ensued, Reyes blacked out. He remembers what happened, though everything is faint.

Following the event, Reyes did everything he could to avoid contact with Watson. He started drinking more, was less sociable, and seemed anxious around others. The soldiers whom Reyes manages noticed that his behavior had changed, and Reyes overheard one of them saying he seems "off his game." Reyes muddled through the remaining four weeks of his deployment and returned to the United States feeling dirty, guilty, and out-of-control.

Reyes considered reaching out to the Army Chaplain or the Military and Family Life Counseling Program, but he doesn't want to be perceived as weak or unable to manage his mental health. He decides to make an appointment with Dr. James Garcia, a spiritually integrated psychotherapist at St. Marks Roman Catholic Church. He doesn't really know what Dr. Garcia does or how his role differs from Father Mendoza's, but Reyes feels better about seeking help within the parish than within the Army.

1 This case study is adapted from a vignette published by the San Diego Military Family Collaborative, accessed March 28, 2024, https://sdmilitaryfamily.org/wp-content/uploads/2018/06/SDMFC-June-2018-Trauma-and-MST-Vignettes.pdf.

Reyes arrives at his appointment with Dr. Garcia and asks if it's possible to make the Sacrament of Reconciliation (Confession). Dr. Garcia tells Reyes that he is not a priest in the Roman Catholic tradition and cannot offer the Sacrament. Dr. Garcia explains that he is welcome to contact Father Mendoza or another priest and provides contact information. Sensing that Reyes is dysregulated, Dr. Garcia asks if he would perhaps like to talk a bit more. Reyes appears hesitant, and Dr. Garcia details the parameters of confidentiality. Seeming relieved, Reyes agrees that it would probably help to talk. Reyes tells Dr. Garcia that he did something "really stupid." Reyes shares how he drank too much and recalls what he can from the encounter with Watson.

Suggested Questions for Reflection

Imagine you are Dr. Garcia. As a spiritually integrated psychotherapist and a licensed professional counselor, you see clients at three area parishes, all located within thirty miles of a major Army base. Three years ago, you completed a three-day training on military sexual trauma (MST), and everything Reyes shares seems to reflect MST.

1. What are the pros and cons of sharing information about MST with Reyes?
2. What are the pros and cons of explaining a stress-trauma continuum to Reyes and offering it as a theoretical frame for his experience?
3. Reyes initially requested the Sacrament of Reconciliation. How can you ask about this in a way that elicits insight into his spiritual beliefs about and/or experiences with the ritual?
4. What could you ask to understand how Reyes's request for the Sacrament of Reconciliation relates to his experience of stress or trauma?

Additional Thoughts for Consideration

In engaging case study 2, you might also reflect upon the following: notions of confession as a narrative act; aspects of moral injury; harmful theological and cultural attitudes regarding male rape; and the potential for toxic masculinity in Reyes or Dr. Garcia.

Case Study 3: Nonprofit and Non-Governmental Organization Care

Everyday hundreds of displaced persons fleeing conflict from four neighboring African countries come through the doors of the global Christian faith-based non-governmental organization (NGO), CARE. CARE is responsible for medical clinics in the displacement camps where they operate. These clinics provide multiple types of support, including medical services and spiritual and psychological care. By its policy, the agency does not proselytize and offers general care to persons of any faith, or no faith. Many of the men, women, and children who come to the clinic have escaped harrowingly close calls with invading forces. Some have experienced sexual assault or seen loved ones killed in front of them. All have been forcibly displaced from their homes and endured the insecurity and hardships of a long journey.

You are the global director of spiritual well-being for CARE. The new CEO for CARE has tasked you with overhauling the training practices for employees who are responsible for providing spiritual support for persons who come through your clinics across the CARE global network. The CEO, himself a physician with an MBA and special training in nonprofit management, took the helm three months ago. He is familiar with post-traumatic stress disorder awareness trainings offered by other NGOs to refugees and internally displaced persons across the global network of camps in which they operate. He says to you, "These men, women, and children have experienced grave trauma. We need spiritual care training that prepares our field teams to provide trauma-based spiritual care practices. I would like for you to design a training program that stresses the impact of trauma on spiritual well-being and provide strategies of care for the field teams that will equip them to offer trauma spiritual first aid."

Suggested Questions for Reflection

1. How might you use concepts like a stress-trauma continuum and post-traumatic growth to expand how the director understands the needs of the refugees that their NGO cares for across the globe?
2. Recognizing that CARE provides resources to people from multiple cultures, sometimes within the same location, how can you best honor cultural customs and traditions while also incorporating

Western biomedical knowledge to inform your understanding of best practices for care where needed and relevant?

3. What spiritual themes from the Christian tradition that are also fundamental to the other Abrahamic or other religious traditions might undergird the ideas of hope and resilience in the face of suffering?
4. How could the workshop design incorporate ways of learning from the participants, especially around matters of culture and traditions?
5. What are the greatest benefits of a training that honors a stress-trauma continuum and other cultural wisdom and practices to:
   a. The NGO as a whole?
   b. Those working in the clinics and camps?
   c. The ultimate recipients of care, the refugees and internally displaced persons?

Additional Thoughts for Consideration

In engaging case study 3, you might also reflect upon the following: how the particular social structures of the Indigenous community inform who needs to be included in the workshop (i.e., the elders, the shamans or other spiritual healers, pastors, political leaders, etc.); how Indigenous laypersons can effectively be incorporated; and how the community's culture and gender biases inform whose stress and trauma is legitimate.

Case Study 4: Hospital Chaplaincy

Imani Moore and her ten-year-old daughter, Jameela, frequently ride their bicycles along a well-worn dirt path through the wooded area behind their home. This was a familiar post-dinner practice and an important time of mother-daughter bonding. One evening while the two were riding along the path, a large branch from a dead tree broke off and fell, striking both Imani and Jameela. A neighbor who lives near the path heard Imani's screams and ran to help them while calling 911. Both were injured, though Jameela took the brunt of the force from the branch which struck her head, instantly knocking her unconscious.

Imani and Jameela were both rushed to Good Samaritan Hospital, a Level 1 trauma center. Jameela was immediately taken into surgery to remove part of her skull to allow her brain to swell. She has suffered severe brain damage, is intubated, and in a medically induced coma. The surgery is complicated and may take six to eight hours. Jameela's prognosis is uncertain.

Imani sustained multiple contusions and two broken ribs but is otherwise unharmed. She was admitted for further monitoring of her neurological status and vital signs. She's had some difficulty breathing, which she attributes to her stress regarding Jameela's condition. To monitor her respiratory function and any delayed signs of a pulmonary contusion, Imani is required to remain in her room as the doctors continue to operate on Jameela. Imani is agitated and angry. She repeatedly tells the nurse that she needs to leave and go to the surgical waiting room.

As Imani's anger escalates, her breathing becomes more labored, and she assures the nurse that she feels "absolutely fine." "It's only because you won't let me go and see my baby," she says. Imani's nurse feels for her and asks the charge nurse if they can reach out to the attending physician. The charge nurse decides to call the Office of Spiritual Support and see if a chaplain can come and speak with Imani. Chaplain Cameron Locke receives the call and goes to Imani who immediately shares that she is Muslim and is "absolutely fine." But Allah has caused her daughter this trauma to test her, and Imani must seek Allah's guidance. She insists upon going to the surgical waiting room to pray and wait for the surgeon.

Suggested Questions for Reflection

Imagine you are Chaplain Locke. Imani is understandably distressed, and, for her own well-being, she needs to remain in her own hospital room for further monitoring. You assure Imani that the surgical team will speak with her as soon as possible. You ask if she would be willing to engage in a spiritually integrated deep breathing exercise that you think can help to regulate her breathing and her sympathetic nervous system. Imani consents, and after the ten-minute exercise she appears calmer.

1. What might you ask Imani to understand how she is narrating the incident?
2. Imani presents with trouble breathing, agitation, irritability, and anger. In considering both her physiological condition and the events

that occurred just four hours prior, what do you think about her presentation in relation to a stress-trauma continuum?

3. You realize that, in this moment, Imani epitomizes the myth of a strong Black woman, "a proud, no-nonsense woman who faces hardship with wisdom, but in the end, she must accept her fate."[2] Would this insight impact how you discuss the theological meaning she is making of the event? Why, or why not?

Additional Thoughts for Consideration

In engaging case study 4, you might also reflect upon the following: issues of medical racism and gaslighting; how medical establishments can pathologize appropriate emotional responses as overly-emotional, noncompliant, or hysterical; how the assessment of the case may differ if Chaplain Locke was cisgender male or cisgender female; and how breathwork and meditation are part of most major religious traditions, yet can be misunderstood as a psychospiritual fad.

---

2 Yvette Cozier, "POV: What 'Strong Black Woman' Means to Me," *BU Today,* accessed March 28, 2024, https://www.bu.edu/articles/2022/pov-what-strong-black-woman-means-to-me/.

BIBLIOGRAPHY

Introduction

American Psychiatric Association. *Diagnostic and Statistical Manual of Mental Disorders*, 5th ed., Text Revision. Washington, DC: American Psychiatric Association, 2022. https://doi.org/10.1176/appi.books.9780890425787.

Cole Jr., Allan Hugh. *Be Not Anxious: Pastoral Care of Disquieted Souls.* Grand Rapids, MI: Eerdmans, 2008.

Dulmus, Catherine N., and Carolyn Hilarski. "When Stress Constitutes Trauma and Trauma Constitutes Crisis: The Stress-Trauma-Crisis Continuum." *Brief Treatment and Crisis Intervention* 3, no. 1 (2003): 27–35. https://doi.org/10.1093/brief-treatment/mhg008.

Greider, Kathleen. "Religious Location and Counseling: Engaging Diversity and Difference in Views of Religion." In *Navigating Religious Difference in Spiritual Care and Counseling: Essays in Honor of Kathleen J. Greider*. Rev. ed. Edited by Jill L. Snodgrass, 17–53. Minneapolis: Fortress Press, 2024.

LaMothe, Ryan. *Care of Souls, Care of Polis: Toward a Political Pastoral Theology.* Eugene, OR: Cascade Books, 2017.

Petersen, Brooke N. *Religious Trauma: Queer Stories in Estrangement and Return*. Lanham, MD: Lexington Books, 2022.

Puhl, Louis J. *The Spiritual Exercises of St. Ignatius: Translation Based on Studies in the Language of the Autograph.* Chicago: Loyola Press, 2021.

Rambo, Shelly. *Spirit and Trauma: A Theology of Remaining.* Louisville, KY: Westminster John Knox Press, 2010.

———. *Resurrecting Wounds: Living in the Afterlife of Trauma.* Waco, TX: Baylor University Press, 2017.

Sanders, Cody J. *Christianity, LGBTQ Suicide, and the Souls of Queer Folk.* Lanham, MD: Lexington Books, 2020.

Scarry, Elaine. *The Body in Pain: The Making and Unmaking of the World.* New York: Oxford University Press, 1985.

Swain, Storm. *Trauma and Transformation at Ground Zero: A Pastoral Theology.* Minneapolis: Fortress Press, 2011.

———. "Embodied Coping in COVID 19 Crisis." YouTube video, 19:38. March 26, 2020. https://www.youtube.com/watch?v=a5QESAGOPJo.

Tillich, Paul. *Systematic Theology*. Vol. 1. Chicago: University of Chicago Press, 1951.

———. *The Courage to Be*. 2nd ed. New Haven, CT: Yale University Press, 2000.

Werdel, Mary Beth. *The Paradox of Trauma and Growth in Pastoral and Spiritual Care: Night Blooming*. Lanham, MD: Lexington Books, 2024.

Chapter 1: Psychospirituality and Trauma

Abrams, Zara. "Stress of Mass Shootings Causing Cascade of Collective Traumas." *Monitor on Psychology* 53, no. 6 (2022): 20. https://www.apa.org/monitor/2022/09/news-mass-shootings-collective-traumas.

American Psychiatric Association. *Diagnostic and Statistical Manual of Mental Disorders,* 5th ed., Text Revision. Washington, DC: American Psychiatric Association, 2022. https://doi.org/10.1176/appi.books.9780890425787.

Anda, Robert F., Laura E. Porter, and David W. Brown. "Inside the Adverse Childhood Experience Score: Strengths, Limitations, and Misapplications." *American Journal of Preventive Medicine* 59, no. 2 (2020): 293–295. https://doi.org/10.1016/j.amepre.2020.01.009.

Barbour, Ian. *Religion and Science*. San Fransisco: HarperSanFrancisco, 1990.

Bennett, Jessica. "If Everything is 'Trauma,' is Anything?" *New York Times*, February 4, 2022. https://www.nytimes.com/2022/02/04/opinion/caleb-love-bombing-gaslighting-trauma.html.

Blake, Michelle. "U.S. Children Carry a Double Burden for Gun Violence and Policy Gaps." *Newsweek*, August 8, 2022. https://www.newsweek.com/us-children-carry-double-burden-gun-violence-policy-gaps-opinion-1730617.

Bonanno, George A., and Anthony D. Mancini. "Beyond Resilience and PTSD: Mapping the Heterogeneity of Responses to Potential Trauma." *Psychological Trauma: Theory, Research, Practice, and Policy* 4, no. 1 (2012): 74–83. https://doi.org/10.1037/a0017829.

Bracken, Patrick. *Trauma: Culture, Meaning & Philosophy*. Hoboken, NJ: Wiley, 2002.

Bueckert, Laura D., and Daniel S. Schipani. "Interfaith Spiritual Caregiving: The Case for Language Care." In *Spiritual Caregiving in the Hospital: Windows to Chaplaincy Ministry*, 245–263. Kitchener, ON: Pandora Press, 2006.

Crocq, Marc-Antoine, and Louis Crocq. "From Shell Shock and War Neurosis to Posttraumatic Stress Disorder: A History of Psychotraumatology."

Dialogues in Clinical Neuroscience 2, no. 1 (2000): 47–55. https://doi.org/10.31887/DCNS.2000.2.1/macrocq.

Danieli, Yael, Editor. *International Handbook of Multigenerational Legacies of Trauma.* New York: Plenum Press, 1998.

Davis, Joseph E. *Chemically Imbalanced: Everyday Suffering, Medication, and Our Troubled Quest for Self-Mastery.* Chicago: University of Chicago Press, 2020.

Doehring, Carrie. "The Challenges of Being Bilingual: Methods of Integrating Psychological and Religious Studies." In *Understanding Pastoral Counseling*, edited by Elizabeth A. Maynard and Jill L. Snodgrass, 87–99. New York: Springer, 2015.

———. "Spiritual Care after Violence: Growing from Trauma with Lived-Theology." Biola University Center for Christian Thought. *The Table*, June 23, 2014. https://cct.biola.edu/spiritual-care-violence-growing-trauma-lived-theology/.

Dulmus, Catherine N., and Carolyn Hilarski. "When Stress Constitutes Trauma and Trauma Constitutes Crisis: The Stress-Trauma-Crisis Continuum." *Brief Treatment and Crisis Intervention* 3, no. 1 (2003): 27–35. https://doi.org/10.1093/brief-treatment/mhg008.

Dyer, Bryan R. "'A Great Conflict Full of Suffering': Suffering in the Epistle to the Hebrews in Light of Feminist Concerns." *McMaster Journal of Theology and Ministry* 12 (2010–2011): 179–198. http://www.mcmaster.ca.proxy-ln.researchport.umd.edu/mjtm/.

Elazar, Daniel J. "Jacob and Esau and the Emergence of the Jewish People." *Judaism* 43, no. 3 (1994): 294–301.

Farley, Edward. *Good and Evil: Interpreting a Human Condition*. Minneapolis: Fortress Press, 1990.

Fassin, Didier, and Richard Rechtman. *The Empire of Trauma: An Inquiry into the Condition of Victimhood.* Translated by Rachel Gomme. Princeton, NJ: Princeton University Press, 2009.

Frueh, B. Christopher, Jon D. Elhai, Anouk L. Grubaugh, Jeannine Monnier, Todd B. Kashdan, Julie A. Sauvageot, Mark B. Hamner, B. G. Burket, and George W. Arana. "Documented Combat Exposure of US Veterans Seeking Treatment for Combat-Related Post-Traumatic Stress Disorder." *British Journal of Psychiatry* 186, no. 6 (2005): 467–472. https://doi.org/10.1192/bjp.186.6.467.

Goto, Toyomi, and John P. Wilson. "A Review of the History of Traumatic Stress Studies in Japan: From Traumatic Neurosis to PTSD." *Trauma, Violence, & Abuse* 4, no. 3 (2003): 195–209. https://doi.org/10.1177/1524838003004003001.

Greider, Kathleen. "Religious Location and Counseling: Engaging Diversity and Difference in Views of Religion." In *Navigating Religious Difference in Spiritual Care and Counseling: Essays in Honor of Kathleen J. Greider*, edited by Jill L. Snodgrass, 11–44. Claremont: Claremont Press, 2019.

Harris, Maxine, and Roger D. Fallot. "Envisioning a Trauma-Informed Service System: A Vital Paradigm Shift." In *Using Trauma Theory to Design Service Systems*, edited by Maxine Harris and Roger D. Fallot, 3–22. Hoboken, NJ: Jossey-Bass/Wiley, 2001.

Herman, Judith. *Trauma and Recovery: The Aftermath of Violence—From Domestic Abuse to Political Terror*. New York: Basic Books, 1992.

Hillstrom, Christa. "The Hidden Epidemic of Brain Injuries from Domestic Violence." *New York Times Magazine*, March 1, 2022. https://www.nytimes.com/2022/03/01/magazine/brain-trauma-domestic-violence.html.

Holton, M. Jan. *Building the Resilient Community: Lessons from the Lost Boys of Sudan*. Eugene, OR: Cascade Books, 2011.

hooks, bell. *Teaching to Transgress: Education as the Practice of Freedom*. New York: Routledge, 1994.

Krupnik, Valery. "Trauma or Adversity?" *Traumatology* 25, no. 4 (2019): 256–261. http://dx.doi.org/10.1037/trm0000169.

LA Blade Digital Staff. "Trauma and Suicide Risk among LGBTQ+ Youth; New Study Released." *LA Blade*, July 29, 2022. https://www.losangelesblade.com/2022/07/29/trauma-and-suicide-risk-among-lgbtq-youth-new-study-released/.

Lowe, Sarah R., and Sandro Galea. "The Mental Health Consequences of Mass Shootings." *Trauma, Violence, & Abuse* 18, no. 1 (2015): 62–82. https://doi.org/10.1177/1524838015591572.

Marsella, Anthony J., Matthew J. Friedman, Ellen T. Gerrity, and Raymond M. Scurfield. "Ethnocultural Aspects of PTSD: Some Closing Thoughts." In *Ethnocultural Aspects of Posttraumatic Stress Disorder: Issues, Research, and Clinical Applications*, edited by Anthony J. Marsella, Matthew J. Friedman, Ellen T. Gerrity, and Raymond M. Scurfield, 529–538. Washington, DC: American Psychological Association, 1996.

McIntosh, Roger, Gail Ironson, and Neal Krause. "Keeping Hope Alive: Racial-Ethnic Disparities in Distress Tolerance are Mitigated by Religious/Spiritual Hope among Black Americans." *Journal of Psychosomatic Research* 144, no. 110403 (2021). https://doi.org/10.1016/j.jpsychores.2021.110403.

Menakem, Resmaa. *My Grandmother's Hands: Racialized Trauma and the Pathway to Mending Our Hearts and Bodies*. Las Vegas, NV: Central Recovery Press, 2017.

Moore, Elena. "The First Gen Z Candidates Are Running for Congress—and Running against Compromise." All Things Considered. *National Public Radio*, July 6, 2022. https://www.npr.org/2022/07/06/1109193929/the-first-gen-z-candidates-are-running-for-congress-and-running-against-compromi.

Nichter, Mark. "Idioms of Distress: Alternatives in the Expression of Psychosocial Distress—A Case Study from South India." *Culture, Medicine and Psychiatry* 5, no. 4 (1981): 379–408. https://doi.org/10.1007/BF00054782.

Pinderhughes, Ellen. "The Multigenerational Transmission of Loss and Trauma: The African-American Experience." In *Living Beyond Loss: Death in the Family*, 2nd ed., edited by Froma Walsh and Monica McGoldrick, 161–181. New York: W. W. Norton, 2004.

Snodgrass, Jill L. "Pastoral Counseling: A Discipline of Unity Amid Diversity." In *Understanding Pastoral Counseling*, edited by Elizabeth A. Maynard and Jill L. Snodgrass, 1–16. New York: Springer, 2015.

Spoont, Michelle R., Nina Sayer, Greta Friedmann-Sanchez, Louise E. Parker, Maureen Murdoch, and Christine Chiros. "From Trauma to PTSD: Beliefs About Sensations, Symptoms, and Mental Illness." *Qualitative Health Research* 19, no. 10 (2009): 1456–1465. https://doi.org/10.1177/1049732309348370.

Stevenson-Moessner, Jeanne. "The Road to Perfection: An Interpretation of Suffering in Hebrews." *Interpretation* 57 (2003): 280–290. https://link.gale.com/apps/doc/A105160684/AONE?u=googlescholar&sid=googleScholar&xid=23be684a.

Stone, Howard W., James O. Duke. *How to Think Theologically*, 3rd ed. Minneapolis: Fortress Press, 2013.

Summerfield, Derek. "A Critique of Seven Assumptions Behind Psychological Trauma Programmes in War-Affected Areas." *Social Science and Medicine* 45, no. 10 (1999): 1449–1462. https://doi.org/10.1016/s0277-9536(98)00450-x.

Swinton, John. *Raging with Compassion: Pastoral Responses to the Problem of Evil.* Grand Rapids, MI: Eerdmans, 2007.

Thornton, Tim. "Cross-Cultural Psychiatry and Validity in DSM-5." In *The Palgrave Handbook of Sociocultural Perspectives on Global Mental Health*, edited by Ross G. White, Sumeet Jain, David M. R. Orr, and Ursula Read, 51–69. New York: Palgrave Macmillan/Springer Nature, 2017.

Thurman, Howard. *Jesus and the Disinherited.* Nashville, TN: Abingdon-Cokesbury Press, 1949. Reprint New York: Beacon, 1996.

Tillich, Paul. *Systematic Theology*. Vol. 1. Chicago: University of Chicago Press, 1951.

Townsend, Loren. *Introduction to Pastoral Counseling*. Nashville, TN: Abingdon Press, 2009.

US Department of Health & Human Services. *US Surgeon General Issues Advisory on Youth Mental Health Crisis Further Exposed by COVID-19 Pandemic*. Washington, DC: GPO, 2021. https://www.hhs.gov/about/news/2021/12/07/us-surgeon-general-issues-advisory-on-youth-mental-health-crisis-further-exposed-by-covid-19-pandemic.html.

van der Kolk, Bessel A., Susan Roth, David Pelcovitz, Susanne Sunday, and Joseph Spinazzola. "Disorders of Extreme Stress: The Empirical Foundation of a Complex Adaptation to Trauma." *Journal of Traumatic Stress* 18, no. 5 (2005): 389–399. https://doi.org/10.1002/jts.20047.

Vaish, Amrisha, Tobias Grossmann, and Amanda Woodward. "Not All Emotions Are Created Equal: The Negativity Bias in Social-Emotional Development." *Psychological Bulletin* 134, no. 3 (2008): 383–403. https://doi.10.1037/0033-2909.134.3.383.

Walker, Jenny. "Suffering with Christ." *Tabletalk* 53 (2020). https://tabletalkmagazine.com/article/2020/10/suffering-with-christ/.

Werdel, Mary Beth, and Robert J. Wicks. *Primer in Posttraumatic Growth: An Introduction and Guide*. Hoboken, NJ: Wiley, 2012.

White, Ross G., Sumeet Jain, David M. R. Orr, and Ursula Reed, eds. *The Palgrave Handbook of Sociocultural Perspectives on Global Mental Health*. New York: Palgrave Macmillan/Springer Nature, 2017.

Chapter 2: A Womanist Psychospirituality

American Association of University Women. *Systemic Racism and the Gender Pay Gap: A Supplement to the Simple Truth*. Washington, DC: American Association of University Women, 2021. https://www.aauw.org/app/uploads/2021/07/SimpleTruth_4.0-1.pdf.

American Psychological Association. "Stress." *APA Dictionary of Psychology*. Washington, DC: American Psychological Association, 2022. https://dictionary.apa.org/stress.

Anderson, Riana Elyse, and Howard C. Stevenson. "RECASTing Racial Stress and Trauma: Theorizing the Healing Potential of Racial Socialization in Families." *American Psychologist* 74, no. 1 (January 2019): 63–75. http://doi.org/10.1037/amp0000392.

Ashley, Wendy. "The Angry Black Woman: The Impact of Pejorative Stereotypes on Psychotherapy with Black Women." *Social Work in Public*

Health 29, no. 1 (2014): 27–34. http://doi.org/10.1080/19371918.2011.619449.

Banks, Martha E., and Stephanie Lee. "Womanism and Spirituality/Theology." In *Womanist and Mujerista Psychologies: Voices of Fire, Acts of Courage*, edited by Thema Bryant-Davis and Lillian Comas-Díaz, 123–148. Washington, DC: American Psychological Association, 2016.

Barlow, Jameta Nicole. "Black Women, the Forgotten Survivors of Sexual Assault." *American Psychological Association*, February 1, 2020. https://www.apa.org/pi/about/newsletter/2020/02/black-women-sexual-assault.

Bryant-Davis, Thema and Lillian Comas-Díaz, eds. *Womanist and Mujerista Psychologies: Voices of Fire, Acts of Courage.* Washington, DC: American Psychological Association, 2016.

Bryant-Davis, Thema, Bemi Fasalojo, Ana Arounian, Kirsten L. Jackson, and Egypt Leithman. "Resist and Rise: A Trauma-Informed Womanist Model for Group Therapy." *Women & Therapy* (July 2021). http://doi.org/10.1080/02703149.2021.1943114.

Carter, Robert T. "Racism and Psychological and Emotional Injury: Recognizing and Assessing Race-Based Traumatic Stress." *The Counseling Psychologist* 35, no. 1 (2007): 13–105. http://doi.org/10.1177/0011000006292033.

Chapman Lape, Jessica. "A Pandemic of Mistreatment: Theories, Practices, and Convergences in Womanist Clinical Pastoral Theology and Black Maternal Healthcare Curing Covid-19." *Journal of Pastoral Theology* 31, no. 2–3 (2021): 128–144. https://doi.org/10.1080/10649867.2021.1929712.

Coleman, Monica A. *Making a Way Out of No Way: A Womanist Theology.* Minneapolis: Fortress Press, 2008.

Collins, Patricia Hill. *Black Feminist Thought: Knowledge, Consciousness, and the Politics of Empowerment.* New York: Routledge, 2000.

Crumpton, Stephanie M. *A Womanist Pastoral Theology against Intimate and Cultural Violence.* London: Palgrave Macmillan, 2014.

Drake-Burnette, Danielle, BraVada Garrett-Akinsanya, and Thema Bryant-Davis. "Womanism, Creativity, and Resistance: Making a Way Out of 'No Way.'" In *Womanist and Mujerista Psychologies: Voices of Fire, Acts of Courage*, edited by Thema Bryant-Davis and Lillian Comas-Díaz, 173–194. Washington, DC: American Psychological Association, 2016. https://doi.org/10.1037/14937-008.

Essed, Philomena. *Understanding Everyday Racism: An Interdisciplinary Theory.* Thousand Oaks, CA: Sage, 1991.

Fins, Amanda. *National Snapshot: Poverty among Women & Families*. Washington, DC: National Women's Law Center, 2020. https://nwlc.org/wp-content/uploads/2020/12/PovertySnapshot2020.pdf.

Hamel, Liz, Lunna Lopes, Cailey Muñana, Samantha Artiga, and Mollyann Brodie. *Race, Health, and Covid-19: The Views and Experiences of Black Americans*. San Francisco, CA: Kaiser Family Foundation, 2020. https://files.kff.org/attachment/Report-Race-Health-and-COVID-19-The-Views-and-Experiences-of-Black-Americans.pdf.

Harrell, Shelly P. "A Multidimensional Conceptualization of Racism-related Stress: Implications for the Well-Being of People of Color." *American Journal of Orthopsychiatry* 70, no. 1 (2000): 42–57. https://doi.org/10.1037/h0087722.

Ingrey, Jennifer C. "Gender oppression." In *The Wiley Blackwell Encyclopedia of Gender and Sexuality Studies*, edited by Wai Ching Angela Wong, Maithree Wickramasinghe, Renée C. Hoogland, and Nancy A. Naples, 353–366. Hoboken, NJ: Wiley, 2016. https://doi.org/10.1002/9781118663219.wbegss324.

Lowcountry Digital History Initiative. "Hidden Voices: Enslaved Women in the Lowcountry and U.S. South." Charleston: Lowcountry Digital History Initiative. https://ldhi.library.cofc.edu/exhibits/show/hidden-voices/resisting-enslavement/reproduction-and-resistance.

Motro, Daphna, Jonathan B. Evans, Aleksander P.J. Ellis, and Lehman Benson, III. "The 'Angry Black Woman' Stereotype at Work." *Harvard Business Review*, January 31, 2022. https://hbr.org/2022/01/the-angry-black-woman-stereotype-at-work.

Nabors, Nina A., and Melanie F. Pettee. "Womanist Therapy with African American Women with Disabilities." *Women & Therapy* 26, no. 3–4 (2003): 331–341. https://doi.org/10.1300/J015v26n03_10.

National Center on Violence Against Women in the Black Community. *Black Women and Sexual Assault*. Washington, DC: National Center on Violence Against Women in the Black Community, 2018. https://ujimacommunity.org/wp-content/uploads/2018/12/Ujima-Womens-Violence-Stats-v7.4-1.pdf.

Neville, Helen A., and Alex L. Pieterse. "Racism, White Supremacy, and Resistance: Contextualizing Black American Experiences." In *Handbook of African American Psychology*, edited by Helen A. Neville, Brendesha M. Tynes, and Shawn O. Utsey, 159–174. Thousand Oaks, CA: Sage, 2009.

New York Times. "The Slave Tragеoy in Cincinnati." February 2, 1856. https://www.nytimes.com/1856/02/02/archives/the-slave-trageoy-in-cincinnati.html.

Owens, Donna M. "Breonna Taylor and Hundreds of Black Women Have Died at the Hands of Police. The Movement to Say Their Names is Growing." *USA Today*, March 11, 2021. https://www.usatoday.com/in-depth/news/investigations/2021/03/11/sayhername-movement-black-women-police-violence/6921197002/.

Ricks, Shawn Arango. "Normalized Chaos: Black Feminism, Womanism, and the (Re)definition of Trauma and Healing." *Meridians* 16, no. 2 (2018): 343–350. https://doi.org/10.2979/meridians.16.2.15.

Ross, Loretta. J. "Trust Black Women: Reproductive Justice and Eugenics." In *Radical Reproductive Justice: Foundations, Theory, Practice, Critique*, edited by Loretta J. Ross, Lynn Roberts, Erika Derkas, Whitney Peoples, and Pamela Bridgewater Toure, 58–85. New York: Feminist Press at the City University of New York, 2017.

Sanchez-Hucles, Janis V. "Womanist Therapy with Black Women." In *Womanist and Mujerista Psychologies: Voices of Fire, Acts of Courage*, edited by Thema Bryant-Davis and Lillian Comas-Díaz, 69–92. Washington, DC: American Psychological Association, 2016.

Walker-Barnes, Chanequa. *Too Heavy a Yoke: Black Women and the Burden of Strength*. Eugene, OR: Cascade Books, 2014.

Washington, Harriet A. *Medical Apartheid: The Dark History of Medical Experimentation on Black Americans from Colonial Times to the Present.* New York: Harlem Moon, 2006.

Westfield, N. Lynne. *Dear Sisters: A Womanist Practice of Hospitality.* Cleveland, OH: Pilgrim Press, 2007.

Williams, Delores S. *Sisters in the Wilderness: The Challenge of Womanist God-talk.* Maryknoll, NY: Orbis Books, 1993.

Chapter 3: The Psychospiritual Trauma of LGBTQ+ People and Communities

American Civil Liberties Union. "Mapping Attacks on LGBTQ Rights in U.S. State Legislatures in 2023." December 21, 2023. https://www.aclu.org/legislative-attacks-on-lgbtq-rights-2023.

Barba, Antonia, Megan A. Mooney, Kalie Giovanni, Megan Clarke, Jennifer Brizzie Grady, and J.A. Cohen. *Identifying the Intersection of Trauma and Sexual Orientation and Gender Identity Part I: Key Considerations.*

Los Angeles: National Child Traumatic Stress Network, 2021. https://www.nctsn.org/resources/identifying-the-intersection-of-trauma-and-sexual-orientation-and-gender-identity-key-considerations.

Brison, Susan J. *Aftermath: Violence and the Remaking of a Self.* Princeton, NJ: Princeton University Press, 2002.

Butler, Catherine, and Angela Byrne. "Queer in Practice: Therapy and Queer Theory." In *Feeling Queer or Queer Feelings? Radical Approaches to Counselling Sex, Sexualities and Genders*, edited by Lyndsey Moon, 89–105. London: Routledge, 2008.

Caruth, Cathy. "Recapturing the Past: Introduction." In *Trauma: Explorations in Memory*, edited by Cathy Caruth, 151–157. Baltimore, MD: Johns Hopkins University Press, 1995.

Choi, Soon Kyu, Bianca D. M. Wilson, Jama Shelton, and Gary Gates. *Serving Our Youth 2015: The Needs and Experiences of Lesbian, Gay, Bisexual, Transgender, and Questioning Youth Experiencing Homelessness.* Los Angeles: The Williams Institute with True Colors Fund, 2015. https://williamsinstitute.law.ucla.edu/wp-content/uploads/Serving-Our-Youth-Update-Jun-2015.pdf.

Crawley, Ashon T. *Blackpentecostal Breath: The Aesthetics of Possibility.* New York: Fordham University Press, 2017.

Cvetkovich, Ann. *An Archive of Feelings: Trauma, Sexuality, and Lesbian Public Cultures.* Durham, NC: Duke University Press, 2003.

Di Nicola, Vincenzo. "Two Trauma Communities: A Philosophical Archaeology of Cultural and Clinical Trauma Theories." In *Trauma and Transcendence: Suffering and the Limits of Theory*, edited by Eric Boynton and Peter Capretto, 17–52. New York: Fordham University Press, 2018. https://doi.org/10.1515/9780823280292-002.

Dulmus, Catherine N., and Carolyn Hilarski. "When Stress Constitutes Trauma and Trauma Constitutes Crisis: The Stress-Trauma-Crisis Continuum." *Brief Treatment and Crisis Intervention* 3, no. 1 (2003): 27–35. https://doi.org/10.1093/brief-treatment/mhg008.

Edelman, Lee. *No Future: Queer Theory and the Death Drive.* Durham, NC: Duke University Press, 2004.

Erikson, Kai. "Notes on Trauma and Community." In *Trauma: Explorations in Memory*, edited by Cathy Caruth, 183–199. Baltimore, MD: Johns Hopkins University Press, 1995.

Felitti, Vincent J., Robert F. Anda, Dale Nordenberg, David F. Williamson, Alison M. Spitz, Valerie Edwards, Mary P. Koss, and James S. Marks. "Relationship of Childhood Abuse and Household Dysfunction to Many of the Leading Causes of Death in Adults: The Adverse

Childhood Experiences (ACE) Study." *American Journal of Preventive Medicine* 14, no. 4 (1998): 245–258. https://doi.org/10.1016/s0749-3797(98)00017-8.

Freeman, Elizabeth. *Time Binds: Queer Temporalities, Queer Histories.* Durham, NC: Duke University Press, 2010.

Freeman, Mark. *Hindsight: The Promise and Peril of Looking Backward.* Oxford: Oxford University Press, 2010.

Freud, Sigmund. "A Letter to an American Mother." *American Journal of Psychiatry* 105 (1935/1951): 786–787. https://doi.org/10.1176/ajp.107.10.786.

Fuss, Diana. "Pink Freud." *GLQ: A Journal of Lesbian and Gay Studies* 2 (1995): 1–9. https://doi.org/10.1215/10642684-2-1_and_2-1.

Griffin, Horace L. *Their Own Receive Them Not: African American Lesbians and Gays in Black Churches.* Cleveland, OH: Pilgrim Press, 2006.

Human Rights Campaign Staff. "For the First Time Ever, Human Rights Campaign Officially Declares 'State of Emergency' for LGBTQ+ Americans; Issues National Warning and Guidebook to Ensure Safety for LGBTQ+ Residents and Travelers.". June 6, 2023. https://www.hrc.org/press-releases/for-the-first-time-ever-human-rights-campaign-officially-declares-state-of-emergency-for-lgbtq-americans-issues-national-warning-and-guidebook-to-ensure-safety-for-lgbtq-residents-and-travelers.

Janssen, Dirk-Jan, and Peer Scheepers. "How Religiosity Shapes Rejection of Homosexuality Across the Globe." *Journal of Homosexuality* 66, no. 14 (2019): 1974–2001. https://doi.org/10.1080/00918369.2018.1522809.

Keeling, Kara. *Queer Times, Black Futures.* New York: New York University Press, 2019.

Kerr, Michael E., and Murray Bowen. *Family Evaluation.* New York: W. W. Norton, 1988.

Kosciw, Joseph G., Emily A. Gretak, Adrian D. Zongrone, Caitlin M. Clark, and Nhan L. Truong. *The 2017 National School Climate Survey: The Experiences of Lesbian, Gay, Bisexual, Transgender, and Queer Youth in Our Nation's Schools.* New York: GLSEN, 2018. https://www.glsen.org/sites/default/files/2019-10/GLSEN-2017-National-School-Climate-Survey-NSCS-Full-Report.pdf.

Lester, Andrew D. *Hope in Pastoral Care and Counseling.* Louisville, KY: Westminster John Knox Press, 1995.

Lothian, Alexis. *Old Futures: Speculative Fiction and Queer Possibility.* New York: New York University Press, 2018.

Meyer, Ilan H. "Prejudice, Social Stress, and Mental Health in Lesbian, Gay, and Bisexual Populations: Conceptual Issues and Research Evidence." *Psychological Bulletin*, 129, no. 5 (2003): 674–697. https://doi.org/10.1037/0033-2909.129.5.674.

Meyer, Ilan H., and David M. Frost. "Minority Stress and the Health of Sexual Minorities." In *Handbook of Psychology and Sexual Orientation*, edited by Charlotte J. Patterson and Anthony R. D'Augelli, 252–266. Oxford: Oxford University Press, 2013.

Miller-Karas, Elaine. *Building Resilience to Trauma: The Trauma and Community Resiliency Models*. New York: Routledge, 2015.

Miller-McLemore, Bonnie J. "The Living Human Web." In *Images of Pastoral Care: Classic Readings*, edited by Robert C. Dykstra, 40–46. St. Louis, MO: Chalice Press, 2005.

Mitchell, Stephen A., and Margaret J. Black. *Freud and Beyond: A History of Modern Psychoanalytic Thought*. New York: Basic Books, 2016.

Muñoz, José Esteban. *Cruising Utopia: The Then and There of Queer Futurity*. New York: New York University Press, 2009.

Mustanski, Brian S., Robert Garofalo, and Erin M. Emerson. "Mental Health Disorders, Psychological Distress, and Suicidality in a Diverse Sample of Lesbian, Gay, Bisexual, and Transgender Youths." *American Journal of Public Health* 100, no. 12 (2010): 2426–2432. https://doi.org/10.2105/ AJPH.2009.178319.

Nelson, Hilde Lindemann. *Damaged Identities, Narrative Repair*. Ithaca, NY: Cornell University Press, 2001.

Pew Research Center. *A Survey of LGBT Americans: Attitudes, Experiences and Values in Changing Times*. Washington, DC: Pew Research Center, 2013. https://www.pewresearch.org/social-trends/2013/06/13/a-survey-of-lgbt-americans/.

Ratcliffe, Matthew, Mark Ruddell, and Benedict Smith. "What is a 'Sense of Foreshortened Future?' A Phenomenological Study of Trauma, Trust, and Time." *Frontiers in Psychology* 5 (2014): 1–11. https://doi.org/10.3389/fpsyg.2014.01026.

Rooney, Caitlin, and Laura E. Durso. *The Harms of Refusing Service to LGBTQ People and Other Marginalized Communities*. November 29, 2017. Washington, DC: Center for American Progress. https://www.americanprogress.org/article/harms-refusing-service-lgbtq-people-marginalized-communities/.

Root, Maria P. P. "Reconstructing the Impact of Trauma on Personality." In *Personality and Psychopathology: Feminist Reappraisals*, edited by Laura S. Brown and Mary Ballou, 229–266. New York: Guilford Press, 1992.

Rose, Gillian. *Judaism and Modernity: Philosophical Essays*. London: Verso, 2017.

Rosky, Clifford. "Anti-Gay Curriculum Laws." *Columbia Law Review* 117, no. 8 (2017): 1461–1522. https://columbialawreview.org/content/anti-gay-curriculum-laws/.

Rubenstein, Mary-Jane. "Afterword—The Transcendence of Trauma: Prospects for the Continental Philosophy of Religion." In *Trauma and Transcendence: Suffering and the Limits of Theory*, edited by Eric Boynton and Peter Capretto, 283–294. New York: Fordham University Press, 2018.

Sanders, Cody J. *Christianity, LGBTQ Suicide, and the Souls of Queer Folk*. Lanham, MD: Lexington Books, 2020.

Sedgwick, Eve Kosofsky. *Epistemology of the Closet*. Oakland, CA: University of California Press, 2008.

Servigne, Pablo, Raphaël Stevens, and Gauthier Chapelle. *Another End of the World is Possible: Living the Collapse*. Medford, MA: Polity Press, 2021.

Stanley, Elizabeth A. *Widen the Window: Training Your Brain and Body to Thrive During Stress and Recover from Trauma*. New York: Penguin Random House, 2019.

The Trevor Project. *National Survey on LGBTQ Youth Mental Health 2022*. West Hollywood, CA: The Trevor Project, 2022. https://www.thetrevorproject.org/survey-2022/assets/static/trevor01_2022survey_final.pdf.

van der Kolk, Bessel A. *The Body Keeps the Score: Brain, Mind, and Body in the Healing of Trauma*. New York: Penguin Books, 2014.

van der Kolk, Bessel A., Alexander C. McFarlane, and Lars Weisaeth, eds. *Traumatic Stress: The Effects of Overwhelming Experience on Mind, Body, and Society*. New York: The Guilford Press, 2007.

Chapter 4: Ontological Psychospirituality

Agamben, Giorgio. *Potentialities: Collected Essays in Philosophy*. Translated by Daniel Heller-Roazen. Redwood City, CA: Stanford University Press, 1999.

———. *The Open: Man and Animal*. Translated by Kevin Attell. Redwood City, CA: Stanford University Press, 2004.

———. *What is an Apparatus? And Other Essays*. Redwood City, CA: Stanford University Press, 2009.

Alford, Fred. *Trauma and Forgiveness: Consequences and Community*. Cambridge: Cambridge University Press, 2013.

Amery, Jean. "Torture." In *Art from the Ashes*, edited by Lawrence Langer. Oxford: Oxford University Press, 1995.

Andrianova, Anastassiya. "Narrating Animal Trauma in Bulgakov and Tolstoy." *Humanities* 5, no. 4 (2016): 84. https://doi.org/10.3390/h5040084.

Antal, Jim. *Climate Church, Climate World: How People of Faith Must Work for Change*. Washington, DC: Rowman & Littlefield, 2018.

Boer, Roland. *Criticism of Heaven: On Marxism and Theology*. Chicago: Haymarket Books, 2009.

Bromberg, Philip. "Treating Patients with Symptoms—and Symptoms with Patience." *Psychoanalytic Dialogues* 11, no. 6 (2001): 891–912.

Brown, Wendy. *Walled States, Waning Sovereignty*. New York: Zone Books, 2010.

Caruth, Cathy. *Unclaimed Experience: Trauma, Narrative, and History*. Baltimore, MD: Johns Hopkins University Press, 1996.

———. *Listening to Trauma: Conversations with Leaders in the Theory and Treatment of Catastrophic Experience*. Baltimore, MD: Johns Hopkins University Press, 2014.

Colebrook, Claire, and Jason Maxwell. *Agamben*. Cambridge, MA: Polity Press, 2016.

Coleman, Athena. "Corporeal Schemas and Body Images: Fanon, Merleau-Ponty, and the Lived Experience of Race." In *Fanon, Phenomenology, and Psychology*. Edited by Leswin Laubscher, Derek Hook, and Miraj U. Desai, 127–138. Oxfordshire: Routledge, 2022.

Crockett, Clayton. *Radical Political Theology*. New York: Columbia University Press, 2012.

Crutzen, Paul, and Eugene Stoermer. "The 'Anthropocene.'" *IGB Global Change Newsletter* 41 (2000): 17–18.

Darwin, Charles. *The Expression of Emotions in Man and Animals*. London: Penguin Classics, 2009.

Des Pres, Terrence. *The Survivor*. Oxford: Oxford University Press, 1976.

Dickinson, Colby. "The Absence of Gender." In *Agamben's Coming Philosophy: Finding a New Use for Theology*, edited by Colby Dickinson and Adam Kotsko, 167–182. Washington, DC: Rowman & Littlefield, 2015.

Fassin, Didier, and Richard Rechtman. *The Empire of Trauma: An Inquiry into the Condition of Victimhood*. Princeton, NJ: Princeton University Press, 2009.

Ferdowsian, Hope, and Debra Merskin. "Parallels in Sources of Trauma, Pain, Distress, and Suffering in Humans and Nonhuman Animals."

Journal of Trauma and Dissociation 12, no. 4 (2012): 448–468. https://doi.org/10.1080/15299732.2011.652346.

Fonagy, Peter. *Attachment Theory and Psychoanalysis*. New York: Other Press, 2001.

Fonagy, Peter, and Mary Target. "Attachment and Reflective Function: Their Role in Self-organization." *Development and Psychopathology* 9, no. 4 (1997): 679–700. https://doi.org/10.1017/S0954579497001399.

Freyd, Jennifer. *Betrayal Trauma*. Cambridge, MA: Harvard University Press, 1996.

Gergely, György, and Zsolt Unoka. "Attachment and Mentalization in Infants." In *Mind to Mind: Infant Research, Neuroscience, and Psychoanalysis*, edited by Sharone Berger, Elliot Jurist, and Arietta Slade, 50–87. New York: Other Press, 2008.

Grand, Sue. *The Reproduction of Evil*. Hillsdale, NJ: Analytic Press, 2000.

Gray, John. *The Silence of Animals*. New York: Farrar, Straus, and Giroux, 2013.

Holmes, Jeremy. *Attachment, Intimacy, Autonomy*. New York: Jason Aronson, 1996.

Holznagel, Hans. "Dire Climate Report Prompts Call for Church Action; UCC Offers Ways to Respond." Last Modified March 7, 2022. https://www.ucc.org/dire-climate-report-prompts-call-for-church-action-ucc-offers-ways-to-respond/.

Janoff-Bulman, Ronnie. *Shattered Assumptions: Towards a New Psychology of Trauma*. Washington, DC: Free Press, 1992.

Johnson, Mark. *The Body in the Mind: The Bodily Basis of Meaning, Imagination, and Reason*. Chicago: University of Chicago Press, 1987.

Keltz, Kyle. *Thomism and the Problem of Animal Suffering*. Eugene, OR: Wipf & Stock, 2020.

Klein, Naomi. *This Changes Everything: Capitalism vs. the Climate*. New York: Simon and Schuster, 2014.

Kolbert, Elizabeth. *The Sixth Extinction: An Unnatural History*. New York: Henry Holt, 2014.

Kompridis, Nikolas. Nonhuman Agency and Human Normativity." In *Nature and Value*, edited by Akeel Bilgrami, 240–260. New York: Columbia University Press, 2020.

Lakoff, George, and Mark Johnson. *Philosophy in the Flesh: The Embodied Mind and its Challenges to Western Thought*. New York: Basic Books, 1999.

LaMothe, Ryan. "The Absence of Cure: The Core of Malignant Trauma and Symbolization." *Journal of Interpersonal Violence* 14, no. 11 (1999): 1193–1210. https://doi.org/10.1177/088626099014011005.

———. *A Radical Political Theology for the Anthropocene Age*. Eugene, OR: Cascade, 2021.

Layton, Lynne. *Toward a Social Psychoanalysis: Culture, Character, and Normative Unconscious Processes*. Oxfordshire: Routledge, 2020.

Lear, Jonathan. *Radical Hope: Ethics in the Face of Cultural Devastation*. Cambridge, MA: Harvard University Press, 2006.

Levi, Primo. *Survival in Auschwitz*. New York: Collier, 1960.

Linzey, Andrew. *Why Animal Suffering Matters: Philosophy, Theology, and Practical Ethics*. Oxford: Oxford University Press, 2009.

London, Jack. *The Unabridged Jack London*. Philadelphia: Running Press, 1981.

Løgstrup, Knud. *The Ethical Demand*. Notre Dame, IN: Notre Dame University Press, 1997.

Meijer, Eva. *Animal Languages*. Cambridge, MA: MIT Press, 2020.

———. *When Animals Speak: Toward an Interspecies Democracy*. New York: New York University Press, 2019.

Melville, Herman. *The Piazza Tales*. Edited by Egbert S. Oliver. New York: Hendricks House, Farrar Straus, 1948.

Mills, Charles. *Black Rights/White Wrongs*. Oxford: Oxford University Press, 2017.

———. *The Racial Contract*. Ithaca, NY: Cornell University Press, 1997.

Patterson, Orlando. *Slavery and Social Death*. Cambridge, MA: Harvard University Press, 1982.

Peirce, Charles. *The Essential Pierce: Selected Philosophical Writings*. Edited by the Peirce Edition Press. Bloomington, IN: Indiana University Press, 1998.

———. *Peirce on Signs: Writings on Semiotic by Charles Sanders Peirce*. Edited by James Hoopes. Chapel Hill, NC: North Carolina University Press, 1991.

Prozorov, Sergei. *Agamben and Politics*. Edinburgh: Edinburgh University Press, 2014.

Puryear, Stephen. "Schopenhauer on the Rights of Animals." *European Journal of Philosophy* 25, no. 2 (2017): 250–269.

Rousseau, Bryant. "In New Zealand Lands and Rivers can be People too (Legally Speaking)." *New York Times*, July 13, 2016. https://www.nytimes.com/2016/07/14/world/what-in-the-world/in-new-zealand-lands-and-rivers-can-be-people-legally-speaking.html.

Scully, Matthew. *Dominion: The Power of Man, the Suffering of Animals, and the Call to Mercy*. New York: St. Martin's Griffin, 2003.

Segal, Hanna. "Notes of Symbol Formation." *International Journal of Psychoanalysis* 38 (1957): 391–397.

Sehgal, Parul. "The Case Against the Trauma Plot." *New Yorker*, January 3, 2022.

Self, Will. "How Everything Became Trauma." *Harper's Magazine*, December 2021. https://harpers.org/archive/2021/12/a-posthumous-shock-trauma-studies-modernity-how-everything-became-trauma/.

Shore-Goss, Robert. *God is Green: An Eco-spirituality of Incarnate Compassion*. Eugene, OR: Cascade Books, 2016.

Singer, Peter. *Animal Liberation*. New York: Harper Collins, 1975.

———. *Ethics in the real World*. Princeton, NJ: Princeton University Press, 2016.

Sollereder, Bethany. *God, Evolution, and Animal Suffering: Theodicy without a Fall*. Oxfordshire: Routledge, 2020.

Spencer, Nick, and Robert White. *Christianity, Climate Change, and Sustainable Living*. London: SPCK, 2007.

Stampfl, Barry. "Theorizing Canine PTSD." *Semiotics* (2012): 159–168. https://doi.org/10.5840/cpsem201216.

Tyson, Paul. *Theology and Climate Change*. Oxfordshire: Routledge, 2021.

Ugilt, Rasmus. *Giorgio Agamben: Political Philosophy*. London: Humanities-E-books, 2014.

van der Kolk, Bessel A., Lars Weisaeth, and Onno van der Hart. "History of Trauma in Psychiatry." In *Traumatic Stress*, edited by Bessel A. van der Kolk, Alexander McFarlane, and Lars Weisaeth, 57–76. New York: Guilford, 1996.

van der Kolk, Bessel A., Onno van der Hart, and Charles R. Marmar, "Dissociation and Information Processing in Posttraumatic Stress Disorder." In *Traumatic Stress*, edited by Bessel A. van der Kolk, Alexander McFarlane, and Lars Weisaeth, 303–330. New York: Guilford, 1996.

Wallace-Wells, David. *The Uninhabitable Earth*. Spokane: Dugan Books, 2020.

Wilson, Edward O. *The Future of Life*. London: Abacus, 2005.

Zeddies, Timothy. "Behind, Beneath, Above, and Beyond: The Historical Unconscious." *Journal of the American Academy of Psychoanalysis* 30, no. 2 (2002): 211–222.

Chapter 5: Psychospiritual Stress, Trauma, and Migration

Bäärnhielm, Sofie, and Mike Mösko. "Cross-Cultural Communication with Traumatised Immigrants." In *Trauma and Migration: Cultural Factors in the Diagnosis and Treatment of Traumatised Immigrants*, edited by Meryam Schouler-Ocak, 39–55. New York: Springer International, 2015.

Caruth, Cathy. *Unclaimed Experience: Trauma, Narrative, and History.* Baltimore, MD: John Hopkins University Press, 1996.

Cho, Eunil David. "Coping with a Double Pandemic of Health Crisis and Anti-Asian Racism in America: The Role of Immigrant Churches." In *Between Pandemonium and Pandemethics: Responses to Covid-19 from Theology and Religions*, edited by Volker Küster and Dorothea Erbele-Küster, 57–86. Berlin: Evangelische Verlagsanstalt, 2022.

Cohen, Judith A., Anthony P. Mannarino, and Laura K. Murray. "Trauma-Focused CBT for Youth Who Experience Ongoing Traumas." *Child Abuse and Neglect* 35, no. 8 (2011): 637–646. https://doi.org/10.1016/j.chiabu.2011.05.002.

Delaney, Harold D., William R. Miller, and Ana M. Bisono. "Religiosity and Spirituality Among Psychologists: A Survey of Clinician Members of the American Psychological Association." *Professional Psychology: Research and Practice* 38, no. 5 (2007): 538–546. https://doi.org/10.1037/0735-7028.38.5.538.

DeLuca, Lawrence A., Marylyn M. McEwen, and Samuel M. Keim. "United States-Mexico Border Crossing: Experiences and Risk Perceptions of Undocumented Male Immigrants." *Journal of Immigrant and Minority Health* 12, no. 1 (2010): 113–123. https://doi.org/10.1007/s10903-008-9197-4.

Diamond, Gary M., Joshua D. Lipsitz, Zvi Fajerman, and Omit Rozenblat. "Ongoing Traumatic Stress Response (OTSR) in Sderot Israel." *Professional Psychology: Research and Practice* 41, no. 1 (2010): 19–25. http://doi.org/10.1037/a0017098.

Eagle, Gillian, and Debra Kaminer. "Continuous Traumatic Stress: Expanding the Lexicon of Traumatic Stress." *Peace and Conflict: Journal of Peace Psychology* 19, no. 2 (2013): 85–99. https://doi.org/10.1037/a0032485.

Ebaugh, Helen Rose, and Janet Saltzman Chafetz. *Religion and the New Immigrants: Continuities and Adaptations in Immigrant Congregations.* Lanham, MD: AltaMira Press, 2000.

Erikson, Kai. *Everything in Its Path: Destruction of Community in the Buffalo Creek Flood.* New York: Simon & Schuster, 1976.

Gone, Joseph P. "Redressing First Nations Historical Trauma: Theorizing Mechanisms for Indigenous Culture and Mental Health Treatment." *Transcultural Psychiatry* 50, no. 5 (2013): 683–706. https://doi.org/10.1177/1363461513487669.

Good, Mary-Jo DelVecchio. "Perspectives on Trauma and Healing from Anthropology and Social and Affective Neuroscience."

Transcultural Psychiatry 50, no. 5 (2013): 744–752, https://doi.org/10.1177/1363461513508174.

Good, Mary-Jo DelVecchio, Paul Brodwin, Byron J. Good, and Arthur Kleinman. *Pain as Human Experience*. Oakland, CA: University of California Press, 1992.

Gregory, Amanda Ann. "Why Forgiveness Isn't Required in Trauma Recovery." *Psychology Today*, February 20, 2022. https://www.psychologytoday.com/us/blog/simplifying-complex-trauma/202202/why-forgiveness-isn-t-required-in-trauma-recovery.

Herman, Judith. "Recovery from Psychological Trauma." *Psychiatry and Clinical Neurosciences* 52, no. S1 (2002): S98–S103. https://doi.org/10.1046/j.1440-1819.1998.0520s5S145.x.

Hirschman, Charles. "The Role of Religion in the Origins and Adaptation of Immigrant Groups in the United States." *International Migration Review* 38, no. 3 (2004): 1206–1233.

Holton, M. Jan. *Longing for Home*. New Haven, CT: Yale University Press, 2016.

Ihimaera, Witi. *The Whale Rider*. London: Penguin Books, 1987.

Kira, Ibrahim. "Etiology and Treatment of Post-Cumulative Traumatic Stress Disorders in Different Cultures." *Traumatology* 16, no. 4 (2010): 128–141. https://doi.org/10.1177/1534765610365914.

Kristeva, Julia. *Intimate Revolt: The Powers and Limits of Psychoanalysis*. New York: Columbia University Press, 2002.

Lahad, Mooli, and Dmitry Leykin. "Ongoing Exposure Versus Intense Periodic Exposure to Military Conflict and Terror Attacks in Israel." *Journal of Traumatic Stress* 23, no. 6 (2010): 691–698. https://doi.org/10.1002/jts.20583.

Lederach, John Paul, and Angela Jill Lederach. *When Blood and Bones Cry Out: Journeys Through the Soundscape of Healing and Reconciliation*. Oxford: Oxford University Press, 2010.

Lester, Rebecca. "Back from the Edge of Existence: A Critical Anthropology of Trauma." *Transcultural Psychiatry* 50, no. 5 (2013): 753–762. https://doi.org/10.1177/1363461513504520.

Luckhurst, Roger. *The Trauma Question*. Oxfordshire: Routledge, 2008.

Luhrmann, Tanya Marie. "Making God Real and Making God Good: Some Mechanisms Through Which Prayer May Contribute to Healing." *Transcultural Psychiatry* 50, no. 5 (2013): 707–725. https://doi.org/10.1177/1363461513487670.

Mercer, Joyce Ann. "Pastoral Care with Children of War: A Community-Based Model of Trauma Healing in the Aftermath of Indonesia's

Religious Conflicts." *Pastoral Psychology* 64, no. 6 (2015): 847–860. https://doi.org/10.1007/s11089-015-0654-4.

Miller, Kenneth E., and Lisa M. Rasco, eds. *The Mental Health of Refugees: Ecological Approaches to Healing and Adaptation*. Mahwah, NJ: Lawrence Erlbaum Associates, 2004.

Nguyen, Viet Thanh, ed. *The Displaced: Refugee Writers on Refugee Lives*. New York: Abrams Press, 2018.

Norris, Fran H., Matthew J. Friedman, Patricia J. Watson, Christopher M. Byrne, Eolia Diaz, and Krzysztof Kaniasty. "60,000 Disaster Victims Speak: Part I. An Empirical Review of the Empirical Literature, 1981–2001." *Psychiatry* 65, no. 3 (2002): 207–239. https://doi.org/10.1521/psyc.65.3.207.20173.

Office of the High Commissioner for Human Rights. "'Intolerable' Tide of People Displaced by Climate Change: UN Expert." *United Nations, Office of the High Commissioner for Human Rights*. https://www.ohchr.org/en/press-releases/2022/06/intolerable-tide-people-displaced-climate-change-un.

Pargament, Kenneth. *Spiritually Integrated Psychotherapy: Understanding and Addressing the Sacred*. New York: Guilford Press, 2007.

Pargament, Kenneth, and Julie J. Exline. *Working with Spiritual Struggles in Psychotherapy*. New York: Guilford Press, 2021.

Perreira, Krista M., and India Ornelas. "Painful Passages: Traumatic Experiences and Post-Traumatic Stress Among Immigrant Latino Adolescents and their Primary Caregivers." *International Migration Review* 47, no. 4 (2013): 1–25. https://doi.org/10.1111/imre.12050.

Porter, Matthew, and Nick Haslam. "Predisplacement and Postdisplacement Factors Associated with Mental Health of Refugees and Internally Displaced Persons: A Meta-Analysis." *JAMA* 294, no. 5 (2005): 602–612. https://doi:10.1001/jama.294.5.602.

Reis, Ria. "Children Enacting Idioms of Witchcraft and Spirit Possession as a Response to Trauma: Therapeutically Beneficial, and for Whom?" *Transcultural Psychiatry* 50, no. 5 (2013): 622–643. https://doi.org/10.1177/1363461513503880.

Rothberg, Michael. "Decolonizing Trauma Studies: A Response." *Studies in the Novel* 40, no. 1 (2008): 224–234. https://doi.org/10.1353/sdn.0.0005.

Saul, Jack. *Collective Trauma, Collective Healing: Promoting Community Resilience in the Aftermath of Disaster*. Oxfordshire: Routledge, 2014.

Slattery, Jeanne M., Joseph M. Currier, Crystal L. Park, and J. Irene Harris. *Trauma, Meaning, and Spirituality: Translating Research into Clinical Practice*. Washington, DC: American Psychological Association, 2017.

Smith, Timothy L. "Religion and Ethnicity in America." *American Historical Review* 83, no. 5 (1978): 1155–1185. https://doi.org/10.2307/1854689.

Stevens, Garth, Gillian Eagle, and Debra Kaminer. "Continuous Traumatic Stress: Conceptual Conversations in Contexts of Global Conflict, Violence and Trauma." *Peace and Conflict: Journal of Peace Psychology* 19, no. 2 (2013): 75–84. https://doi.org/10.1037/a0032484.

Straker, Gillian, and The Sanctuaries Counselling Team. "The Continuous Traumatic Stress Syndrome: The Single Therapeutic Interview." *Psychology in Society* 8 (1987): 48–78.

Toussaint, Loren, Sowmya Kshtriya, Ani Kalayjian, Erinn Cameron, and Daria Diakonova Curtis. "Christian Religious Affiliation is Associated with less Posttraumatic Stress Symptoms through Forgiveness but not Search for Meaning after Hurricane Irma and Maria." *Psychology of Religion and Spirituality* 15, no. 1 (2022): 79–82. https://doi.org/10.1037/rel0000454.

Office of the High Commissioner for Human Rights. "Refugees from Ukraine Recorded Across Europe." October 11, 2022. https://data.unhcr.org/en/situations/ukraine.

van der Kolk, Bessel. *Psychological Trauma*, Washington, DC: American Psychiatric Publishing, 2003.

Visser, Irene. "Decolonizing Trauma Theory: Retrospect and Prospects." *Humanities* 4, no. 2 (2015): 250–265, https://doi.org/10.3390/h4020250.

Warner, R. Stephen, and Judith G. Wittner, eds. *Gatherings in Diaspora: Religious Communities and New Immigration*. Philadelphia: Temple University Press, 1998.

Zibulewsky, Joseph. "Defining Disaster: The Emergency Department Perspective." *Baylor University Medical Center Proceedings* 14, no. 2 (2001): 144–149. https://doi.org/10.1080/08998280.2001.11927751.

Chapter 6: Psychospirituality and Genocidal Rape

American Psychiatric Association. *Diagnostic and Statistical Manual of Mental Disorders,* 5th ed., Text Revision. Washington, DC: American Psychiatric Association, 2022. https://doi.org/10.1176/appi.books.9780890425787.

Barstow, Anne Llewellyn, ed. *War's Dirty Secret: Rape, Prostitution, and Other Crimes Against Women*. Cleveland, OH: Pilgrim Press, 2000.

Bastick, Megan, Karin Grimm, and Rahel Kunz. *Sexual Violence in Armed Conflict: Global Overview and Implications for the Security Sector.*

Geneva: Geneva Centre for the Democratic Control of Armed Forces, 2008. https://www.dcaf.ch/sites/default/files/publications/documents/sexualviolence_conflict_full.pdf.

Becker, Daniel F., Stevan M. Weine, Dolores Vojvoda, and Thomas H. Mcglashan. "Case Series: PTSD Symptoms in Adolescent Survivors of 'Ethnic Cleansing.' Results from a 1-Year Follow-up Study." *Journal of the American Academy of Child and Adolescent Psychiatry* 38, no. 6 (1999): 775–781. https://doi.org/10.1097/00004583-199906000-00027.

Bell, Duncan. "Introduction: Memory, Trauma and World Politics." In *Memory, Trauma and World Politics: Reflections on the Relationship between the Past and the Present*, edited by Duncan Bell, 1–29. London: Palgrave Macmillan, 2006.

Bergoffen, Debra B. *Contesting the Politics of Genocidal Rape: Affirming the Dignity of the Vulnerable Body*. New York: Routledge, 2012.

Bonilla, Natalia Suarez. "Rape, Blaming the Victim and Social Control in Paramilitary Enclaves: An Approach to the Case of Colombia." In *Rape in Wartime: Genders and Sexualities in History*, edited by Raphaelle Branche and Fabrice Virgili, 79–89. London: Palgrave Macmillan, 2012.

Brewin, Chris R. "The Nature and Significance of Memory Disturbance in Post-traumatic Stress Disorder." *Annual Review of Clinical Psychology* 7 (2011): 203–227. https://doi.org/10.1146/annurev-clinpsy-032210-104544.

Brewin, Chris R., Ruth A. Lanius, Andrei Novac, Ulrich Schnyder, and Sandro Galea. "Reformulating PTSD for DSM-V: Life after Criterion A." *Journal of Traumatic Stress* 22, no. 5 (2009): 366–373. https://doi.org/10.1002/jts.20443.

Brownmiller, Susan. *Against Our Will: Men, Women and Rape*. New York: Simon and Schuster Publishers, 1975.

Card, Claudia. "Rape as a Weapon of War." *Hypatia* 11, no. 4 (1996): 5–18. https://doi.org/10.1111/j.1527-2001.1996.tb01031.x.

Crowe, David M. *War Crimes, Genocide, and Justice: A Global History*. London: Palgrave Macmillan, 2013.

de Vito, Daniela, Aisha Gill, and Damiel Short. "Rape Characterised as Genocide." *Sur: International Journal on Human Rights* 6, no. 10 (2009), 28–51.

Ericson, Maria. "Reconciliation and the Search for a Shared Moral Landscape: Insights and Challenges from Northern Ireland and South Africa." *Journal of Theology for Southern Africa* 115 (2003): 19–42.

Evaldsson, Anns-Karin. "Grass-roots Reconciliation in South Africa." PhD diss., University of Gothenburg, 2007.

Fernandez, Ana, Patricia Moreno-Peral, Edurne Zabaleta-del-Olmo, Juan Angel Bellon, Jose Manuel Aranda-Regules, Juan Vicente Luciano, Antoni Serrano-Blanco, and Maria Rubio-Valera. "Is There a Case for Mental Health Promotion in the Primary Care Setting? A Systematic Review." *Preventive Medicine* 76 (2015): S5–S11. https://doi.org/10.1016/j.ypmed.2014.11.019.

Govier, Trudy. "What is Acknowledgement and Why is it Important?" Paper presented at OSSA Conference, University of Windsor, May 15, 1999. https://scholar.uwindsor.ca/cgi/viewcontent.cgi?article=1845&context=ossaarchive.

Greenwald, Ricky. "Eye Movement Desensitization and Reprocessing (EMDR): A New Kind of Dreamwork?" *Dreaming* 5, no. 1 (1995): 51–55. https://doi.org/10.1037/h0094423.

Hill, Matthew, David Campanale, and Joel Gunter. "'Their Goal is to Destroy Everyone': Uighur Camp Detainees Allege Systematic Rape." *BBC News*, February 2, 2021. https://www.bbc.com/news/world-asia-china-55794071.

Horowitz, Donald L. *Ethnic Groups in Conflict.* Berkeley, CA: University of California Press, 1985.

Isgandarova, Nazila. "Effective Islamic Spiritual Care: Foundations and Practices oflmams and Other Muslim Spiritual Caregivers, Imams and Other Muslim Spiritual Caregivers." DMin thesis, Wilfrid Laurier University, 2011.

———. "Rape as a Tool against Women in War: The Role of Spiritual Caregivers to Support the Survivors of an Ethnic Violence." *CrossCurrents* 63, no. 2 (2013): 174–184. https://doi.org/10.1111/cros.12022.

Joubert, Natacha and John Raeburn. "Mental Health Promotion: People, Power and Passion." *International Journal of Mental Health Promotion* 1, no. 1 (1998): 15–22.

Luthar, Suniya S., Dante Cicchetti, and Bronwyn Becker. "The Construct of Resilience: A Critical Evaluation and Guidelines for Future Work." *Child Development* 71, no. 3 (2000): 543–562. https://doi.org/10.1111/1467-8624.00164.

Marzillier, John. *The Trauma Therapies.* Oxford: Oxford University Press, 2014.

Mertus, Julie. "Truth in a Box: The Limits of Justice through Judicial Mechanisms." In *The Politics of Memory, Truth, Healing and Social Justice,* edited by Ifi Amadiume and Abdullahi An-Na'im, 142–61. New York: Bloomsbury, 2000.

Mullins, Christopher W. "'He Would Kill Me with His Penis': Genocidal Rape in Rwanda as a State Crime." *Critical Criminology* 17, no. 1 (2009): 15–33. https://doi.org/10.1007/s10612-008-9067-3.

Murthy, R. Srinivasa, and Rashmi Lakshminarayana. "Mental Health Consequences of War: A Brief Review of Research Findings." *World Psychiatry* 5, no. 1 (2006): 25–30.

Peterman, Amber, Tia Palermo, and Caryn Bredenkamp. "Estimates and Determinants of Sexual Violence against Women in the Democratic Republic of Congo." *American Journal of Public Health* 101, no. 6 (2011): 1060–1067. https://doi.org/10.2105/AJPH.2010.300070.

Rosner, Rita, Steve Powell, and Willi Butollo. "Posttraumatic Stress Disorder Three Years After the Siege of Sarajevo." *Journal of Clinical Psychology* 59, no. 1 (2003): 41–55. https://doi.org/10.1002/jclp.10116.

Rūmī, Jalāl al-Dīn Rūmī. *The Essential Rumi*. Translated by Coleman Barks with John Moyne. New York: HarperCollins, 1996.

Selimovic, Johanna Mannergren. "Perpetrators and Victims: Local Responses to the International Criminal Tribunal for the Former Yugoslavia." *Focaal* 57 (2010): 50–61. https://doi.org/10.3167/fcl.2010.570104.

Shapiro, Francine. *Eye Movement Desensitization and Reprocessing (EMDR) Therapy: Basic Principles, Protocols and Procedures*. 3rd ed. New York: Guilford Press, 2017.

Shaw, Rosalind. "Memory Frictions: Localizing the Truth and Reconciliation Commission in Sierra Leone." *International Journal of Transitional Justice* 1, no. 2 (2007): 183–207. https://doi.org/10.1093/ijtj/ijm008.

Siegel, Judith M., Susan B. Sorenson, Jacqueline M. Golding, M. Audrey Burnham, and Judith A. Stein. "The Prevalence of Childhood Sexual Assault: The Los Angeles Epidemiologic Catchment Area Project." *American Journal of Epidemiology* 126, no. 6 (1987): 1141–1153. https://doi.org/10.1093/oxfordjournals.aje.a114752.

Simich, Laura, Brenda Roche, and Leigh Ayton. "*Defining Resiliency, Constructing Equity*." Toronto: Wellesley Institute, 2012. http://wellesleyinstitute.com/wp-content/uploads/2012/03/Defining-Resiliency-Constructing-Equity1.pdf.

Sossou, Marie-Antoinette, Carlton D. Craig, Heather Ogren, and Michelle Schnak. "A Qualitative Study of Resilience Factors of Bosnian Refugee Women Resettled in the Southern United States." *Journal of Ethnic & Cultural Diversity in Social Work* 17, no. 4 (2008): 365–385. https://doi.org/10.1080/15313200802467908.

Stewart, Miriam. J., and Lynn Langille. "A Framework for Social Support Assessment and Intervention in the Context of Chronic Conditions and Caregiving." In *Chronic Conditions and Caregiving in Canada*, edited by Miriam J. Stewart, 3–28. Toronto: University of Toronto Press, 2000.

Tedeschi, Richard G., Jane Shakespeare-Finch, Kanako Taku, and Lawrence G. Calhoun. *Posttraumatic Growth: Theory, Research, and Applications*. New York: Routledge, 2018. https://doi.org/10.4324/9781315527451.

Totten, Samuel, and Paul R. Bartrop. *Dictionary of Genocide*. Westport, CT: Greenwood, 2007.

United Nations. *Convention on the Prevention and Punishment of the Crime of Genocide*. Paris: United Nations, 1951. https://www.un.org/en/genocideprevention/documents/atrocity-crimes/Doc.1_Convention%20on%20the%20Prevention%20and%20Punishment%20of%20the%20Crime%20of%20Genocide.pdf.

———. *International Tribunal for the Prosecution of Persons Responsible for Serious Violations of International Humanitarian Law Committed in the Territory of the Former Yugoslavia since 1991*. United Nations, 1993. https://www.icty.org/x/cases/kunarac/tjug/en/kun-tj010222e.pdf.

———. *Report of the Independent International Commission of Inquiry on Ukraine* (A/77/533). Ukraine: United Nations, 2022. https://documents-dds-ny.un.org/doc/UNDOC/GEN/N22/637/72/PDF/N2263772.pdf?OpenElement.

———. *The Rule of Law and Transitional Justice in Conflict and Post-Conflict Societies: Report of the Secretary-General*. United Nations, 2004. https://www.unhcr.org/us/media/rule-law-and-transitional-justice-conflict-and-post-conflict-societies-report-secretary.

Walsh, Froma. "A Family Resilience Framework: Innovative Practice Applications." *Family Relations: Interdisciplinary Journal of Applied Family Science* 51, no. 2 (2002): 130–137. https://doi.org/10.1111/j.1741-3729.2002.00130.x.

Wilson, Richard A. *The Politics of Truth and Reconciliation in South Africa: Legitimizing the Post-Apartheid State*. Cambridge: Cambridge University Press, 2001.

Woolner, Leah, Myriam Denov, and Sarilee Kahn. "'I Asked Myself If I Would Ever Love My Baby': Mothering children born of genocidal rape in Rwanda." *Violence Against Women* 25, no. 6 (2019): 703–720. https://doi.org/10.1177/1077801218801110.

Chapter 7: The Psychospirituality of Historical Trauma in South Korea

Alexander, Jeffrey. *Trauma: A Social Theory.* Medford, MA: Polity Press, 2012.

American Psychiatric Association. *Diagnostic and Statistical Manual of Mental Disorders,* 5th ed., Text Revision. Washington, DC: American Psychiatric Association, 2022. https://doi.org/10.1176/appi.books.9780890425787.

Bonanno, George A. *The Other Side of Sadness: What the New Science of Bereavement Tells Us About Life After Loss.* New York: Basic Books, 2009.

Bonanno, George A., and Anthony D. Mancini. "Beyond Resilience and PTSD: Mapping the Heterogeneity of Responses to Potential Trauma." *Psychological Trauma: Theory, Research, Practice, and Policy* 4, no. 1 (2012): 74–83. https://doi.org/10.1037/a0017829.

Bonanno, George A., Courtney Rennicke, and Sharon Dekel. "Self-Enhancement Among High-Exposure Survivors of the September 11th Terrorist Attack: Resilience or Social Maladjustment?" *Journal of Personality and Social Psychology* 88, no. 6 (2005): 984–998. https://doi.org/10.1037/0022-3514.88.6.984.

Brave Heart, Maria Yellow Horse. "The Historical Trauma Response Among Natives and Its Relationship with Substance Abuse: A Lakota Illustration." *Journal of Psychoactive Drugs* 35, no. 1 (2003): 7–13. https://doi.org/10.1080/02791072.2003.10399988.

Brave Heart, Maria Yellow Horse, and Lemyra M. DeBruyn. "The American Indian Holocaust: Healing Historical Unresolved Grief." *American Indian and Alaska Native Mental Health Research* 8, no. 2 (1998): 56–78. https://doi.org/10.5820/aian.0802.1998.60.

Brock, Rita Nakashima, and Gabriella Lettini. *Soul Repair: Recovering from Moral Injury After War.* Boston: Beacon Press, 2012.

Crawford, Allison. "'The Trauma Experienced by Generations Past Having an Effect in Their Descendants': Narrative and Historical Trauma Among Inuit in Nunavut, Canada." *Transcultural Psychiatry* 51, no. 3 (2013): 1–31. https://doi.org/10.1177/1363461512467161.

Duran, Eduardo, and Bonnie Duran. *Native American Postcolonial Psychology.* Albany, NY: State University of New York Press, 1995.

Evans-Campbell, Teresa. "Historical Trauma in American Indian/Native Alaska Communities: A Multilevel Framework for Exploring Impacts on Individuals, Families, and Communities." *Journal of*

Interpersonal Violence 23, no. 3 (2008): 316–338. https://doi.org/10.1177/0886260507312290.

Eyerman, Ron. "Cultural Trauma: Emotion and Narration." In *The Oxford Handbook of Cultural Sociology*, edited by Jeffrey C. Alexander, Ronald N. Jacobs, and Philip Smith, 564–582. Oxford: Oxford University Press, 2012.

Fassin, Didier, and Richard Rechtman. *The Empire of Trauma: An Inquiry into the Condition of Victimhood*. Princeton, NJ: Princeton University Press, 2009.

Galea, Sandro, Heidi Resnick, Jennifer Ahern, Joel Gold, Michael Bucuvalas, Dean Kilpatrick, Jennifer Stuber, and David Vlahov. "Posttraumatic Stress Disorder in Manhattan, New York City, after the September 11th Terrorist Attacks." *Journal of Urban Health: Bulletin of the New York Academy of Medicine* 79, no. 3 (2002): 340–353. https://doi.org/10.1093/jurban/79.3.340.

Galea, Sandro, David Vlahov, Heidi Resnick, Jennifer Ahern, Ezra Susser, Joel Gold, Michael Bucuvalas, and Dean Kilpatrick. "Trends of Probable Post-Traumatic Stress Disorder in New York City after the September 11 Terrorist Attacks." *American Journal of Epidemiology* 158, no. 6 (2003): 514–524. https://doi.org/10.1093/aje/kwg187.

Gone, Joseph P. "Redressing First Nations Historical Trauma: Theorizing Mechanisms for Indigenous Culture as Mental Health Treatment." *Transcultural Psychiatry* 50, no. 5 (2013): 683–706. https://doi.org/10.1177/1363461513487669.

Gordon, Avery F. *Ghostly Matters: Haunting and the Sociological Imagination*. Minneapolis: Minnesota University Press, 1997.

Graham, Larry Kent. *Moral Injury: Restoring Wounded Souls*. Nashville, TN: Abingdon Press, 2017.

Kellermann, Natan P. F. "Psychopathology in Children of Holocaust Survivors: A Review of the Research Literature." *Israeli Journal of Psychiatry Related Science* 38, no. 1 (2001): 36–46.

———. "Transmission of Holocaust Trauma: An Integrative View." *Psychiatry* 64, no. 3 (2001): 256–267. https://doi.org/10.1521/psyc.64.3.256.18464.

Kirmayer, Laurence J., Joseph P. Gone, and Joshua Moses. "Rethinking Historical Trauma." *Transcultural Psychiatry* 51, no. 3 (2014): 299–319. https://doi.org/10.1177/1363461514536358.

Kim, Tong Ch'un. 전쟁과 사회. [*War and Society*]. Seoul: Tolbegae, 2000.

———. 미국의 엔진, 전쟁과 시장. [*The Engine of the USA: War and Market*]. Paju: Changbi, 2004.

———. 이것은 기억과의 전쟁이다. [*This is a War Against Memories*]. Paju: Sagyejeol, 2013.

———. 전쟁정치. [*War Politics*]. Seoul: Gil, 2013.

———. 대한민국 잔혹사. [*The History of Cruelty in the Republic of Korea*]. Seoul: Hangyure, 2013.

———. 반공자유주의- 우리를 병들게 하는 낙인. [*Anticommunist Liberalism: The Stigma That Makes Us Dysfunctional*]. Seoul: Pilyohanchaek, 2021.

Kim, Tong Ch'un and Myeong Hee Kim. 트라우마로 읽는 대한민국. [*Reading Korea Through Trauma*]. Seoul: Yeoksabipyeongsa, 2014.

Konkuk University Institute for Humanities and Unification. 코리언의 역사적 트라우마. [*The Historical Trauma of Koreans*]. Seoul: Seonin, 2012.

———.역사가 우리에게 남긴 9가지 트라우마. [*The Nine Traumas History Left Us*]. Hanam: Paradigm Book, 2015.

———. 식민/이산/분단/전쟁의 역사와 코리언의 트라우마. [*The History of Colonization/Dispersion/Division/War and the Korean Trauma*]. Seoul: Seonin, 2015.

———. 구술로 본 코리언의 역사적 트라우마. [*The Korean Historical Trauma Examined Through Oral Histories*]. Seoul: Seonin, 2015.

———. 분단트라우마치유를 위한 고통의 공감과 연대. [*Empathy and Solidarity for Healing Division Trauma*]. Seoul: Hankukmunhwasa, 2016.

———.국가폭력 트라우마의 치유. [*The Trauma of State Violence and its Healing*]. Hanam: Paradigm Book, 2018.

LaCapra, Dominick. *History and Memory after Auschwitz.* Ithaca, NY: Cornell University Press, 2000.

———. *History and Reading: Tocqueville, Foucault, French Studies.* Toronto: University of Toronto Press, 2000.

———. *History in Transit: Experience, Identity, Critical Theory.* Ithaca, NY: Cornell University Press, 2004.

———. *Representing the Holocaust: History, Theory, Trauma.* Ithaca, NY: Cornell University Press, 1994.

———. 치유의 역사학으로: 라카프라의 정신분석학적 역사학. [*Toward Therapeutic Historiography: LaCapra's Psychoanalytic Study of History*], edited and translated by Yeongsu Yuk. Seoul: Pureun Yeoksa, 2008.

———. *Writing History, Writing Trauma.* Baltimore, MD: Johns Hopkins University Press, 2001.

Lévinas, Emmanuel. "Transcendence and Height." In *Basic Philosophical Writings*, edited by Adriaan Theodoor Paperzak, Simon Critchley, and Robert Bernasconi, 11–32. Bloomington, IN: Indiana University Press, 1996.

Park, Ch'an Sŭng. 마을로 간 한국전쟁: 한국전쟁기 마을에서 벌어진 작은 전쟁들. [*Korean War Enters the Villages: Small Battles in Rural Villages during the Korean War Period*]. Paju: Dolbege, 2010.

Park, Hee-Kyu Heidi. "Postcolonializing Practical Theological Methodology as Cartography of Boundary Dynamics." *International Journal of Practical Theology* 22, no. 1 (2018): 58–68. https://doi.org/10.1515/ijpt-2016-0037.

Rambo, Shelly. *Spirit and Trauma: A Theology of Remaining.* Louisville, KY: Westminster John Knox, 2010.

Smelser, Neil J. "Psychological and Cultural Trauma." In *Cultural Trauma and Collective Identity*, edited by Jeffrey C. Alexander, Ron Eyerman, Bernhard Giesen, Neil J. Smelser, and Piotr Sztompka, 31–59. Oakland, CA: University of California Press, 2004.

Summerfield, Derek. "The Invention of Post-Traumatic Stress Disorder and the Social Usefulness of a Psychiatric Category." *British Medical Journal* 322, no. 7278 (2001): 95–98. https://doi.org/10.1136/bmj.322.7278.95.

Tedeschi, Richard G., and Lawrence G. Calhoun. "Posttraumatic Growth: Conceptual Foundations and Empirical Evidence." *Psychological Inquiry* 15, no. 1 (2004): 1–18. https://doi.org/10.1207/s15327965pli1501_01.

Ulanov, Ann Belford. *Finding Space: Winnicott, God, and Psychic Reality.* Louisville, KY: Westminster John Knox Press, 2001.

Winnicott, Donald Woods. *The Child, the Family, and the Outside World.* 2nd ed. New York: Perseus, 1992.

———. "Transitional Objects and Transitional Phenomena: A Study of First Not-Me Possession." *International Journal of Psychoanalysis* 34, no. 1 (1953): 89–97.

Yu, Sŏn Yŏng. 식민지 트라우마. [*Colonial Trauma*]. Seoul: Pureun Yeoksa, 2017.

Chapter 8: A Buddhist Psychospirituality of Trauma

Anderson, Tonny Elmose, Yael Lahav, Hanne Ellegaard, and Claus Manniche. "A Randomized Control Trial of Brief Somatic Experiencing for Chronic Low Back Pain and Comorbid Post-Traumatic Stress

Disorder Symptoms." *European Journal of Psychotraumatology* 8, no. 1 (2017). https://doi.org/10.1080/20008198.2017.1331108.

Bhikkhu, Thanissaro. *First Things First: Essays on the Buddhist Path*. Mountain View, CA: Creative Commons, 2018.

———. "Jhana." Access to Insight, 2005. https://www.accesstoinsight.org/ptf/dhamma/sacca/sacca4/samma-samadhi/jhana.html.

———. *With Each & Every Breath: A Guide to Meditation*. Valley Center, CA: Metta Forest Monastery, 2013.

Bodhi, Bhikkhu. "The Transformations of Mindfulness." In *Handbook of Mindfulness: Culture, Context, and Social Engagement*, 3–15. New York: Springer, 2016.

Briere, John, and Catherine Scott. *Principles of Trauma Therapy: A Guide to Symptoms, Evaluation, and Treatment*. 2nd ed. Thousand Oaks, CA: Sage, 2014.

Brom, Danny, Yaffa Stokar, Cathy Lawi, Vered Nuriel-Porat, Yuval Ziv, Karen Lerner, and Gina Ross. "Somatic Experiencing for Posttraumatic Stress Disorder: A Randomized Controlled Outcome Study." *Journal of Traumatic Stress* 30, no. 3 (2017): 304–312. https://doi.org/10.1002/jts.22189.

Compson, Jane. "Meditation, Trauma and Suffering in Silence: Raising Questions about How Mediation is Taught and Practiced in Western Contexts in Light of a Contemporary Trauma Resiliency Model." *Contemporary Buddhism* 15, no. 2 (2014): 274–297. https://doi.org/10.1080/14639947.2014.935264.

Epstein, Mark. *The Trauma of Everyday Life*. London: Penguin Books, 2014.

Follette, Victoria M., Deborah Rozelle, James W. Hopper, John Briere, and David Rome, ed. *Mindfulness-Oriented Interventions for Trauma: Integrating Contemplative Practices*. New York: Guilford Press, 2015.

Gleig, Ann. "American Dharma: Buddhism Beyond Modernity." In *American Dharma*. New Haven, CT: Yale University Press, 2019. https://www-degruyter-com.dtl.idm.oclc.org/document/doi/10.12987/9780300245042/html.

Goenka, Satya Narayana. *Discourse Summaries*. Onalaska, WA: Pariyatti Publishing, 2000.

Herman, Judith Lewis. *Trauma and Recovery: The Aftermath of Violence—From Domestic Abuse to Political Terror*. New York: Basic Books, 2015.

Kuhfuß, Marie, Tobias Maldei, Andreas Hetmanek, and Nicola Baumann. "Somatic Experiencing—Effectiveness and Key Factors of a Body-Oriented Trauma Therapy: A Scoping Literature Review." *European*

Journal of Psychotraumatology 12, no. 1 (2021). https://doi.org/10.1080/20008198.2021.1929023.

Levine, Peter A. *In an Unspoken Voice: How the Body Releases Trauma and Restores Goodness*. Berkeley, CA: North Atlantic Books, 2010.

———. "Polyvagal Theory and Trauma." In *Clinical Applications of the Polyvagal Theory: The Emergence of Polyvagal-Informed Therapies*, edited by Stephen W. Porges and Deb Dana, 3–26. New York: W. W. Norton, 2018.

———. *Waking the Tiger: Healing Trauma*. Berkeley, CA: North Atlantic Books, 1997.

Miller-Karas, Elaine. *Building Resilience to Trauma: The Trauma and Community Resiliency Models*. Oxfordshire: Routledge, 2015.

Ogden, Pat and Janina Fisher. *Sensorimotor Psychotherapy: Interventions for Trauma and Attachment*. CSM ed. New York: W. W. Norton, 2015.

Payne, Peter, Peter A. Levine, and Mardi A. Crane-Godreau. "Somatic Experiencing: Using Interoception and Proprioception as Core Elements of Trauma Therapy." *Frontiers in Psychology* 6 (2015). https://doi.org/10.3389/fpsyg.2015.00093.

Sayadaw, Ledi. *Manual of Mindfulness of Breathing: Anapana Dipani*. Sri Lanka: Buddhist Publication Society, 2000.

Sayadaw, Mahasi. *Practical Insight Medication: Basic and Progressive Stages*. Sri Lanka: Buddhist Publication Society, 1991.

Sujato, Bhikkhu. *A History of Mindfulness, How Insight Worsted Tranquility in the Satipatthana Sutta*, 2nd ed. n.p., Santipada: 2012.

———, trans. "An Arrow." In *Linked Discourses: A Plain Translation of the Saṁyutta Nikāya*. n.p., SuttaCentral, 2018. https://suttacentral.net/sn36.6/en/sujato.

———, trans. "Dukkhasutta." In *Linked Discourses: A Plain Translation of the Saṁyutta Nikāya*. n.p., SuttaCentral, 2018. https://suttacentral.net/sn12.43/en/sujato.

———, trans. "Dutiyacetanāsutta." In *Linked Discourses: A Plain Translation of the Saṁyutta Nikāya*. n.p., SuttaCentral, 2018. https://suttacentral.net/sn12.39/en/sujato.

———. *How Early Buddhism Differs from Theravada*. n.p.: Publisher at the End of the World, 2022.

———, trans. "Spiritual Discourse (Nirāmisasutta)." In *Linked Discourses: A Plain Translation of the Saṁyutta Nikāya*. n.p., SuttaCentral, 2018. https://suttacentral.net/sn36.31/en/sujato.

Treleaven, David Allan. "Meditation and Trauma: A Hermeneutic Study of Western Vipassana Practice Through the Perspective of Somatic

Experiencing." PhD diss., San Francisco: California Institute of Integral Studies, 2012.

U Ba Khin, Sayagyi, and Satya Narayana Goenka. *Sayagyi U Ba Khin Journal: A Collection Commemorating the Teaching of Sayagyi U Ba Khi.* India: Vipassana Research Publications, 2017.

Chapter 9: A Reframed Psychospirituality of Stress and Trauma

American Psychiatric Association. *Diagnostic and Statistical Manual of Mental Disorders.* 5th ed., Text Revision. Washington, DC: American Psychiatric Association, 2022. https://doi.org/10.1176/appi.books.9780890425787.

Bonanno, George A. "The Resilience Paradox." *European Journal of Psychotraumatology* 12, no 1 (2021): 1942642. https://doi.org/10.1080/20008198.2021.1942642.

Bonanno, George A., Courtney Rennicke, and Sharon Dekel. "Self-enhancement Among High-Exposure Survivors of the September 11th Terrorist Attack: Resilience or Social Maladjustment?" *Journal of Personal Social Psychology*, 88, no. 6 (2005):984–98. https://doi.org/10.1037/0022-3514.88.6.984.

Bonanno, George A., Maren Westphal, and Anthony D. Mancini. "Resilience to Loss and Potential Trauma." *Annual Review of Clinical Psychology,* 7 (2011): 511–535. https://doi.org/10.1146/annurev-clinpsy-032210-104526.

Caruth, Cathy. *Unclaimed Experience: Trauma, Narrative, and History.* Baltimore, MD: Johns Hopkins University Press, 1996.

Chopp, Rebecca S. *The Power to Speak: Feminism, Language, and God.* Chestnut Ridge, NY: Crossroad, 1991.

Dulmus, Catherine N., and Carolyn Hilarski. "When Stress Constitutes Trauma and Trauma Constitutes Crisis: The Stress-Trauma-Crisis Continuum." *Brief Treatment and Crisis Intervention* 3, no. 1 (2003): 27–35. https://doi.org/10.1093/brief-treatment/mhg008.

Freese, John B. "A Buddhist Psychospirituality of Trauma: A Critical Correlation of Vipassana Meditation and Somatic Experiencing." In *Reframing Trauma: A Psychospiritual Theory and Theology*, edited by M. Jan Holton and Jill L. Snodgrass, 180–204. Minneapolis: Fortress, 2025.

Geertz, Clifford. *Interpretation of Cultures: Selected Essays.* New York: Basic Books, 1973.

Herman, Judith. *Trauma and Recovery: The Aftermath of Violence—from Domestic Abuse to Political Terror*. New York: Basic Books, 1997.

———. *Truth and Repair: How Trauma Survivors Envision Justice*. New York: Basic Books, 2023.

Holmes, Barbara A. *Joy Unspeakable: Contemplative Practices of the Black Church*. 2nd ed. Minneapolis: Fortress Press, 2017.

Holton, M. Jan. *Longing for Home: Forced Displacement and Postures of Hospitality*. New Haven, CT: Yale University Press, 2016.

Johnson-Jennings, Michelle, Shanondora Billiot, and Karina Walters. "Returning to Our Roots: Tribal Health and Wellness through Land-Based Healing." *Geneology* 4, no. 3 (2020): 91. https://doi.org/10.3390/genealogy4030091.

LaMothe, Ryan. "Ontological Psychospirituality: The Stress and Trauma of Other Species." In *Reframing Trauma: A Psychospiritual Theory and Theology*, edited by M. Jan Holton and Jill L. Snodgrass, 87–108. Minneapolis: Fortress, 2025.

Lartey, Emmanuel Y. "Be-ing in Relation." In *Postcolonial Images of Spiritual Care: Challenges of Care in a Neoliberal Age*, edited by Emmanuel Y. Lartey and Hellena Moon, 17–29. Eugene, OR: Pickwick Publications, 2020.

Lartey, Emmanuel Y., and Helena Moon, eds. *Postcolonial Images of Spiritual Care: Challenges of Care in a Neoliberal Age*. Eugene, OR: Pickwick Publications, 2020.

Lester, Rebecca. "Back from the Edge of Existence: A Critical Anthropology of Trauma," *Transcultural Psychiatry* 50, no. 5 (2013): 753–762. https://doi.org/10.1177/1363461513504520.

Levine, Peter A., *In an Unspoken Voice: How the Body Releases Trauma and Restores Goodness*. Berkeley, CA: North Atlantic Books, 2010.

Mann, Thomas W. *The Book of the Torah*. 2nd ed. Eugene, OR: Cascade Books, 2013.

Menhinick, Keith A. and Cody J. Sanders. "The Psychospiritual Trauma of LGBTQ+ People and Communities: Depathologizing Queer Lives and Experiences." In *Reframing Trauma: A Psychospiritual Theory and Theology*, edited by M. Jan Holton and Jill L. Snodgrass, 57–84. Minneapolis: Fortress, 2025.

Park, Crystal L., "Meaning Making Following Trauma," *Frontiers in Psychology*, 13 (2022): 844891, https://doi.org/10.3389/fpsyg.2022.844891.

Root, Maria P. P., "Reconstructing the Impact of Trauma on Personality." In *Personality and Psychopathology: Feminist Reappraisals*, edited by Laura S. Brown and Mary Ballou, 229–266. New York: Guilford Press, 1992.

Strawn, Brent A. *Honest to God Preaching: Talking Sin, Suffering, and Violence*. Minneapolis: Fortress Press, 2021.

Swinton, John. "From Inclusion to Belonging: A Practical Theology of Community, Disability and Humanness." *Journal of Religion, Disability & Health* 16, no. 2 (2012): 172–190. https://doi.org/10.1080/15228967.2012.676243.

Tedeschi, Richard G., and Lawrence G. Calhoun. *Trauma and Transformation: Growing in the Aftermath of Suffering*. Thousand Oaks, CA: Sage, 1995.

Tillich, Paul. *The Courage to Be*. 2nd ed. New Haven, CT: Yale University Press, 2000.

———. *Systematic Theology*, vol. 2, *Existence and The Christ*. Chicago: The University of Chicago Press, 1957.

Werdel, Mary Beth. *The Paradox of Trauma and Growth in Pastoral and Spiritual Care: Night Blooming*. Lanham, MD: Lexington Books, 2024.

Westfield, N. Lynne. *Dear Sisters: A Womanist Practice of Hospitality*. Cleveland, OH: Pilgrim Press, 2007.

Conclusion

Cozier, Yvette. "POV: What 'Strong Black Woman' Means to Me." *BU Today*. Accessed March 28, 2024. https://www.bu.edu/articles/2022/pov-what-strong-black-woman-means-to-me/.

INDEX